A BRIEF HISTORY OF

FRANCE

Cecil Jenkins

RUNNING PRESS
PHILADELPHIA · LONDON

ROBINSON

Constable & Robinson Ltd
3 The Lanchesters
162 Fulham Palace Road
London W6 9ER
www.constablerobinson.com

First published in the UK by Robinson,
an imprint of Constable & Robinson, 2011

A copy of the British Library Cataloguing in Publication
Data is available from the British Library

UK ISBN: 978-1-84529-868-5

1 3 5 7 9 10 8 6 4 2

First published in the United States in 2011 by Running Press Book Publishers

9 8 7 6 5 4 3 2 1

Digit on the right indicates the number of this printing

Library of Congress Control number: 2010928995
US ISBN: 978-0-7624-4120-4

Running Press Book Publishers
2300 Chestnut Street
Philadelphia, PA 19103-4371

Visit us on the web!
www.runningpress.com

Typeset by TW Typesetting, Plymouth, Devon
Printed and bound in the EU

CONTENTS

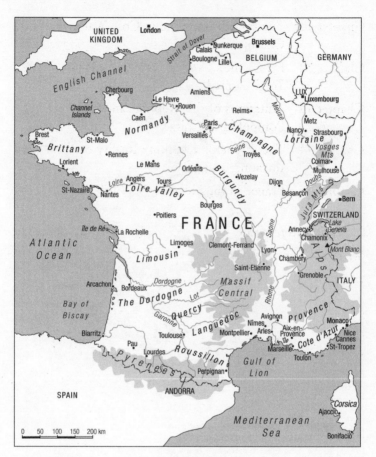

Modern France

The Expansion of France

Key
The small royal domain of Hugues Capet in 1000
Acquisitions up to 1500, in reign of Louis XII
Territorial gains up to 1600, start of Bourbon dynasty with Henri IV
Subsequent additions up to the present.

INTRODUCTION

Why a history of France? What does it tell us? About the France of today, about Europe – about ourselves?

That there is widespread interest in France goes without saying, since it is the most visited tourist destination in the world. Of course, it has the attraction of a highly advanced country, with an excellent infrastructure, which yet offers a sense of space and rural charm. It is after all the largest country in Europe, with extensive plains, forests and mountain ranges, as well as splendid beaches on two contrasting coastlines. Since it stretches from northern to southern Europe, it also offers considerable climatic and regional diversity – from Normandy to the Côte d'Azur, and from Brittany with its Celtic heritage to the Germanic picturesqueness of Alsace in the east. Yet beyond all this, the attraction for many is a longstanding *idea* of France, an almost mythical view of the country seen through a prism in which historical and cultural associations merge with the idea of a specific lifestyle.

There are the reflections triggered by Louis XIV's bedchamber at Versailles, the gloomy Conciergerie in Paris which was the last stop for those due to be guillotined under the Terror, Napoleon's tomb in the Invalides, the vast cemeteries of immaculate graves of those killed in the two world wars. There are also the many heritage sites – from the Roman monuments of Arles or Orange, through the great medieval cathedrals of Amiens or Chartres, to the royal palaces of Fontainebleau or Chambord and a whole complex of buildings in Paris, ranging from the Église de la Madeleine to the École Militaire. And then of course there is the richness of the art, from the mysterious cave paintings of the Dordogne to the Louvre or the striking new Musée des Arts Premiers. The importance of French painting of the nineteenth and twentieth centuries can be measured by the fact that the basic terms used in modern art – Impressionism, Art Nouveau, Fauvism, Surrealism – are French. More recently, France has developed the strongest cinema industry in Europe and produced both modern film theory and the influential New Wave of directors such as Jean-Luc Godard or Claude Chabrol.

However, this idea of France, which to a degree is a myth of Paris, is also seen as distinguishing the French lifestyle. It combines the idea of refinement with simplicity. You may have traditional high French fashion, with its household names like Pierre Balmain or Yves Saint Laurent, but you also have the shop assistant who can effortlessly achieve elegance through a certain sense of self or a way with a scarf. French cuisine may be renowned for its sophistication, but the passion for food of a country that runs to 246 different kinds of cheese is visible in every village. For staid Edwardians as for inter-war Americans, the City of Light was also the city of love in which they found emotional self-expression. For those English people who move to the French provinces today, as for others before them, France has seemed to offer freedom from the constraints and complexities of post-industrial society, a more *natural* lifestyle, in fact a kind of alternative civilization. That is indeed how the former president Chirac tended to present his country, in opposition to materialistic 'Anglo-Saxon' society. But, since those buying French houses are essentially buying them from locals abandoning the provinces to look for work or greater amenities in the cities, are they looking for a traditional way of life that is dying? Are they pursuing an illusion?

Not that the 'Anglo-Saxons' have ever had a very clear view of the French – or vice versa. Britain and France have been close rivals for centuries, which is why the English, notoriously, love France but not the French. They tangled in the dynastic struggle of the Hundred Years War, there was the religious conflict after England became Protestant, the British opposition to the Revolution, the prolonged Napoleonic Wars, fierce colonial rivalry right up to the Entente Cordiale of 1904 and mutual suspicion thereafter. Closely comparable in importance – still today, as nuclear powers, members of the Security Council and with their economies jostling for fifth rank in the world – each became the mirror image of the other, a *bête noire*. So the British traditionally saw the French as foppish, cowardly and none too clean, while the French equally happily saw the British as perfidious, brutal and arrogantly opportunist. And while in recent times the hostility has subsided, the two countries have adopted opposing economic models, with the British – at least until the recent recession raised some doubts – tending to see France as strike-bound and over-regulated and the French viewing Britain as a laissez-faire unequal society.

Inevitably, as the competing power in the West became the United States rather than Britain, a similarly ambiguous anti-Americanism overtook French Anglophobia. France had of course supported the American Revolution, but the US opposed France's colonial aims, did not join the League of Nations, withdrew from European involvement after the First World War and initially supported Vichy rather than de Gaulle, while the very fact that it saved France politically and economically after the Second World War reinforced the sense of dependency on this powerful new social and cultural model so different from France's own. So the French, however defensively, now saw the United States as a new kind of shallow, materialistic society destined to dominate the world, while the Americans – especially after France refused to support the invasion of Iraq – tended to see the French as pretentious, ungrateful and cowardly. Of course there is a love–hate element to these anxieties and popular prejudices but, comical as they can seem, they do not make for understanding.

To understand the France of today it is necessary to understand its historical development. To understand the French concern for their republican social model you have to go back to the Revolution; to understand the structure of education you have to go back to Napoleon; to have any sense of the power of Racinian drama you have to grasp the tensions in the world of Louis XIV; to understand the development of the language you have to go back to Roman Gaul. The fact that France has had such a dramatic history – oscillating between revolution and reaction, clericalism and secularism, left and right – does not derive from temperament. It derives from France's geographical position on the continent of Europe with enemies on all sides, so that the French identity has been conditioned by a whole series of conflictual relationships – with Ancient Rome, the Holy Roman Empire, Italy and the Vatican, Germany and Spain – as well as by imperial rivalry with Britain and the US.

Frenchness is largely a historical construct, as indeed is the country itself, for the present neat 'hexagon' developed over centuries in an essentially unplanned fashion and was only completed with the return of Alsace-Lorraine after the Second World War. And French national feeling, in a country where barely 10 per cent of the inhabitants spoke French before the Revolution, is largely the effect of Napoleonic conscription and the introduction of free schooling with patriotic indoctrination by the Third Republic. But underlying these changes there are significant, often ironic continuities as when the central importance of the State – which differentiates France so markedly from Britain and the US – persists despite apparent contradiction across quite different regimes, from absolute monarchy through the Revolution and Napoleonic empire up to the Fifth Republic of today.

Yet French history is also part and parcel of the history of Europe and the world. For France has played a strikingly representative role in Western and world history, through its central part in such key events as the Wars of Religion, the French Revolution of 1789, the European revolutions of 1848 and the two world wars of the last century, as well as through its worldwide colonial presence and continuously important place in art and thought. With its exceptionally long traceable history going back beyond the Greeks and Romans towards the cave painters of the Dordogne, it is integral to the development of civilization in Europe.

And its history reminds us that civilization does not come cheap – the higher level of social organization brought by Rome was bought with much slaughter of Gauls; the high spirituality of the medieval cathedrals was an attempt to transcend a world of suffering and casual cruelty that was swept by the Black Death; the world-changing Declaration of Human Rights came out of the same historical nexus as the revolutionary Terror. It also reminds us that France and Britain were the two great world powers only 100 years ago, it reminds us of the impermanence of things. And as the balance of planetary forces slides slowly away from the West, it brings an urgency to France's efforts to maintain its presence and its culture in a changing world.

I

CRO-MAGNON MAN, ROMAN GAUL AND THE FEUDAL KINGDOM

Among the glories of France are the mysterious painted caves of the Dordogne and the Pyrenees, which bear witness to the revolutionary step change in human development that began in the latter part of the ice age, or Upper Paleolithic period, some 35,000 years ago. As the Neanderthal people faded away, their *Homo sapiens* successors proceeded to demonstrate their superior skills with startling representations of bison or mammoths or wild horses which leave the urbanized viewer of today not only impressed but troubled. For, while 35,000 years represent a mere moment in geological time, our inability to identify clearly with these early ancestors or to understand what went on in these deep dark caves is disturbing.

The mystery is only increased by the fact that for thousands of years so many of these caves kept their dark secrets to themselves – the famous Lascaux was discovered by boys looking for their lost dog in 1940, the important

Chauvet-Pont-d'Arc was found only in 1994 and the Vilhonneur cave, also in the Dordogne, in late 2005. It is true that traces of Paleolithic art have been found across Europe as far as Russia, as well as on other continents, including Australia, but the most prominent examples have been discovered in the limestone Franco-Cantabrian region, notably in the Dordogne, the Pyrenees and at Altamira in northern Spain. There are almost 200 prehistoric sites in the Dordogne alone and it is largely through exploration carried out there in the Vézère valley that prehistoric studies developed in the nineteenth century. This discipline is consequently largely French in origin and the town of Les Eyzies-de-Tayac, with its National Museum of Prehistory, can proudly bill itself not only as the world capital of prehistory but as having been one of humanity's capitals long before the Assyrians or the Pharaohs existed.

These cave systems, normally formed in the limestone by underground water channels, are often very extensive. Pech Merle, for instance, is 2 kilometres in length while Rouffignac, with its 158 depictions of mammoths, has no fewer than 8 kilometres of galleries. While the part exposed to daylight at the entrance may well have afforded shelter to these hunter-gatherers, it is clear that they did not use the dark interiors as dwelling-places, especially since they might have had to share the accommodation with the very large bears which hibernated there. So it is significant that the paintings are not to be found towards the opening of the caves, but rather in the dark recesses of them – in the case of Niaux in the Ariège, for example, as far as a kilometre from the entrance. Since they had to be executed with some difficulty by the light of lamps burning animal fat, which would have made these shadowy tunnels even more disquieting, this was therefore neither a casual pastime nor art as decoration but something more significant – and harder to interpret.

These are not landscapes, there is no depiction of natural features such as hills or trees or vegetation. Nor are they scenes of everyday life, whether of group or individual activity, or portrayals of an event. In fact they are almost exclusively single images without context. The overwhelming majority are of animals, sometimes in black outline only and sometimes polychrome using red, brown, yellow and occasionally white and combining the use of a hard point with colours brushed or blown on through a hollow tube. The images, whether of whole animals or of parts only, can be startlingly forceful and lifelike, demonstrating skilful control of line and clever use of the hollows and bulges in the rock face. And above all – like the bulls in Lascaux or the polychrome bison at Niaux – they tend to be disproportionately large. While the emphasis varies from cave to cave, the animals depicted include horses, bison, mammoths, deer, wild oxen, lions, bears and wolves, though there is a tendency to situate the predatory carnivores in the most remote part of the cave. Essentially, these are dark palaces of animals, strange Paleolithic bestiaries, for there is nothing on show to compete with them – certainly not humans, who barely figure at all.

Women are not represented as such but only as the female principle, by a sign symbolizing the female sex organ which, together with a tendency to depict some animals as pregnant, would support the idea of a fertility cult also implied by such contemporary artefacts as the famous *Venus of Willendorf* found in Austria. Men, too, are absent, except in very rare instances as when in Pech Merle there is a crude line drawing of a hunter lying on his back with spears protruding from him, or more mysteriously as in Lascaux where as a mere stick drawing he is also lying prone, perhaps dead but with penis erect, before a threatening bison which he may have wounded since its entrails are trailing downwards. What is going on here? Since there is a strong emphasis on hunting the larger, predatory animals rather than those that appear to have regularly provided food, does the sexual excitement of the hunter somehow merge with the shared death of man and beast in a primitive, magical sense of life? Are these places, as a prominent expert suggests, temples for community worship with sacred sanctums open only to sorcerers or shamans in the deepest recesses of the cave?[1]

The fact is that, although various theories have been advanced, we just do not know any more than we know how to interpret certain enigmatic signs: hand prints or hand outlines, rows of dots sometimes made by hand prints, also lines, triangles and quadrilateral drawings. Are these ideograms, elements of a cultish system of meaning? Or are the hand prints to be seen simply as signatures, the quadrilaterals as animal traps and the red ochre dots – as an American study suggests – as blood drops from a wounded animal being stalked by the knowing hunter in the snow?[2] It is not easy to say. However, there are two things that we can say. The first is that these representations are at once stylized and functional. The emphasis on outline and a characteristic outward twisting of antlers or forelegs are definitional in that they identify the animal both from the side and from the front. The separate detailed studies of heads and hooves, like the sometimes disproportionate attention given to significant parts of the animal's body, serve the same purpose, as also do the tricks used to achieve perspective or movement.

These images state what the hunter needs to know and do so in celebratory fashion. If there is no attention paid to the grouping of images, and if animals are drawn pell-mell on top of others, it is because of the hunter's obsessive concentration on the specific characteristics of the single animal. If the ice age hunter-gatherer has no mastery in life over these large dangerous beasts that may also represent the greater forces beyond his control, he can achieve a symbolic mastery of them in art. But this in itself means that, as his virtual absence from the picture other than as a mere cipher indicates, he is as yet unable to conceive of himself as living with them on equal terms.

*   *   *

If it is not easy to see the cave painters clearly, since they did not portray themselves, neither is it easy to see the Gauls clearly. Because their tradition was essentially oral and they left no significant written records, they have been viewed largely through the distorting prism of others – indeed the very name by which they are known was given them by the Romans. The first self-interested version was that of Julius Caesar, who in his account of the Gallic Wars presents them as credulous barbarians, the more dangerous in that they are temperamentally unstable and unpredictable. Since then, at succeeding moments in France's volatile history, they have been dragooned into the service of quite conflicting causes claiming to represent the true continuity of the French nation – their leader Vercingétorix has been annexed for propaganda purposes by the emperor Napoleon III, by anti-German Third Republic politicians, by pro-German spokesmen for the collaborationist Vichy regime in the Second World War and then by anti-German post-war school books. Since historians, novelists and artists have reflected the same fluctuating interpretations, the picture remains blurred.[3] And then there is one other famous Gaul who has been pressed into the service of a political message.

For, to lay blur upon blur, there is the fact that for so many people today the Gauls are viewed through the comic lens of the Astérix cartoon stories of René Goscinny and Albert Uderzo, which have now been translated into almost 100 languages. You might innocently think that their attraction lies in the fact that they combine the cartoon features that appeal to children – clever drawings, farcical situations and violent knockabout – with the take-off of school history and the knowing allusions that can be picked up by adults. Certainly the political message might not seem to be immediately obvious in these comic accounts of Gaul under Roman occupation, based on the conceit that there is one unconquerable village that is still holding out, even though it is squeezed between the sea and four hapless

Roman garrisons with names like Laudanum and Aquarium. It is true that it is described as a mad village, but it can afford to be mad since its secret is a magic potion concocted by the local druid who, doubtless because he takes a broader view of things, is called Panoramix, briskly translated in English as Getafix. And it is this elixir which gives our hero Astérix a temporary burst of superhuman strength to meet all eventualities.

Astérix may be tiny and funny-looking as warriors go, but he is as bold and cunning as any Odysseus and he has a sturdy companion in the gigantic lumbering Obélix, who has overdone it with the magic potion and is now embarrassingly stuck with superhuman strength. With this pillar of a man beside him and Obélix's obsessional dog Idéfix – nicely rendered in English as Dogmatix – Astérix can not only foil Julius Caesar's legions but take on the great wide world beyond, leaving behind the attractive Panacea since his warrior destiny leaves no room for commitment. And the humour lies in the puns, the implausible situations, the anachronisms and the exaggeration of national or regional stereotypes – the British, for example, are appropriately dull, formal, serve everything with mint sauce and drive their chariots on the wrong side of the road. Meanwhile individual cartoon figures look uncannily like politicians or film stars, such as 'Laurensolivius' or Arnold Schwarzenegger, while the 'crazy' Romans converse portentously in Latin sayings lifted straight from the list of classical expressions in the *Petit Larousse* dictionary. Since it seems clear that these comic books satirize the absurdities of the French and everybody else, it takes an effort to see Astérix patriotically representing Gaullist France standing up to the Americans, as some did in the 1960s. And it is doubtful whether the comparison with this tiny Mickey Mouse of a hero would have left the august and transcendently tall general particularly amused.

So what can reasonably be said about the Gauls? First that they were Celts living since at least 600 BC in the area roughly corresponding to present-day France, Belgium and northern Italy. The Celts had spread across Europe during the Iron Age and indeed had sacked Rome in 390 BC, the smouldering memory of which would later colour the Romans' ambition to conquer Gaul. This was a semi-nomadic people graduating slowly towards a more settled agricultural society, a collection of tribes with no overarching sense of a fixed territory or nationhood. The social order consisted of a warrior aristocracy given to swagger and pillage, a powerful class of druids combining the functions of priest, educator and lawgiver, and dependent commoners including enslaved war captives.

Since there was a considerable number of tribes each with its own king – and the name of many a French town is derived from that of the local tribe – conflicts were inevitable, especially given the romantic temperament of people inclined to hunting, carousing and colourful display. In this essentially oral culture, the tradition was transmitted not only by druids but by bards and it was fused with an all-pervading polytheistic, animistic religion attributing sacred qualities to natural features and encompassing reincarnation and human sacrifice. Yet these 'barbarians' were also ingenious people, who practised surgery, excelled at metalwork and jewellery, had solar and lunar calendars, and are credited with the invention of soap, the wine barrel and the coat of mail. And, as recent archaeological investigation has shown, their architecture did not consist solely of round thatched huts, but included elegant buildings with tiled roofs and well-ordered public squares.[4]

The Romans had in fact been preceded in Gaul by the Greeks, who founded the trading post Massalia (the present-day Marseille) around 600 BC, and it was through their alliance with this important port that the Romans became engaged in Gaul. In 123 BC they established the fortress of Aquae Sextiae (Aix-en-Provence) and within a few years had achieved control of the Upper Rhône valley and set up the colony of Narbo Martius (Narbonne). Once engaged, however, they gradually found themselves having to cope not only with the local tribes but with Germanic invasions from the east which were a potential threat to northern Italy. It was such a Germanic incursion which brought Caesar to Gaul in 58 BC. He dealt with that and subsequent attempts in no uncertain fashion, but was led in the process to occupy the whole of Gaul, which unsettled the tribes and led eventually to the serious rebellion begun by Vercingétorix, (c. 72–46 BC) an imposing young nobleman from the Arverni tribe – which gave its name to the Auvergne – in 52 BC.

Having managed to band together the fractious tribes and inflict an initial defeat on Caesar, Vercingétorix successfully practised a scorched earth policy to deprive him of supplies, but was caught out by the refusal of the Bituriges to destroy their prized fortified capital Bourges and reluctantly agreed that they should defend it. They held out during a month-long siege with the reckless bravery that Caesar records with an admiration that did not prevent him from massacring the inhabitants – all 40,000 of them apart from some hundreds who had got out in time to join Vercingétorix.

Later in that same year, Caesar trapped Vercingétorix and his troops in the fortified town of Alésia, near present-day Dijon, and in the hope of starving them into submission set up the most elaborate siege works to prevent a breakout. As the Gauls, with food for no more than a month, attacked these ferociously, he strengthened them with further spiked ditches and embankments and then, to counter a relieving force consisting, as he claimed, of 8,000 cavalry and 250,000 foot soldiers, he set up similar defences facing outwards. The relief force arrived and attacked fiercely with the support of the defenders from the town, but their bravery and enthusiasm proved no match for Roman organization and the relief force broke up and fled. Meanwhile the starving inhabitants had come out to throw themselves on the mercy of the Romans, offering themselves as slaves, but had been left to rot in no-man's-land. In this situation Vercingétorix had little option but to throw his arms at the feet (not agonizingly *on* the feet, as the irreverent Astérix version has it) of this formidable Roman general in the scarlet cloak – who merely records in his matter-of-fact way that 'the leaders were brought, Vercingétorix handed over and the arms thrown down', adding that 'he distributed the remainder of the captives as prizes to his soldiers, one to each man'.[5]

It may well be that the defeat of Vercingétorix, contrary to the romantic legend, was a blessing for Gaul, that it was a great advance, as Voltaire was to argue, to be drawn away from druidic superstition, to become part of the Roman world and to have the protection for the next three centuries of the Pax Romana. Roman Gaul was given an administrative structure of four provinces, a capital at Lugdunum (Lyon), and a unifying infrastructure of new roads. The Romans built towns and promoted the growth of a new middle class of merchants and tradesmen. In short, they brought what, by the standards of the time, represented modernity and civilization – an indication of the stability of the new order being the emergence of Latin as the basis of French. Yet if all this was a blessing, it was a blessing that came in heavy disguise. It may be that up to a million people died over the seven years of the Gallic Wars, with another million enslaved as well as tribes dislocated and hundreds of towns destroyed. The cost of civilization and the price of peace were high.

As to Vercingétorix, he had to wait until Caesar had leisure to deal with him, for the victor had other wars to win – against Pompey, in Egypt and in Africa. It was five years before he found time to get back to Rome and organize a sequence of four lavishly expensive triumphs celebrating his victories. For the first of these Vercingétorix was brought out from the dark dungeon in the Tullianum prison where he had been mouldering all this time and made to stumble in chains in the parade through streets filled with cheering, jeering crowds. After which demonstration of power he was returned to prison and disposed of, doubtless in the usual manner, by strangulation – a less distinguished death than that of Caesar by assassination in the Senate less than two years later.

Yet for all its power the Roman Empire itself could not last indefinitely in the face of the chaotic migrations of peoples and shifts of world-view that were to take place during the first millennium of this era, releasing instability and violence that would bring down Rome and plunge western Europe into the Dark Ages.

For the next couple of centuries, however, so long as the good times lasted, Roman Gaul compared favourably with other parts of the Empire. The south in particular was something of a showcase because of its agricultural produce, its craft exports and the stately public buildings that can still be seen in Nîmes or Arles or Orange today. As for Paris, although known as Lutetia until the early fourth century AD and although its inhabitants had burnt it down rather than surrender to Caesar, it developed similarly into a well-ordered Roman town. And so Romanized over time did the inhabitants become that they gradually abandoned Gaulish in favour of Vulgar or spoken Latin – apart from place names there is only a handful of Celtic derivations in French today – and were ready to defend the new order against intermittent barbarian attacks from the east.

However, an incursion by the Franks in AD 257 and another in AD 354–5 by the Alemanni, who got as far as Lyon, were merely the prelude to a prolonged series of wholesale invasions by Germanic peoples, which began dramatically on the last day of the year AD 406 with a broad advance across the ice on the frozen Rhine. These peoples had been driven eastward by the pressure of the Huns advancing from Asia and threatening not only Gaul but

Rome itself – which was sacked again, by Visigoths in AD 410 and by Vandals in AD 455. Gaul, with a composite army under a Roman general, still possessed enough coherence to defeat Attila the Hun in an exceptionally bloody battle near Troyes when he invaded in AD 451, but by the end of that century, with the collapse of the Roman Empire itself in AD 476 compounding the death, destruction and chaos wrought by the invasions, Gallo-Roman civilization had almost been wiped out.

The one institution left standing, ironically, was the Christian Church. The Romans had in fact shown considerable tolerance towards the religious practices of the conquered territories, largely because other polytheistic systems offered no great threat and, as Tacitus observed, could be absorbed. But monotheistic Christianity was fundamentally different and, if the Empire engaged in heavy persecution of this new religion that was eating into Rome itself, it is because it saw it as a threat to the State – the plebeian or slave offered equality in an afterlife might be less inclined to accept the social order in this life. Accordingly, in Gaul as elsewhere, there were some notable martyrs – St Blandine fed to the lions with forty-seven others at Lyon in AD 177 and St Denis beheaded after appalling torture a century later. However, the persecutions came to a natural end with the conversion to Christianity of the emperor Constantine himself in AD 313, so that the Church remained the only structure which transcended Gaul itself and the sole repository of literacy and tradition.

The figure who emerged from the anarchy to create a Frankish kingdom was Clovis (AD 481–511), leader of one of the Salian Frankish tribes and king of the Merovingian dynasty centred on Tournai. Clovis, if he brought together the Church and the temporal power, was not himself a saintly individual – though, in these barbaric times, we would hardly have heard of him if he had been. In AD 486, with the support of the neighbouring Salian kings, he became master of northern Gaul by defeating the last Roman commander there at Soissons – and then simplifying life by assassinating his own allies in the endeavour. It is of Clovis that the famous story of '*le vase de Soissons*' is told. While about to share out by lot the riches pillaged from the churches, Clovis yields to the plea of a bishop to return one special silver chalice and asks his men to let him have it over and above his share of the spoils. They all agree with the exception of one, who says it is unfair and angrily smashes his axe into the chalice. A year later, seeing the same man on parade, Clovis reminds him of the incident – and of the respect due to the Church – by splitting his head with an axe.

Clovis's pursuit of power was relentless. He neutralized the Ostrogoths by marrying one of his sisters to their king and, having failed to conquer Burgundy, he formed an alliance with it instead in order to defeat the Alemanni at Tolbiac and take over their territory in the east. At which point, famously, he converted to Christianity and was baptized by Bishop Remigius at Reims.

It is true that his wife was Christian and that, having experimentally invoked her God on one occasion to help him win a battle, he had found that the magic worked. But he had also been under pressure from Bishop Remigius, who had boldly written to this pagan teenager as soon he came to power 'an astonishing letter', as one historian of the period rightly calls it, almost commanding him to defer to his bishops.[6] Clearly, just as Remigius understood the need for the Church to have the protection of a viable secular power, Clovis realized the advantage of having the support and validation of the Church. Once he had added most of Aquitaine to his conquests and established Paris as the capital of his new kingdom, he founded an abbey and gratefully accepted honours from the Church. And, while that did not deter him from systematically killing off several potential rivals among the Franks, relatives included, he convoked a synod of Catholic bishops just before he died in AD 511.

Is there a mystery about the unsatisfactory outcome of this death? For, unscrupulous or not, Clovis had accomplished extraordinary things. He had not only conquered Gaul and unified the Franks but, by allying himself with the Church, he had contributed towards the fusion of the Franks with the culture of Roman Gaul. And that fusion was beginning to take place, notably through intermarriage between the elites. The Franks were gradually accepting Latin as the language of administration and culture and moving over to everyday spoken Latin or Romance while still mixing it with their original Germanic speech. It is this fusion that becomes the *langue d'oïl*, the northern dialect from which modern French derives, as opposed to the *langue d'oc*, the dialect of the south where the Latin basis was stronger – *oïl* and *oc* being the two versions of the modern French *oui*.

Clovis's unifying achievements were therefore significant, but then, initiating a sequence that would be repeated over the next three centuries, he appeared to throw it all away. For at his death he divided his territory between his four sons and there began the pattern of division, reunification and further division that would cause conflict and weaken the Merovingian kings – several of them simple-minded or underage into the bargain – to the point that they became known as '*les rois fainéants*' or 'do-nothing kings' and were finally replaced by their own lieutenants, or 'mayors of the palace', who set up a new Carolingian dynasty in the year AD 754. And even beyond that the pattern continued to an extent that is almost comical, with the cartoon-like sobriquets bestowed on some of these kings – Pépin the Short, Charles the Fat, Louis the Stammerer – reminding us almost of the world of Astérix. So why this pattern of alternating unification and division?

There is no mystery. It is rather that we tend with hindsight to look at the issue teleologically or back-to-front and assume unconsciously that these rulers glimpsed the eventual possibility of a France not unlike the nicely balanced hexagon we know today. We may therefore tend to see anything that hinders the forward movement towards a modern centralized state in terms of decline or failure. But if Clovis and other kings followed the Frankish form of succession, it was because they were concerned with personal and family power, while the external body they had to consider was not the state – there were no states in our sense – but the Church. In the chaotic Europe of the period, there was no vision or necessity leading inevitably to France as it exists today but, on the contrary, a great deal of chance – as the career of Charles Martel illustrates.

A giant of a man in more ways than one, Charles Martel (*c.* AD 727–41), known as Charles the Hammer because of his military prowess, was a resourceful 'mayor of the palace' who fought his way to power in a war of succession. An excellent administrator, he was also a brilliantly inventive general who established his authority over all three of the squabbling kingdoms into which the Frankish realm had been divided. But the achievement for which he has been hailed as the saviour of European civilization by a range of historians from Gibbon to Henri Pirenne was his victory at the Battle of Tours in AD 732 over an invading Muslim army marching northwards from Spain.

Thoroughly prepared, with 30,000 men, Charles took the enemy by surprise on high ground of his choosing, which forced its cavalry to attack uphill against the square formation of his massed infantry. This was a rare example of infantry being effective against cavalry, although when the Muslims broke off after the death of their commander it was doubtless also with an eye to saving their booty. It was perhaps one of the decisive battles in world history since, had he failed to roll back the Islamic expansion which had already swept over Spain, the history of France and Europe might have been very different indeed. But there was nothing inevitable about the victory, which was very much against the odds and achieved only through the exceptional strategic skill of this particular individual.

In the event the relations between Frankish rulers and the Church became so close as to be an alliance when Charles Martel's son Pépin the Short, having ousted the nominal king, got the Pope not only to accept his *coup d'état* but to consecrate his new Carolingian dynasty. And his own son Charlemagne (*c.* AD 768–814) would be seen as the model Christian ruler, the shield and sword of the Church, indeed as the towering figure in the Europe of this period, who brought the Dark Ages to at least a temporary end – a towering figure in more ways than one, incidentally, in that unlike his father he was exceptionally tall. Having secured his own position in the usual manner by eliminating potential rivals among his relatives, he proceeded to expand his kingdom by invading Lombardy, Bohemia and northern Spain, then held by the Moors – a campaign which would later be celebrated in the famous twelfth-century verse-chronicle *La Chanson de Roland* (*The Song of Roland*). He also made repeated attempts to Christianize the pagan Saxons by making them an offer they could not comfortably refuse: convert or die. Some failed to grasp the merits of the offer and were executed – over 4,000 on one day in one instance – but the method proved effective, though it did raise an eyebrow or two in court circles.

In AD 799, Pope Leo III came under attack from members of the Roman nobility who resented his accession to the papacy. In an attempt to disqualify him they sent a gang to tear out his eyes and cut out his tongue, but Leo escaped in time and fled to seek help from Charlemagne. Although unimpressed by the Pope, Charlemagne sent a delegation which restored him to the papal throne and followed this up with a personal visit to Rome, where on Christmas Day 800 Leo crowned him emperor. Charlemagne claimed that he did not know this was to happen, but that seems unlikely. If the Pope gained by securing his position, this spectacular consecration of the leader of a confederation of Germanic tribes also enhanced Charlemagne's status enormously. From his capital in Aachen, or Aix-la-Chapelle, he now controlled a Frankish empire stretching from the Atlantic to Bavaria and from the North Sea to the Mediterranean. And this formal alliance with the Church would establish the idea of a Holy Roman Empire which would run through the Middle Ages. It may be true, as wicked little Voltaire typically remarked, that this agglomeration of a Holy Roman Empire was 'neither holy, nor Roman nor an empire', but it was an aspiration that was to run through the war-torn Middle Ages – and feed the idea of a united Europe later entertained, however differently, by Napoleon and the European Union of today.[7]

Meanwhile, Charlemagne was playing his role with impressive energy. He created a central administration, enlisting clerics – the only literate group – as civil servants. He sent imperial envoys throughout the realm, held yearly assemblies of court officials, magistrates and nobles, introduced legal reforms, standardized weights and customs tolls, and dispensed judgements on matters of public order. He issued decrees relating to church structures and religious education – social, legal and religious issues being regarded as not inherently different. He also made great efforts to raise the cultural level of his court, improving his own literacy by learning Latin, founding an academy for the education of young Frankish knights, and inviting the English theologian Alcuin to Aachen to become his religious and educational adviser. In fact he brought about a Carolingian renaissance. It is true that his empire could not compare with the real Roman Empire as regards the basic features – political institutions, permanent army or roads infrastructure – that provide solidity and continuity. Nevertheless the achievements of this strong and determined man were remarkable. Which did not prevent the legacy from falling apart yet again.

Though before he died in AD 814 he had decreed that the realm should be divided between his three sons, it came down intact to his son Louis the Pious by the simple accident that the other two died before their father. But when Louis in his turn divided the kingdom between his own three sons on his death in AD 840, he predictably precipitated civil war. Yet this regular splitting of the kingdom, the destructive discontinuity caused by the alternation of unification and disintegration, was only half of the problem. It was not simply that the system was over-dependent on the strong leader like Charles Martel or Charlemagne who could only be expected to crop up occasionally; the reality was that the more this strong leader succeeded in unifying and enlarging his realm, the more he ran into its inherent contradictions. For the days of the one-man rule of the tribal chieftain who could regard his realm as personal property to be divided up among his heirs as he chose were fading. And the larger the realm, the larger the difficulties. Charlemagne, ironically, by his very success in increasing so dramatically the size of his kingdom, had tested the system to destruction.

The division of Charlemagne's kingdom had profound consequences for the future not only of France but of Europe – and, incidentally, the Strasbourg Oaths of AD 842 by which two of Louis's sons, Louis the German and Charles the Bald, sealed their alliance against their brother Lothair, was the first official document in the then current form of French. The Treaty of Verdun of the following year divided the territory into a western third approximating broadly to the future France, an eastern third which would correspond to the German-speaking area east of the Rhine, and an intermediate strip extending from the Netherlands down the Rhine towards the Mediterranean. This partition helped to create the destructive tensions that would arise in the future between France and Germany over control of what in effect was an ambiguous buffer zone between them.

Meanwhile, the inheritance of Charles the Bald (AD 840–77) would become the basis of the medieval kingdom of France. However, since the partition had been made largely on grounds of administrative convenience, the borders of his kingdom were somewhat artificial. Also, the old pattern of division, partial reunification and further division persisted, so that the kings would remain weak and the kingdom unstable. And the instability was much increased during these ninth and tenth centuries by further Arab attacks from the south and, above all, by the invasion and effective colonization of Normandy from the north by the much-feared Norsemen.

It was precisely in response to this fragmentation of authority and to a general sense of anarchy and insecurity that the feudal system developed. Of course under Charlemagne the system existed whereby he made grants of land – the essential asset of value at this time – to his vassals in exchange for their sworn loyalty and their services to him as warriors or administrators. However, the system began increasingly to be replicated at regional and local levels, with castles – simple defensive wooden structures initially – sprouting up across the land. So a nobleman also bound to himself as vassals men of rank who served as *chevaliers*, or armoured knights on horseback – it is from the code of behaviour of this self-consciously stylish class that the idea of chivalry derives. And the principle of interdependence operated down through the ranks, in that these high-born vassals might have their own local vassals, while the peasants worked and fought for their lord when required in return for his protection.

It was in fact a complete system of legal and property relationships, implying protection and maintenance on one side in exchange for service and obedience on the other. But, while it responded to the insecurity of the time, it tended to weaken the kings, especially as the fiefs granted to vassals gradually became hereditary and therefore the vassals themselves became more independent. Increasingly, there were powerful regional noblemen capable of challenging royal power. The king could try to hold their loyalty through further grants of land or booty but, since these tended to depend on waging war, that could destabilize the situation further. He therefore had to rely to a great extent on soft power, moral authority gained through a sense of tradition and through the validation of the Church.

So it was not a strong kingdom that Hugues Capet (*c.* AD 987–96), a nobleman from the Île-de-France, took over from the failing Carolingian dynasty. It had no ethnic or linguistic coherence, with Franks, Bretons and others speaking a variety of languages ranging from German in the north-east to Basque in the south-west – quite apart from the difference in the Romance-speaking areas between *langue d'oïl* and *langue d'oc*. In practice, Hugues's writ only ran in his own central area of the Île-de-France and the Orléanais. Indeed, if he ventured beyond it he risked being kidnapped for ransom, for the rest of the kingdom was controlled by the rulers of the virtually independent regions, such as the Duc d'Aquitaine, the Duc de Normandie or the Comte d'Auvergne. Add to that the lack of a common currency or legal system and the general disorder of the times and it is easy to imagine the problem of ruling over such a fragmented kingdom. Hugues did in fact have to fight various power battles during his reign and he survived a plot against him in AD 993, though his position was too weak to enable him to punish the perpetrators.

Even so, he had certain advantages. For a start, he had been elected by an assembly of nobles, which gave him some authority. Also, he had been consecrated King of the Franks with the strong support of the Church – indeed the Archbishop of Reims had largely been responsible for engineering his election. And, while the central area which he directly controlled from Paris was relatively small, it was one of the richest in the kingdom. Moreover, on coming to the throne he immediately had his son crowned as his successor on the pretence that he intended to undertake a campaign against Moorish incursions in Spain and that there needed to be a king on the throne during his absence. All this enabled him to consolidate his family's rule and inaugurate a Capetian dynasty which would last until 1328. And, while other branches of the line would take over in France, the Capetian dynasty has lingered on with King Juan Carlos of Spain and the Comte de Paris, as well as in the ancestry of Queen Elizabeth II of Great Britain.

By the end of the first millennium, clearly, there was not yet a kingdom directly resembling what we know as France. Nor could there be until these weak Capetian kings succeeded in redressing the imbalance between themselves and their over-mighty vassals. If only in retrospect, however, the arrival of the Capetians may be seen as the start of the long process leading by default towards an independent French kingdom.

2

A NATION BORN IN BLOOD

The world of the Middle Ages never really seems remote in France; it lingers on in the many towns where the cathedral is the central defining feature, as in Chartres or Senlis. It is a natural part of the scene in the old quarters of towns such as Sarlat or Avignon, as it is spectacularly present in the fortified walled cities of Loches or Carcassonne. In Paris itself, quite apart from the cathedral of Notre Dame or the Sainte Chapelle, it has left echoes in the Latin Quarter, so called because Latin was the lingua franca for students of the Sorbonne in the Middle Ages and indeed for several centuries thereafter. Academic titles such as *baccalauréat* (higher school certificate) and *licence* (BA) date from that time, as do certain traditional courtesies, titles of nobility and the practice of investiture.

Of course the whole period has been bathed in the soft light of romance over the centuries by troubadours and historical novelists, to say nothing of Hollywood. It evokes stylized images of noble kings and gracious queens, of pious faces in stone or stained glass, of chivalrous Crusaders heroically confronting the infidel, of armoured knights galloping towards each other with threatening lances on royal jousts, of chaste ladies looking down from the slit windows of castle towers upon pining lovers in doublet and hose with one leg of one colour, one leg of another and impossibly elongated pointed shoes. But what was it like to be living at such a time – a time of stark contrasts, when spirituality co-existed with refined cruelty and the religious aspiration expressed in the great cathedrals sought to offer certainty to people living short lives subject to the vagaries of harvests, plague and intermittent war?

While the quality of life depended on economic and cultural development, that in turn depended largely on the extent to which the feudal kingdom could provide peace and stability. But it was 100 years and more before the Capetian kings began to gain some control over a kingdom that was constituted on three levels in a kind of confused jigsaw. There was the royal domain itself, the Île-de-France and the Orléanais; there were the apanages, lands given to sons of one king or another over the years – which reverted to the throne if the incumbent, or kinglet, died without issue. And then there were large provincial fiefdoms like Guyenne or Flanders which were formally part of the kingdom but which were virtually independent. The problem for successive kings, who throughout the eleventh century could not control the disorder in their own inner domain, was once again not to create a unitary French state – that dream had not yet been dreamt – but simply to make this feudal system work. And they did not have a strong hand to play.

They now had the moral authority acquired through their sanctification by the Church in the traditional coronation in Reims, strengthened by the belief in the king's miraculous ability to cure scrofula, or the 'king's evil'. The king was politically the suzerain, or feudal overlord, to all the nobles in the kingdom. But he had little leverage over increasingly independent vassals enjoying their now hereditary estates in their imposing new castles. Again, the old practice of dividing estates among the sons, which had created so many problems with the royal succession, caused continual private wars among the minor nobles who had often little else to do but strike knightly attitudes.

So the eleventh century was a time of brigandage, feuding and general anarchy and it was left to the Church to try to limit the bloodshed by instituting a 'Truce of God'. This condemned fighting between Wednesday evening and Monday morning – and fighting by priests, monks and women on any day of the week – but in effect legitimized fighting on the other three days of the week. And Pope Urban II was still criticizing violence among the nobility and trying to turn 'robbers into knights' when, at the Council of Clermont in 1095, he issued his passionate call to believers to go forth and wrest back from the Muslim infidels the holy city of Jerusalem.

This was the first of the eight Crusades from Europe that were to take place over the next two centuries, and which were to have important consequences. They unified the Christian world by providing a global cause and channelling destructive energies outwards towards a common enemy demonized as the infidel. They stimulated economic development by opening up trade routes and also introduced new concepts into European culture. The Capetian kingdom gained in prestige from the First Crusade in particular, since it had been proclaimed in France and since it contributed to the enterprise such leading figures as Godefroi de Bouillon and Hugues le Grand, the brother of King Philippe I (1060–1108). Not that the Crusaders were all knights – in fact the majority of the 40,000 or so who 'took up the cross' were peasants who were attracted to the adventure of a lifetime presented in such apocalyptic terms. Of course, as is the way with holy wars where absolute conviction necessarily defines the opponent as evil or worthless, this three-year expedition was a murderous affair on both sides. The Crusaders, to whom Pope Urban had promised remission of sins for any who died in the endeavour, pillaged, massacred Jewish and Muslim civilians, and performed other atrocities in the standard fashion of the time. However, the Crusades helped to strengthen the Capetian dynasty, not just by associating it with a noble myth but in more practical ways.

For the Crusades had the unintended consequence of weakening the power of the nobles, since a number were killed or died in foreign lands, while others were all but ruined by the cost of kitting out a private army for an expedition lasting years. Meanwhile, the craftsmen and traders who had equipped them had done quite nicely out of it. Indeed a new trading class was emerging which resented the constraints of the feudal system, while craftsmen were forming themselves into guilds and organizing free towns in an attempt to escape the payment of feudal dues. Thus the throne now had a potential ally in the new commercial class of the growing towns and the first to take advantage of this was the spectacularly fat but energetic Louis VI, le Gros (1108–37), who began to grant royal charters to towns and in return received support from their militias in his effort to control the general disorder. For twenty years he was largely occupied with suppressing brigandage, besieging the robber barons in their castles and punishing wrongdoers. Well advised by his childhood friend Abbé Suger, he also had the Church and the peasantry on his side and by the time he passed the baton to his son, the very pious Louis VII (1137–80), the job of establishing the king's authority had largely been accomplished.

Yet the strengthening of the monarchy began to bring out two larger problems which would become more pressing in the thirteenth and fourteenth centuries. The first was the relationship with the Vatican and the extent of its control

over the French Church. Louis, pious though he was, refused
to accept the Pope's nominee in preference to his own
candidate as Archbishop of Bourges, which brought a papal
interdict and led to a war with the Comte de Champagne, in
the course of which Louis was involved in the murder of
more than 1,000 people, burnt to death in the church at Vitry.
Consumed by guilt, he sought to redeem himself by going on
a Crusade – though the fact that he was accompanied by his
wife, Aliénor (Eleanor) of Aquitaine and a bevy of her ladies
did not exactly endear him to the Pope.

Aliénor was an attractive, feisty and forceful lady at a time
when women's roles were very secondary and it is not
surprising that she should feature in many historical films
and novels.[1] Coming at the age of fifteen from the more
relaxed, sophisticated Aquitaine court in Poitiers, she felt
that she had been married off to a monk rather than a king
and was seen as wayward and flighty. On their catastrophic
Crusade, she quarrelled with Louis over strategy and was
assumed to have had an affair with her young uncle
Raymond of Antioch – whose severed head, after his defeat,
was presented on a platter to the Caliph of Baghdad. Upon
their eventual return, since she had also produced no sons,
the marriage was dissolved – which is where the second
problem emerges.

Almost at once she married the young Henry Plantagenet,
who within two years would become King Henry II of
England. However, she retained her title to the duchy of
Aquitaine, which meant that the Angevin dynasty – so called
because Henry was also the Comte d'Anjou – now
controlled England, Normandy and the whole coastal area
right down to the Pyrenees. Henry was still the vassal of his
feudal overlord Louis, but the mismatch between the feudal
system and the actual power relationship would challenge
the Capetian kings throughout the thirteenth century – and
indeed would throw up dynastic conflicts that would take
300 years to resolve.

Philippe Auguste (1180–1223), the son of Louis VII, was a cunning and determined character. Sharply aware of the rising Angevin threat, he fought for over thirty years against the forces of three successive Angevin kings: Henry II, Richard the Lionheart and King John. By the end he had acquired Normandy, Brittany, Anjou, Maine, Poitou and Touraine, conquests which he consolidated at the Battle of Bouvines in 1214 – in effect establishing his kingdom as a leading European power. He also made considerable improvements at home, professionalizing his administration, creating financial stability and protecting the interests of the rising middle class of the towns. He had the main streets of Paris paved, continued the construction of Notre Dame and built the central market of Les Halles while, by granting a charter to the Sorbonne, he recognized that it was now the intellectual centre of medieval Christendom.

In his canny fashion Philippe Auguste contrived to be too busy to respond to the Pope's appeal to lead the Crusade against the Cathars. This holy war, against other Christians this time, was proclaimed by Pope Innocent III in 1209 in order to suppress the heretical Cathars or Albigensians – so called after the southern town of Albi. The Cathars were peaceful, but were Manichean in outlook, emphasized the moral teaching of Christ rather than the resurrection and – a crucial factor in the Pope's eyes – rejected the sacraments. In effect they were denying the whole ministering role of the Church, which they also saw as too worldly, and to that extent might be seen as early Protestants.

The Pope's proclamation brought many thousands of knights and peasants, encouraged by the guarantee of remission of sins and the possibility of seizing land from the Cathars, to descend on Languedoc under the leadership of Simon de Montfort.[2] An early episode was the slaughter of the inhabitants of Béziers during which the papal legate Arnald Amalric, when asked who should be spared, is said to have replied 'Kill them all, God will recognize his own.'

Simon himself, ferociously devout and devoutly ferocious, tortured and killed, and had the eyes torn out of those he allowed to live. Since all this, not surprisingly, provoked resistance, the affair dragged on for decades until the Vatican brought in the Inquisition to crush it, by which time up to a million people may have been killed across the south. Meanwhile the Crusade had turned inevitably into a war of conquest – of which the winners, in the end, were the crafty Philippe Auguste and his successors, who absorbed Languedoc.

However, the reign which is seen as the high point of a golden thirteenth century is that of Louis IX (1226–70), sanctified after his death as St Louis and a legendary figure for French schoolchildren. Tutored by his dominant mother Blanche of Castile, he was an ascetically pious figure much given to the hair shirt, fasting and practising humility by washing the feet of his nobles. This did not prevent him from jealously protecting his independence from the Vatican, as though anticipating the later concept of the absolute monarch as deriving his authority directly from God. And the absolutist severity of his religious belief, once again, dictated his ready approval of the Inquisition's use of torture and confiscation against the Cathars, as of the slaughter of infidels in the Crusades. He himself went eagerly on two Crusades, the first of which he financed by expelling Jews for usury and confiscating their lands. Both were disastrous failures, since he had to be ransomed after capture on the Seventh Crusade and died of fever on the Eighth in 1270. But they added to the lustre of a king who, however stark his religious zeal, blended severity with justice and did much good for his kingdom.

For he reformed the courts in an attempt to provide more equal justice and encouraged the use of Roman law. He forced the nobles to fulfil their obligations, improved the administration of taxes and founded the Quinze-Vingts hospital for the poor in Paris. He patronized the arts, encouraged the spread of Gothic cathedrals and built the magnificent Sainte Chapelle as his court chapel.

He was as shrewd and successful in strengthening his kingdom. In 1259, in an attempt to put an end to longstanding claims and counter-claims, he ceded Limoges, Cahors and Périgueux to Henry III of England in return for Henry's renunciation of any claim to Normandy, Anjou, Maine, Poitou or Touraine. He also exchanged his claim to Roussillon and Barcelona for the King of Aragon's claim to Provence and Languedoc. All this led him to be seen as the ideal Christian prince and his kingdom, at a time of relative peace and prosperity, as the most prestigious in Christendom.

It was left to Louis IX's grandson Philippe IV (1285–1314), called le Bel or the Fair on account of his cold good looks, to tackle the underlying problem of the relationship with the Vatican and to see the kingdom into a troubled fourteenth century. With nothing saintly about him other than his hair shirt, Philippe changed the rules of the game in more ways than one. He proceeded to govern less like the head of a feudal kingdom than that of a centralized monarchy, with more general taxation and a state bureaucracy which tended to sideline the nobles. This, together with military expenses and ambitious rebuilding schemes, demanded ever more money. So he dispossessed the money-lending Lombards and then the Jews, before taxing the clergy, whereupon he was threatened with excommunication by Pope Boniface VIII, who believed kings to be accountable to himself.

Philippe's answer was to send a diplomatic hit squad to rough up the Pope and to have the papacy transferred to Avignon, with a tame new Pope in the form of Clément V. This not only asserted the independence of the French Church, but helped when in his search for money he set out with the connivance of Clément to destroy the wealthy order of the Knights Templar, which had unwisely refused to finance a war with England. This was achieved through the Inquisition, with elaborate torture to extract patently false confessions, the sad paradox being that, as one writer puts it, 'the most frightening of the inquisitors were the incorruptible ones, who tortured purely and simply for the love of God'.[3] A flavour of Philippe's style may be given by his treatment of two clandestine young lovers of his daughters-in-law – who were publicly flayed, castrated, disembowelled, beheaded and then strung up by their armpits. None of this was pretty, but by the end of his reign he had largely achieved political control of the Church and had moved the feudal kingdom towards something approaching a more integrated modern monarchy.

The gradual increase in security over the three centuries up to Philippe's death in 1314 had encouraged both economic and cultural development. Of course it was still an agricultural economy and work in the fields was harsh, with only oxen available as draught animals and – before the arrival of New World plants such as potatoes, maize and tomatoes – a limited range of crops. The cereal-based diet was poor, harvests could fail, and there was no protection from smallpox or typhoid. Even so, with broadly benign climatic conditions, the clearing of forests for planting, the introduction of crop rotation and an improvement in yields, the situation had improved to the point where the population had trebled to around 15 million. The energy was to be found in the rapidly growing towns, centres of local and often through trade, with their markets, their specialized craftsmen, their fairs, their jugglers, their pickpockets, their prostitutes and their itinerant beggars. By the thirteenth century there was also a rising middle class of educated servants of the throne, as administrators or magistrates. The towns, however cramped and insanitary the conditions, were where the future lay.

Culture and education in this period depended essentially on the Church. The two greatest monastic orders of the Middle Ages, the Benedictines and the more austere Cistercians, arose in Burgundy. The Benedictines, in particular, had much to do with the spread of churches across the country and originated the highly influential Cluniac Reforms, named after their abbey at Cluny, designed to remove corruption from the Church and protect it from secular interference. The university of Paris grew out of the cathedral school of Notre Dame and competing schools such as Ste Geneviève and the college founded in 1257 by Robert de Sorbon, who would give his name to the Sorbonne in the mid-sixteenth century.

Luminaries of this period when Paris had become the leading centre for theological studies include the prolific St Thomas Aquinas and the charismatic Peter Abelard – whose tragic love affair with his student Héloïse, for which her uncle had him castrated, has inevitably led to fictional treatments which perhaps obscure his importance as a scholastic thinker.[4] As for literature, while there were pious stories celebrating the Virgin and semi-liturgical plays on biblical themes, there were also secular works in the form of heroic verse-chronicles such as *La Chanson de Roland*, or didactic narrative poems such as the lengthy *Le Roman de la Rose* (*The Romance of the Rose*) – in which Love instructs the would-be courtly Lover not to stand around with his mouth open and to serve and honour ladies at all times. Happily perhaps, these invited bourgeois take-offs such as the *Le Roman de Renart* (*The Romance of Renart the Fox*) or satirical verses such as those of Rutebeuf.

Still, the iconic image of the French Middle Ages is doubtless the Gothic cathedral. And it is true that the religious fervour which expressed itself in the cruelties of the Inquisition or the massacres of the Crusades also expressed the direct opposite in these powerfully aspirational buildings. If Gothic was a derisive term used by Renaissance artists for a style they thought barbarous, it is because it represented a startling departure from the Romanesque style, with its round arches, to be found in the basilicas of Toulouse or Vézelay. The new style responded to the idea of the Abbé Suger, who pioneered it at St Denis, of *lux continua* or unbroken light. This called for a new understanding of vertical and lateral thrusts and, above all, for a strikingly bold venture into the structural possibilities of the pointed arch and the ribbed vault, the aim being to reduce the stone structure to a skeletal framework.

The style took time to develop and it is probably with thirteenth-century cathedrals such as Reims or Amiens that it achieved its purest form, before mutating into the flamboyant Gothic style of the fourteenth century. Suger's *lux continua* was achieved, modulated through vast new areas of stained glass, so that the cathedral could now speak with three complementary voices: the towering new height of the nave, the sculpture on portals, columns or choir screens, and the coloured images on the stained glass. And this created a whole new glass industry in such centres as St Denis and Poitiers, driven by the desire to improve translucency and to develop new colours – such as the famous 'Chartres blue'.

What then, to take this particular example of Chartres, did the cathedral mean to the people of the town? First of all, as the only stone building other than the castle, it was an enormously dominant structure which could be seen from far away across the rich plain of Beauce. It was an important place of pilgrimage since it housed the Sancta Camisia, a garment said to have belonged to the Virgin Mary and to have been miraculously preserved from fire. And since the pilgrims came mainly on important feast days, when big fairs were held, they brought good business – though the cathedral portals in any event served as a marketplace for traders selling their various wares. Inevitably the basilica, dedicated in the presence of Louis IX, also represented the throne, with kings and queens alongside religious figures in its statuary. In addition Chartres had a cathedral school, it served as a sleeping-place for pilgrims, as a hospital in times of pestilence and as a place where journeymen came to be hired – in short it was the town centre.

Yet it also superbly fulfilled its religious purpose. For the illiterate faithful, unable to understand the Latin, the building itself was the message. The soaring nave echoing to the plainsong; the richness of the vestments, the magnificence of the silver on the altar, the glorious stained glass that told the Bible story in scenes animated magically from without by the changing light of day, the sweet Madonna and Child in the startling Blue Virgin window – to people of brief, harsh and uncertain lives this holy place was the very threshold of heaven. Even more profoundly, in the realism and humanism of the stone statuary, where they could see humble faces just like their own, they could sense that they themselves shared equally in this transcendence which reconciled God and man – that this religion of dread and vengeance was also a religion of charity and of love.

Unfortunately, the fourteenth century was going to throw up challenges which neither the Church nor the feudal system itself could meet. First there was the Great Famine, due to cold and wet winters from 1314 to 1317, which left bad harvests unable to support the increasing population. It hit the towns hardest, causing food shortages and rising prices, while desperate people roamed around, burning, looting or killing Jews. Next there was the epidemic, possibly of anthrax, which killed much of the livestock in 1318, leaving weakened immune systems to be attacked by epidemics of leprosy and typhoid. All this was set against the background of the collapse of the Capetian royal succession, a further demonstration of the danger of running a political system as a family business. For Philippe Le Bel's three sons died so fast that they only managed fourteen years on the throne between them. So in 1328 the crown passed – after an exceptional process of election by notables – to Philippe's nephew Philippe de Valois (1328–50), thereby starting a new Valois dynasty. The throne should strictly have gone to Philippe le Bel's grandson, the sixteen-year-old Edward III,

King of England, but to have a French king subordinate to the English throne was unacceptable. Edward did pay due homage to the new king, Philippe VI, at the coronation in Reims, but relations worsened and, after various tit-for-tat provocations, Philippe declared in 1337 that Edward had forfeited Aquitaine because of rebellion, triggering the Hundred Years War.

This was a war of succession within an overextended feudal system and as such, given that Edward had support from other vassals in the north and south-west, it was a kind of civil war. It was also a straggly affair that dragged on confusedly in intermittent fashion for 116 years. Initially, it seemed that Philippe as the leader of the richer and far more highly populated country would win comfortably, but he was defeated in the naval Battle of Sluis and then in the land Battle of Crécy (1346), when the English longbowmen made short work of lumbering French knights in their heavy armour. In the following year Edward captured Calais, but Philippe was too weak to confront him and, when he withdrew to plan a counter-attack and invasion of England, he failed to raise the money. As if that was not bad enough the greatest disaster of all arrived, one that was to have lasting consequences: the Black Death.

The Black Death, which was to ravage Europe as far as Ireland and Sweden and kill around a third of the population, arrived from the east in Marseilles in January 1348. By the month of June it had spread north to Paris and beyond. It struck so fast that, as the chronicler Jean de Venette reported, 'it was almost impossible to bury the dead ... He who was well one day was dead the next and being taken to his grave.'[5] His account of the symptoms, sudden swellings in the armpit or in the groin, tends to support the standard view that this was a bubonic plague. At all events, with 800 people a day dying in Paris at one stage, it was devastating. And it was mysterious. It swept through the city, disappeared, came back for more victims in 1349, then disappeared again the following year. It would kill every member of a monastery or village and for some capricious reason spare just one. But it was no respecter of hierarchy: it killed high and low, priest and sinner, man and woman, young and old, even the animals in the fields. And no remedy would work.

Lancing the boils, bloodletting or purging did not work. Nor did aromatic herbs or rosewater or the alchemists' potions. Neither did beseeching the Virgin, or killing those agents of the Devil, the cats, or killing lepers and beggars, or burning those age-old enemies of Christendom, the Jews. Not even the new breed of well-paid 'plague doctors', like sinister figures from a Venetian carnival in their protective garb and long bird-like masks, could stop the carnage. In this pre-scientific age – 600 years before the plague bacillus was identified – the problem could not be conceptualized, let alone resolved. There was no point in wondering whether it was due to 'bad air' released by an earthquake or to a recent alignment of the planets, since God aligned the planets and controlled the earthquakes. In the enclosed, absolutist mental world of the Middle Ages it could only, as the Pope duly recognized, come from God and, given that God was all-good, it could only be God's punishment for mankind's sin. But since the Church, with its closed communities, had if anything been hit harder than others, was this God's judgment on the Church? It is little wonder that the Church should have been outshone in penitence by the new, highly disciplined body of Flagellants, who gave ceremonial form to the collective moral hysteria by processing from town to town, savagely scourging themselves in a ritual demonstration of their awesome capacity to suffer for the guilt of being. Had the long-announced Judgement Day arrived?

The tragic irony was that, in this society without sanitation or running water and in which people rarely washed or changed their clothes, the remedies merely fed the disease. Bloodletting reduced the victim's resistance. Since the bacillus was carried by the flea associated with the black rat, it hardly helped to kill the 'evil' cats that could have killed the rats. If the Jews were less affected, it was because their religious practices made them more scrupulous about cleanliness. As for the Flagellants, in moving from town to town they were simply spreading the disease. In this dire situation people did what they could: prayed, shunned others, locked themselves in their houses, fled to the countryside or the forest. Some, to live a little before their number came up, squandered all they had on wine, women or whatever – if this was the End of the World, why not go out with a flourish? It was a catastrophe which discredited the Church, dislocated the feudal system and enthroned Death as the meaning of life in tomb sculpture, as in the grinning skeletons dancing with the living in the new artistic fashion of the *danse macabre*.

Certainly it provided a resonant background to the interminable dynastic Hundred Years War, which continued as a free-for-all across the devastated land, with hard-pressed nobles trying to kidnap other nobles for ransom or grab their lands, while roving mercenary bands passed the time between engagements by pillaging, looting and raping. And the war was going badly for the French, with a heavy defeat by the Black Prince at Poitiers in 1356, in the course of which Philippe de Valois's successor, the frivolous Jean II, Le Bon (1350–63), was taken prisoner and sat out the fighting in royal comfort in England while his son scrabbled around for the large ransom – which helped to provoke a serious middle-class rising under Étienne Marcel in Paris and a peasant revolt in the Île-de-France.

It was only with the accession of the frail, but wise and cultivated Charles V, Le Sage (1364–80) that the situation improved. Restoring dignity to the court – his father Jean had over-promoted his gay lover only to see him murdered – he also employed proper generals like Bernard Du Guesclin instead of nobles in search of glory, set up a regular professional army of paid soldiers and chose to use hit-and-run tactics instead of set battles. At his death in 1380, he left the English with no more than Calais and Aquitaine, though the schism in the Church which would last for another forty years meant that there were now two popes – one in Avignon backed by the French and one in Rome supported by the English.

But the feudal system was taking a long time to die. For all his achievements, Charles showed that he was still locked into the old mindset by providing his three brothers with large fiefs as apanages. Which by itself was a recipe for internal conflict, even without the circumstance that his son Charles VI (1380–1422) was only twelve when he came to the throne, had no taste for kingship, went mad at twenty-four and was a plaything in the hands of his squabbling uncles and his dissolute wife Isabeau.

The court soon resolved itself into two warring factions, the loyalist Armagnacs and the Burgundians, who favoured a fusion with England. In an effort to force the issue, Henry V of England invaded, destroyed the flower of French chivalry at the Battle of Agincourt in 1415 and, by the Treaty of Troyes of 1420, not only had himself declared heir to the throne but had the king's son Charles designated a bastard and formally disinherited. But no sooner had the treaty been signed than both Charles VI and Henry V were dead, which left the loyalists saluting as their new king the nineteen-year-old Charles VII (1422–61) and the Burgundians hailing the one-year-old Henry VI. So in addition to two popes there would now be two kings – and civil war. Which is where the legendary Joan of Arc enters the scene.

The Maid of Orléans was a myth in her own time and has been seen as something of a mystery ever since – which has enabled her to be adopted for political propaganda purposes by right, left and centre, if most recently by the Front National, which congregates annually before her gilded statue in the Rue de Rivoli. However, she becomes much less mysterious when placed back in her medieval context, even if the bare facts of her short life of nineteen years are strange enough. An illiterate but shrewd country girl who heard the voices of various saints telling her she had been chosen to expel the English from France, she put on male clothing for protection and made her way in 1429 to Chinon to see Charles VII. Since the English and their Burgundian allies controlled almost all of the north, including Paris and Reims, the king, indecisive and suspicious as he was, was in dire straits. Having given him a secret message from her voices – probably that he was not a bastard, though even his own mother Isabeau had said that he was – she was questioned at length by priests and had her virginity checked. She was then attached in April 1429 to a small force sent to attempt to relieve the besieged city of Orléans, a key stronghold on the Loire without which Charles would be unable to proceed to the traditional coronation at Reims.

The listless English army having left a gap in their defences, her unit was easily able to enter the city with fresh supplies. The over-cautious commander Jean d'Orléans regarded her as something of a nuisance, excluded her from war councils and tried to keep her out of the action, but Joan was irrepressible. She inspired the troops, kept them from swearing, dictated defiant ultimatums to the enemy in which she described herself as 'Joan the Maid, the envoy of the King of heaven', and took part in several actions, in one of which she was lightly wounded. There is no doubt that her courage and conviction as standard-bearer – she is not thought to have fought with a sword – made a decisive contribution to the lifting of the siege, which was achieved in nine days. But while her magic seemed to go on working for a while, she was captured by the Burgundians the following year, sold on to the English and, under pressure from the clerics of the Sorbonne, tried in Rouen as a heretic. She performed well in a prolonged battle of wits, but was condemned and burnt at the stake – to be rehabilitated in 1456 and made a saint in 1920.

So what was the source of Joan's extreme strength of conviction? In the first place, her childhood was spent in a rare loyalist enclave in a pro-Burgundian part of the Vosges, leaving her vivid memories of seeing raiders torch her village that defined the enemy for her very early on. Secondly, the experience of voices and visions was common in the Middle Ages, especially among illiterate people whose mental activity was largely conducted through images and projections, so they were doubtless real not only to her but to her interrogators – the question being rather whether they came from God or the Devil. It is significant that she first heard the voices at the impressionable stage of puberty, when they were commanding her to preserve her virginity, so that in accepting the mission she was like a girl perceiving a vocation to be a bride of Christ – which explains the emotional force of her conviction. Joan was playing for the highest of high stakes and, indeed, seems to have nourished the ultimate dream of freeing the country of the English and making the king the emperor of all Christendom so that he could reconquer the Holy Land and initiate a new millennium of purity and justice. It was this that enabled her to grasp so clearly the essential political imperative: that Charles could only impose himself by having his kingship sanctified by coronation at Reims. And it was in an attempt to invalidate his new religious status that her interrogators had to try to prove that he had been inspired by a heretic.

If Joan was a mystery to her contemporaries it is because, as the distinguished medievalist Colette Beaune points out, she crossed the boundaries between the standard roles.[6] This was a society where, as in older traditional societies today, people were not perceived as individuals but were defined by fixed categories: noble or peasant, man or woman, saint or sinner. A woman – and a peasant woman at that – might be a nun or a prophet, but not a knight or a warrior. By blurring these polar distinctions, and doing so successfully, Joan so disturbed the order of things that the question inevitably arose as to whether she was a saint or a witch – and it was this ambiguity, together with her astonishing success, that contributed to the legend.

Yet she disturbed the order of things in another, unintended way. For, while there were Frenchmen on both sides in this dynastic war of succession, she always referred to the enemy as the English and, indeed, in her rehabilitation trial of 1456 it was assumed that she had been engaged in a war of national liberation from the English. What she symbolized was a new patriotism, a new sense of essential difference from what would from now on be the 'hereditary enemy', in fact the emergence of a nation from the wreckage of the old feudal order. And this new status was formalized by Charles VII, once he began to capitalize on his victory, when he forced the Vatican in 1438 to accept the Gallican principle of the financial and organizational independence of the French Church.

However, patriotism is sentiment and, in order to be effective, the nation has to be organized as a state. And if the French nation comes out of the bitterness and bloodshed of the war, so too does the French State. For to win the war required a superior army, which required money, which meant taxes, which called for a central authority able to impose and collect them, which implied the creation of an administration akin to that of a modern state. In fact this pattern conforms to what the prominent sociologist Norbert Elias calls 'a structural change in Western society as a whole'.[7] And it was under the pressure of such circumstances that Charles VII proceeded to create a permanent royal army with artillery and English-style infantry and – with the support of the middle class of the towns – put down a rebellion of nobles who wished to retain their right to raise their own armies. He also extended the royal monopoly on raising taxes and set up the organization to achieve this, creating in the process – as with the military – a new administrative nobility dependent on the throne. On this basis, having made a separate truce with the Burgundians, he won back Paris and Aquitaine, cleared the English out of France, leaving them only Calais, and effectively put an end to the war. And since his successor Louis XI (1461–83) annexed Burgundy and scrapped the apanages, the country began to look like the France of today.

So by the end of the fifteenth century France, while it was increasingly centralist with no equivalent to the English parliament, had become a much more modern type of monarchy. It had happened partly through the actions of a succession of kings and partly in spite of them. What was clear, however, was that the old mutual obligations of the feudal system had broken down, the apanages had gone, the great nobles were no longer kinglets in their estates, there was a rising middle class, and with the labour shortage following the Black Death the common people no longer knew their place and were demanding higher wages. And with the discovery of America suggesting that the world was a larger place, the enclosed world of the Middle Ages with its pieties, its pogroms and its desperate intensities was already, as though it had been the childhood of the nation, fading into the past.

3

RENAISSANCE, REFORMATION AND THE WARS OF RELIGION

The sixteenth century was a turning point which marks a significant shift towards modernity. The whole continuum of medieval Christendom, with its belief in its own centrality, was shaken by a series of discoveries and innovations which opened up the prospect of a new Europe, a new world and, indeed, a new view of the cosmos.

A fundamental change was that, with the spread of printing, both the Church and the kings were beginning to lose their control of knowledge, even if book publication remained formally subject to royal authorization. Printing had begun in Paris by 1470 and there was already a score of printers in the country by 1500. Between then and the end of the century 25,000 books would be printed in Paris and 15,000 in Dijon, while there were other printing shops elsewhere. This meant not only that works were now accessible to a broader audience, but that the opportunity had been created for the circulation of printed propagandist tracts and seditious lampoons. The medium itself conveyed the message that there could now be a greater exchange of ideas in society.

And there would be no shortage of new ideas to challenge Church orthodoxy: that there were other continents with different civilizations, that the world was round and, most subversive of new-fangled notions – which Copernicus revealed only with great caution in 1543 and for which Galileo would be tried for heresy by the Inquisition almost a century later – that the Earth revolved around the sun. With new translations of the Bible from the original Hebrew showing up errors and inconsistencies in the Latin version – and with Martin Luther's translation into German being the first that non-scholars could actually read in their own language – the Church's authority came under question. As an organization it also came in for heavy criticism, following Luther's fierce attack in 1517 on the worldliness of the papacy and the corruption involved in the selling of salvation. The resulting Reformation would lead to a serious split in the Christian world whereby Spain became Catholic, England Protestant and France had its own wars of religion.

For the sixteenth century saw the beginnings of a new Europe of nations in which these three would constitute a trio of competing forces, each of which would largely define its national identity in contradistinction to the other two. France would gain from the Italian Renaissance and would have such striking kings as François I (1515–47) and Henri IV (1589–1610). England, with the protracted Wars of the Roses finally behind it, would have a strong new Tudor monarchy under such formidable figures as Henry VIII (1509–47) and Elizabeth I (1558–1603) and would become a potential rival following the break with Rome. Spain would become a unified and rigorously Catholic nation through the marriage in 1469 of Ferdinand of Aragon and Isabella of Castile – whose confessor was the implacable Torquemada, head of the Spanish Inquisition. It had also asserted its identity through the expulsion of the Jews and the elimination of the Muslim threat with the conquest of Granada.

Yet, if Spain itself was unified, the old absurdities of the dynastic system – family relationships claiming the right to dictate the fate of large and diverse territories – would stretch its rule confusedly across Europe. For in 1516 Charles V, whose mother tongue was French though he had been brought up in Flanders, inherited the throne of Spain and its Italian possessions through his mother, inherited Flanders and Burgundy through his father, inherited Austria through his grandfather Maximilian and, on Maximilian's death, was elected Holy Roman Emperor (1519–58) – to become the notional master of a complex and rapidly evolving Europe at the grand old age of nineteen. Which meant that tension between the three competing powers – especially since their three long-serving leaders in the first half of the century, Charles V, François I and Henry VIII, were direct contemporaries – was guaranteed.

And this was the more the case in that this new age of nations was already announcing the age of empires. In the different world that was opening up Europeans were beginning to span the globe. England had been early in the field when the Venetian John Cabot, sponsored by Henry VII, landed in 1497 on Cape Breton Island in Nova Scotia, but it only really got into the game with the voyages of Sir Francis Drake and others towards the end of the sixteenth century and with the founding of the East India Company in 1600. As it was, the early running was made by Spain and Portugal. Before the century began the Portuguese, following the lead of Prince Henry the Navigator, had colonized Madeira, the Azores and the Cape Verde islands, had set up trading stations on the west coast of Africa and had rounded the Cape to reach as far as India. On this basis they quickly built up to an extensive overseas empire including Angola, Brazil and Mozambique, which led to Lisbon becoming the premier port for trade in silk, spices and slaves.

As for Spain, which would annex Portugal in 1580, the sixteenth century would of course become its Golden Age, though the gold would be tarnished by the devastating defeat of the Armada inflicted by the English Navy in 1588. Meanwhile, the Castilian conquistadors, driven on this exotic new crusade by the desire to find fame and gold while converting heathens to the Catholic faith, were cutting swathes through the indigenous peoples of South America. With Cortes destroying the Aztec empire in Mexico and Pizarro dealing similarly with the Incas of Peru, Europe was now exporting its religion, its violence and its deadly diseases, to which the native peoples had no immunity, to what would become Europeanized as Latin America.

But where was France in all this? At the start of the century its kings were facing the other way, doing what they still thought kings were supposed to do and chasing old dreams of military glory in Italy. This had begun at the end of the previous century with Charles VIII (1483–98), known as the Affable, who was affable to a fault but not very bright. In pursuit of a thin claim to the kingdom of Naples through his Angevin grandmother, he marched into Italy in 1494 and captured Naples, but provoked an anti-French coalition and had to withdraw without his booty. He was prevented from trying again by large debts and by the fact that he forgot to duck when approaching a low door at Amboise, hit his head on the lintel, went into a coma and died at the age of twenty-eight.

The torch then passed to Louis XII (1498–1515), a popular if intriguing king whose sensible policies at home were eclipsed by the folly of his Italian adventures. In pursuit of a vague claim through a grandfather, he captured Milan in 1499 and was then emboldened to claim Naples, but had to renounce his claim after two serious defeats. Quite un-daunted, he led a coalition that conquered Venice but, when it became clear that he wanted to try again to capture Milan, the coalition dissolved into an anti-French Holy League which defeated him at Ravenna and by 1512 he had lost the lot. This did not prevent him from losing it all over again in a further failed attempt to capture Milan the following year, which ended with his borders being overrun by the English, the Swiss and the Spanish. He succeeded in resolving the situation by buying them off with gold and by marrying Mary Tudor, the famously attractive eighteen-year-old sister of Henry VIII, though his over-ambitious efforts at the age of fifty-two to produce a son and heir to continue his forlorn quest in Italy were said to have contributed to his death three months later.

What was the reason for this obsession with Italy, apart from the fact that such a fragmented area of minor kingdoms and city states offered easier opportunities for military glory? Why should Louis's successor, his son-in-law François I, the emblematic king of the French Renaissance, have also got bogged down there in his turn? The fact is that they were caressing the dream, already obsolete in this new Europe of nations, of becoming a latter-day Charlemagne, the first step being to become head of the old Holy Roman Empire. François started in great style with a victory at Marignano, which he followed up with a concordat with the Pope consolidating his control over the French Church and its riches. With his prestige thus enhanced, he was in fact the obvious candidate to become Holy Roman Emperor, but the prize was stolen from under his nose by the younger Charles V, who was able to pay larger bribes with the help of backers such as the Fugger banking family, who handled the Vatican's financial affairs.

Since France was now caught in a vice between Spain, the Netherlands and Burgundy – territories now under the control of Charles V, who could deploy troops within 100 miles of Paris – the conflict with Spain over the Italian kingdoms was no longer just about glory but about survival. François failed to get the support of Henry VIII at the famous Field of the Cloth of Gold encounter in 1520, but tried again to capture the Duchy of Milan, only to be wounded and taken prisoner at the Battle of Pavia in 1525, then humiliatingly held captive by Charles in Madrid until he paid a heavy ransom and made territorial concessions – later repudiated. This rivalry with Spain and the Habsburgs, with intermittent and rather inconclusive wars, would not only dominate François's foreign policy for the next twenty years, but would continue beyond his death until a peace treaty of 1559.

Meanwhile, if France had virtually no territorial gains to show for the unending military adventures in Italy, this hardly affected the popularity of François I. While this may have been because war was accepted as a normal kingly activity, it was also because François was a charismatic figure. Tall and glamorous, with a heroically long nose, he was intelligent, cultivated, responsive, charming to ladies – the very image of chivalrous royalty. Also, while the frontier areas had suffered, the wars in fact helped to promote internal peace in the rest of the kingdom. It was after all better for the fighting to be taking place somewhere else, especially as the wars sucked in mercenaries and brigands who for decades had been troubling the kingdom. And of course domestic peace favoured the economic revival which had been going on since the end of the previous century.

Despite occasional epidemics and bouts of famine, notably in the 1520s, the loss of population caused by the Black Death had been restored by the middle of the century. There was a considerable increase in agricultural production, due to land clearance for cultivation, to a wider range of cereals such as buckwheat and maize – which came from Mexico via Spain – and to a steady improvement in yields. While it was still basically an agricultural economy, there was a concomitant increase in manufacturing and in trade. The towns were booming – Rouen had its printing and weaving mills while Lyon, in addition to its silk industry, was for most of the century the main banking centre. And while the ports could not compete with Lisbon or Antwerp due to France's tardiness in developing international trade – though François did dispatch Jacques Cartier and others to Canada with the standard instruction to look for gold and promote the Catholic faith – the port of Bordeaux was exporting wines to England and the Low Countries.

Furthermore, through the insistent claims they made upon the treasury, the wars once again helped to strengthen the state. If the centralizing of power was a continuing process, it is because it was not easy to achieve in a large kingdom in which provinces had their own customs and dialects, and where it could take ten days to travel from Paris to Bordeaux. There was no real parliamentary institution to balance royal power – the provincial *parlements* were mere talking shops, while the States-General, where the nobility, clergy and the commoners were supposed to meet in separate conclave, were only convoked at the king's will, and thus almost never. In this situation, the kings were already moving towards the absolute monarchy that would reach its high point with Louis XIV in the following century.

However, it was the need for money which led François I to continue perfecting the machinery of State. He reorganized the treasury, the audit office, the board of excise and other agencies, appointing competent central and provincial administrators to run them. By the highly significant Statute of Villers-Cotterêts he had French replace Latin in all official documents and ordered that for the first time all births and ancestry details be registered. Having acquired through his concordat with the Pope the right not only to appoint bishops but to dispose of much of the Church's revenues and even its property, he was in a position not only to raise funds but to reward those whom he wished to bind to his service – though he soon began to raise money by selling offices of the Crown with a lifetime tenure, adding thereby to the alternative nobility, the administrative 'nobility of the robe'. He also set up a series of loans, whether organized through bankers or through the administrations in the towns. By these means the throne tapped – rather too heavily as would later emerge – into the rising prosperity of the kingdom.

Yet the principal positive effect of France's prolonged military escapades was the impact on the country of the Italian Renaissance. For decades the returning warriors had been bringing back statues, pictures, silverware, books and new ideas of art and architecture. Charles VIII and Louis XII had already brought back artists and François I followed by importing such leading figures as Cellini, Andrea del Sarto and Leonardo da Vinci – who brought with him the *Mona Lisa* among other works. Since François also employed agents in Italy to acquire paintings by Italian masters, he was building towards the royal collection that would end up in the Louvre. Similarly, he used agents to acquire rare books and manuscripts and appointed as librarian of the royal collection the prominent classicist and philologist Guillaume Budé.

A humanist with discreet Protestant leanings, Budé built up the royal library at François's favourite palace of Fontainebleau, helped by a decree that ensured it would be given a free copy of every book published in France and, here too, the collection was eventually removed to Paris to become the nucleus of the Bibliothèque Nationale. Equally important, Budé not only convinced François to ignore the demand of the Sorbonne theologians in 1533 that he forbid printing in France, but persuaded him – to their dismay – to establish the independent centre for scholarly teaching and research that is known today as the prestigious Collège de France. It is difficult to overestimate the importance of François's contribution to French cultural life at this time.

With a royal disregard for the cost, he also had a passion for architecture. As the old fortified style could no longer guarantee safety in a siege since the development of artillery, the medieval castles were ready for replacement or adaptation to the more open-faced Italian Renaissance style. In Paris, to which he brought back the royal administration and which now developed as the capital of an increasingly centralized state, he rebuilt the Louvre and promoted the construction of a new city hall.

But it is for his impact on the châteaux of the Île-de-France and the Loire that he is doubtless most remembered. He renovated the Château d'Amboise, where he had spent his childhood, and added the richly decorated staircase which bears his name to the Château de Blois, a favourite royal palace which he later abandoned for Fontainebleau, where he had the existing medieval building replaced by two new structures linked by a gallery decorated by Rosso Fiorentino, the first such gallery to be built in France. He brought in many other Italian artists, who have since become known as the First School of Fontainebleau, and the traditional religious subjects gave way to classical mythical themes. Fontainebleau, where he installed his official mistress Anne, Duchesse d'Étampes, became his favourite royal residence between expeditions to Italy. However, it is probably the châteaux of the Loire valley, where the lazy landscape and an unusual quality of light enhancing the blue slate roofs add a special charm, that for most people typify the romance and the royal splendour of this period.

The real gems to many French eyes are the smaller châteaux. Azay-le-Rideau, on an island in the Indre tributary so that on all sides it is reflected in the river, harmoniously combines the moat, turrets and other features of the medieval castle with the symmetry and grandeur of an Italian palace and has a magnificent monumental staircase – with the salamander, François's ubiquitous emblem, much in evidence. Then there is the enchanting Chenonceau, which François seized from his treasurer Thomas Bohier because of unpaid debts to the Crown and which has the particular appeal of a grand gallery spanning the Cher tributary. Here again the style is composite, with the neoclassical simplicity of the gallery matching the charm of earlier ornate features such as sculptures on the roofs and balustrades. Chenonceau is rich in historical associations. It saw the first firework display in France and saw some verbal firework displays in the long rivalry between Catherine de Médicis, the wife of François's less charming successor Henri II (1547–59), and Diane de Poitiers, Henri's mistress.

Yet the most eye-opening of all the many châteaux in this region is doubtless the enormous Italianate fantasy which François built at Chambord – partly in order to be close to a pretty unofficial mistress, Anne de Thoury. It is possible that Leonardo da Vinci may have had a hand in the design of this dream palace in which the medieval features – the great bastion towers on the corners, the walls and the partial moat – have become purely decorative gestures towards a disappearing past. It is by far the largest of the châteaux in the Loire valley, with its 440 rooms and its 365 fireplaces, not to mention its vast park filled with red deer. Most noticeable are the famous double helix staircase and, above all, the astonishing roof crowded with chimney stacks, pepperpot turrets, dormer windows and all sorts of teasing features designed to make it look like the skyline of Constantinople – a fabulous village in the sky, ideal for secret meetings and gossip as well as for viewing the activities in the park.

Chambord was an engaging folly, a gigantic hunting lodge that was rarely visited because it was too remote, with no supporting hinterland to maintain a lavish court which at times numbered 10,000 people, and because its open windows and loggias were better suited to the warmth of Italy. But here as elsewhere the salamander emblem summons up images of this glamorous Renaissance prince himself – charming the many noble ladies who graced the scene, hunting the deer here or in the forest of Fontaine-bleau, or talking art with Leonardo da Vinci into the night.

It is hardly surprising that this iconic pleasure-loving human-ist king should have tempted so many writers and film-makers.[1] And it is doubtless inevitable that they should emphasize his amorous adventures rather than the sad truth that his health never really recovered from his incarceration in Madrid, that his last years were marred by syphilis, and that his extravagant ways had emptied the treasury and weakened the economy.

'France, mother of the arts, of arms and of laws' sang the poet Joachim du Bellay in the mid-1550s in his hymn to the new Renaissance France.[2] It is true that he was languishing in Rome as the diplomatic dogsbody of his cantankerous uncle the cardinal when the real action and career advan-tages were back at the French court, and it is true that this was before the Wars of Religion had really set in. Nevertheless this is a striking testimony to a new sense of nationhood and even to a belief that France could aspire to become the new Rome. For the impact of the Renaissance went well beyond architecture and art into poetry – a field in which François himself had dabbled. Du Bellay had already published his resounding *Défense et illustration de la langue française* (*Defence and Illustration of the French Language*), the manifesto of a group of poets, including the more famous Ronsard, which became known as La Pléiade. They aimed both to rival the ancients by the mastery of Greek and Roman poetic forms and to raise French to the dignity of Latin by enriching it with new words derived largely from those languages. This elitist approach was open to the criticism that it unduly latinized the language, but it established French – now the official legal language – as being also the language of high culture.

If the Pléiade poets had to fight a little literary war to establish their new approach, the new Renaissance human-ism, in the context of a Church under threat from new ideas, had sterner battles to fight in the area of religion and intellectual methodology. Humanism today suggests agnosticism or atheism, a rationalist approach which looks for truth not in revelation or religious authority but in human reason and scientific inquiry. In this transitional period of the sixteenth century, however, the meaning was not so clear. Essentially, as the term itself suggests, it marked a shift of emphasis, even within a religious worldview, from God to man. Human beings were no longer seen as crushed by an all-powerful God and by sin, but as having the freedom to develop their own ideas on the basis of experience. With God still seen as creator of the universe and its laws, but not as the observer and judge of every single human act, there was room for a new optimism about human possibilities that nourished a sense of renewal in many fields of activity. Inevitably, however, this Renaissance or rebirth of activity presented a challenge to the Church – and at various levels.

It was a challenge at a fundamental level insofar as the discoveries of the original Christian texts undermined the authority of Church orthodoxy and insofar as the discoveries of Copernicus and others implied knowledge beyond its ken – revelation was giving way before inquiry. More immediately, it was a challenge at the political level because of widespread dismay at the worldliness and corruption not only at the local level but in Rome itself, where the popes had essentially become political leaders. Of the three successive popes between 1492 and 1521, Alexander VI was a Borgia notorious for his extravagance and nepotism who had four illegitimate children; Julius II, the 'warrior Pope' made a cardinal at eighteen, was apparently gay though he had also fathered children; Leo X, a cardinal at thirteen and also gay, decreed the selling of indulgences for the rebuilding of St Peter's basilica.

The fact that some of the money also went on paintings by Raphael or Michelangelo did not impress Martin Luther, who was shocked by this buying and selling of salvation.

While his original intention was to try to reform the institution, he ended up by denying its claim to play a mediating role through the sacraments, arguing that God could only be approached through personal faith and thereby undercutting the whole authority of the Church. This split was doubtless an inevitable development, since the humanists' rejection of medieval scholasticism was combining with the rise of printing and the growth of nationalism to break up the Catholic world – a process which was merely confirmed by the Vatican's Council of Trent, begun in 1545, which introduced some reforms but made no concessions to Protestantism.

Of course, as can be seen with its two most influential figures, there were significant differences within the broad Protestant movement itself. Erasmus from Rotterdam spent six years as a monk, became a priest and studied theology in Paris. This experience led him to write the powerful satire *Encomium Moriae* (in French *Éloge de la folie*; *In Praise of Folly*), in which the 'Goddess of Folly' slates theologians, monks and other authority figures such as lawyers for their pedantry, stupidity and pretentiousness. He also, as through his fresh translation of the Greek New Testament, became a central figure in the revival of learning, advocating 'the philosophy of Christ' as opposed to sterile scholasticism. While he did not ask for the sacraments on his deathbed, he still hoped that the Church could reform itself and did not endorse the growing Reformation movement – not that this prevented his works being condemned by the Council of Trent.

The equally influential Jean Calvin, on the other hand, took a different path. Thrown out of the Church when a theology student at the Sorbonne, he became a lawyer, employing the new humanist method of going directly to the original document and applying historical and grammatical analysis rather than relying on encrusted commentary. Forced to flee Paris following his conversion to a Protestant viewpoint, he spent most of his life in Geneva, where he set up a famous academy. He became associated essentially with the pessimistic doctrine of predestination, which of course conflicted with the Church's view of free will, and he was a key figure in the development of the more austere strand of Protestantism.

However varied they might be, the rise of communities of French Protestants – generally known as the Huguenots, after the Swiss–German *Eidgenossen*, meaning confederates – began inevitably to be seen as a political problem. Indeed François I, despite his openness to the ideas of the Renaissance, had started to act against the rising Protestant movement as early as 1534, when he found a tract attacking the Mass nailed to his own bedroom door. Since he was officially 'His Most Christian Majesty', a Catholic king by divine right, he thought this was going too far and he initiated the persecution of religious minorities or 'heretics' which was to be enthusiastically developed by his son Henri II (1547–59), a stammering introvert who became king by accident following the death of his older brother. Henri turned up the heat with his sinister *chambres ardentes*, lit only by torches even in daytime since the windows were blacked out, in which justice for heretics was dispensed by means of torture, forced confessions and the finality of the stake.

This was a rehearsal for what would be known as the Wars of Religion, which would last until the end of the century and in which the old dream of military glory in Italy would be submerged by the reality of war at home. Of course, as is usual with such wars, they were not simply about conflicting interpretations of the same religion, although the religious overlay tended as always to demonize the opponent and serve as justification for the treachery, the assassinations and the looting that took place on both sides. Basically this was an intermittent baronial civil war between great families of different provinces allying themselves, for fundamental or tactical reasons, with the Church and throne on one side or with the new Protestant movements on the other. And the struggle between the leading Catholic family of the Guises on the one hand and the Protestant Bourbons on the other became in effect a battle for a weakened throne.

Needless to say, the international context was significant in this divided Europe emerging out of medieval Christendom and nobody exemplifies this more than Henri II's wife, Catherine de Médicis of the Florentine family, the niece of two different popes and, eventually, the mother-in-law of Philip II of Spain. Catherine was unpopular in her own time, being seen as the ruthless Machiavellian power behind the throne, and opinion is still divided about her today.[3] But she was an intelligent woman who has to be seen in the context of the period – with its religious violence, the weakness of its dynastic monarchy as a political system, and a climate of opinion in which it was perfectly respectable for a Catholic queen to have the astrologer Nostradamus as adviser and court physician.

Catherine was orphaned within weeks of her birth in Florence, taken hostage by a rebellious faction at eight, threatened with death during a siege at ten and married to Henri II at fourteen – the consummation of the marriage being duly supervised by François I himself. But the death of her sponsor the Pope meant the loss of the hoped-for political leverage, her dowry was not great, she was not pretty, she had no royal blood and she was sidelined by the glamorous Diane de Poitiers, the mother-figure turned mistress doted upon by Henri. Even more threatening for a queen, for the first eleven years of the marriage she was childless, despite the prescribed remedies of drinking mule's urine and applying cow dung to her private parts – until she went on to produce a stream of children. With all that, she loved Henri and was desolate when he died of a jousting lance in the brain, but she soon sidelined Diane de Poitiers in her turn and settled down to supervise the three sons who would form a succession of rather inadequate kings.

François II (1559–60), who came to the throne at fifteen and died within the year of tuberculosis, was married off to the future and ill-fated Scottish queen Mary Stuart, an easily manipulated member of the powerful Guise family, which moved into the Louvre and used its dominant position to attack the Protestant Bourbons. Catherine suspected the motives of this overbearing Spanish-backed ally the Duc de Guise and tried to build bridges between the two sides, but she had her hands full trying to prop up a throne now occupied by her ten-year-old son Charles IX (1560–74) and the Wars of Religion began with the massacre of Protestants at Wassy in Champagne in 1562. When the Duc de Guise was assassinated to her delight in the following year she was able to rule on her own, but there was no stopping the tit-for-tat attacks. She was soon swallowed up in the politics of it all and she was at least complicit in the appalling St Bartholomew's Eve Massacre of August 1572.

Catherine had organized the marriage of her daughter Marguerite de Valois to the Protestant prince Henri de Bourbon-Navarre – a marriage not welcomed by the Pope or the mostly Catholic people of Paris. The arrival in the city of a large number of Protestant wedding guests provided a tempting opportunity for the Catholic Guise faction to liquidate the Protestant leaders – though the bridegroom would be spared on condition that he renounced his belief. Six days after the wedding, on the eve of St Bartholomew, the planned assassination of the Protestant leaders began. It degenerated over the next few days into wholesale massacre and pillage, with perhaps 3,000 Protestants murdered in Paris and bodies being flung into the Seine. The massacre spread to Lyon, Bordeaux, Rouen and other centres, leaving an estimated 25,000 dead in all. This was a key moment in the war between Catholics and Protestants and Pope Gregory, as if to underline the European dimension of the conflict, celebrated it with a Jubilee and a commemorative medal featuring an avenging angel smiting the Protestants with his sword.

When Charles died of tuberculosis at twenty-four two years later, the throne fell to Catherine's favourite son, Henri III (1574–89), who was intelligent but who scandalized many with his bevy of gay favourites and his frivolity. Catherine was now faced with trying to support a moderate Catholic bloc against a resurgent Protestant faction on the one hand and, on the other, confronting a fiercely absolutist new Catholic Holy League backed by Spain and led by the next Duc de Guise, which was actively planning to seize the throne. The threat became dramatic when her remaining son died in 1584 and it was realized that, since the homosexual Henri III would provide no issue, the eventual next in line would be Henri de Bourbon-Navarre, the Protestant leader himself – who had reneged on his forced conversion.

Through the confused fighting that followed over the next five years, this Protestant heir presumptive, the future Henri IV (1589–1610), was to come into his inheritance the hard way. He first defeated Henri III's forces in battle, only to become his ally after the king's assassination of his other dangerous rival the Duc de Guise provoked a rising against the Crown in Paris – at which point the throne fell to him when Henri III was himself assassinated by a Dominican friar. But France had become a cauldron of hatred, he still had the Holy League against him and he had years of fighting to come. Yet Henri IV was not only intelligent and decisive, but a mature and sensible individual who had seen the devastation caused by forty years of warfare. Having already changed religion several times as circumstances required, he decided to cut the Gordian knot by formally converting to Catholicism – with the legendary quip that if that was all it required to win over Paris he would turn up at Mass: 'Paris vaut bien une messe'. While that lost him many Protestants, he gradually took over the country through a judicious combination of military force, negotiation and large bribes, and by giving Protestants a measure of religious freedom with the Edict of Nantes. So the new

Bourbon monarchy would be Catholic by political decision. If it was a somewhat artificial solution to the conflict, it ended the war with Spain and brought an exhausted country a measure of peace.

What did major French writers of the time such as François Rabelais and Michel de Montaigne make of this world in which the monolithic control of the Church over belief and culture had come under threat? In which the earth might merely be a planet revolving around the sun and in which, as we today might discover aliens in outer space, Europeans were finding exotic peoples in distant lands whose heathen otherness was incomprehensible and unacceptable? In which the hopes of humanism faded into civil war and the new sense of nationhood led to brutal conflict between Catholic and Protestant factions for control of the State? In which writing, like living itself, could be a risky business – in which Rabelais saw his printer burnt at the stake and Montaigne saw five of his six children die in infancy? The influential historian Lucien Febvre, while he perhaps tends to under-play the curiosity for new knowledge, reminds us usefully that we should not read a sixteenth-century work through present-day eyes, arguing that every aspect of life was steeped in religion, that with no clear distinction between the natural and the supernatural in people's minds there was as yet no proper philosophical or scientific language, and that we should therefore recognize 'the limits of non-belief in the sixteenth century'.[4]

The rumbustious writings of Rabelais, a highly learned former monk and physician steeped in the humanist tradition, tend to bear this out. Starting with a take-off of an existing tall tale about 'the great and enormous giant Gargantua', he produced an astonishingly inventive and entertaining hotchpotch of cartoon-like exaggeration, satire, buffoonery, wordplay, pastiche, scatological humour, reflections on education and what have you – blending the grotesque with comic precision, as when Gargantua urinates and floods the Parisians down below, 'drowning two hundred and sixty thousand, four hundred and eighteen of them, not counting women and little children'.[5] While no very explicit message emerges from all this exuberance – unless it is the motto of his imagined commune, 'Do what you want' – he is clearly satirizing institutional religion and arguing for freedom of conscience. And, if he still believes in God, his view that nature and the body itself are good leaves no room for the fundamental ideas of sin and redemption. It is as though he blows up the medieval world from within but can see no world beyond it.

As for Montaigne, the very choice of the highly personal essay – a form which he pioneered – is indicative of a withdrawal from the standard organized worldview into the scepticism and pessimism engendered by the long religious wars. In such an uncertain world, 'one should always have one's boots on and be ready to leave'. While also believing in God, he paradoxically defends his belief on the basis of the inadequacy of human reason. And he comes close, quite exceptionally, to modern cultural relativism in 'Des Cannibales', his famous essay on cannibals, when he says that 'we simply call barbarous those customs that are different from our own; it seems indeed that in our search for truth and reason we cannot see beyond the ideas and conventions of our own country'.[6] Even to speculate about the possible arbitrariness of European Christian civilization was to come dangerously close to thinking the unthinkable for a man of his time.

4

THE GRAND CENTURY OF THE SUN KING

For the French, the seventeenth century comes under the sign of *gloire et grandeur*: glory and greatness. It is *le grand siècle, le siècle de Louis XIV* or *Louis le Grand*, otherwise known as *le Roi-Soleil*, the Sun King, through association with Apollo, the Greco-Roman god of the sun. At Versailles, where he constructed a whole new royal town some nineteen kilometres from Paris, the avenues radiate out from the great château like beams from a star, while the ceremonial King's Bedroom was in the exact geometrical centre of the main building, so that all the activity of ministers and courtiers revolved around him as though he were the queen bee in a giant hive. What this symbolized, of course, was the centralization of power in the hands of one anointed absolute monarch answerable only to God. And, certainly, the *gloire* and the *grandeur* everywhere in evidence in this great palace – with its harmonious composition of architecture and landscape, its Hall of Mirrors, its well-tamed gardens sloping down to the lake – are eloquent of the prestige of the French monarchy at this time. The tourist of today may note the absence of running water and fixed sanitation, or gawp a little at Hyacinthe Rigaud's famous full-length portrait of the king, almost buried in full wig and ermine-lined robes but showing a fine leg in his white silk hose and red high heels, yet this was a commanding king at a time of French hegemony in Europe. This was also, as the portraits of Pascal or Racine or Molière attest, a time of French cultural ascendancy in Europe. This was where wit, refined manners and high fashion were to be found. Louis le Grand, in the centre of his stunning new palace, was at the hub of European civilization.

How then did France reach such a peak after the devastation caused by the Wars of Religion and in the face of so many continuing difficulties? For Henri IV was murdered in 1610 by the Catholic fanatic Ravaillac, causing the religious tensions to linger on. And this would once again reveal an inherent weakness of the dynastic system, since his successor Louis XIII (1610–43) would become king at thirteen and his successor, Louis XIV (1643–1715), at the age of five. This would again leave the throne vulnerable to unruly nobles, so that there would be a complicated sequence of rebellions culminating with the Frondes of 1648–53. In addition, France would be involved in the broad European conflict known as the Thirty Years War (1618–48) and in a struggle with Spain and the Habsburgs which was merely exacerbated by intermarriage between the two houses – another feature of the dynastic system by which war between nations could be fused with a family squabble. So how in these circumstances did France rise to the dominance it enjoyed under Louis XIV? One reason was simply that France was now a large, territorially unified and potentially very rich country which, with its 20 million inhabitants, had a larger population than those of its rivals Spain and England

– with 8 and 5 million respectively – put together. If the past twenty years had been marked by bad harvests, the early decades of the new century, at least until the return of the plague in 1627–8, would bring much more favourable conditions. Above all, however, Louis XIV's path to power would be smoothed by a series of strong and competent figures, beginning with Henri IV himself and his minister Sully.

Henri IV's no-nonsense manner, his novel concern that 'every labourer should be able to have a chicken in the pot on a Sunday', his belief in peace and religious tolerance, and doubtless also his amorous adventures, led him to be seen as '*le bon roi Henri*'. With a small team of ministers, of whom the most effective was the Duc de Sully, he set about creating prosperity by promoting both agriculture and manufacturing. To restore the nation's finances, he raised money by charging those who had bought official positions as magistrates or tax collectors an annual fee for the right to hold them on a hereditary basis. While this was laying up problems for his successors by creating an administrative class independent of the Crown, the money was used by Sully to stabilize the currency and create a strong treasury balance. Meanwhile he drained swamps, built a new network of elm-lined roads and constructed bridges and canals.

Henri did much to improve Paris by completing the Pont Neuf, laying out sixty-eight new streets and building the handsome Place Royale, or Place des Vosges as it was renamed after the Revolution. He was keen to develop industry, notably tapestry, silk and other trades, and when he built the Grande Galerie of the Louvre, he invited skilled artisans to set up shop there. He provided the army with fresh cannon, strengthened frontier forts and was an enthusiastic sponsor of expeditions to develop trade with both the Far East and America, notably financing the venture that saw Samuel de Champlain create the colony of New France in Canada. It was a real misfortune for the country that Henri should have been cut down in the Rue de la Ferronnerie by a deluded regicide – who was tortured, then torn apart by four horses in the prescribed manner – for he and Sully had laid down the template for a successful Bourbon monarchy. And the advantage would largely be thrown away by his wife Marie de Médicis when she became regent for her nine-year-old son, Louis XIII.

Marie's marriage had been less than ideal, since Henri had only married her because he needed her dowry to pay debts and had made her put up with the presence at court of his arrogantly proprietorial mistress – whom she now gleefully banished. Marie was capricious, neither bright nor politically aware, and she also had a poor relationship with her rather disturbed and sickly son. To make matters worse, she quickly fell under the influence of her foster-sister Leonora Galigaï's husband, Concino Concini – an Italian adventurer whom she made a field-marshal though he had never seen a battlefield. Sully was dismissed, the reserves he had built up began to be squandered and Concini proceeded to feather his own nest. Seeing the throne so weakened, the princes of the blood and the great nobles became rebellious and had to be bought off at great expense, forcing Marie to try to raise money by summoning the States-General – an experiment which simply revealed the tensions between the three orders and would only ever be repeated under duress just before the Revolution in 1789.

Equally threatening to the peace of the realm, Marie came under pressure from the papal legate to take steps against the Protestants and was drawn towards the Spanish Habsburg dream of creating a universal Catholic kingdom in Europe. This led her to marry off Louis at the age of fourteen to the Habsburg princess Anne of Austria, daughter of King Philip III of Spain – a marriage destined for disaster not just because Louis would turn out to be homosexual, but because he was seething at Marie's refusal to let him take over the reins on reaching his majority at thirteen.

It was by a palace coup against his own mother, therefore, that Louis XIII took over at the age of fifteen in 1617. Acting through his old adviser the Duc de Luynes, he had Concini assassinated, Leonora Galigaï burnt as a witch and Marie banished to the Château de Blois. While this seemed to put an end to the pro-Habsburg, pro-Spanish policy, the religious tensions lingered on, with a Protestant rising in the south-west over the forced handover of Protestant premises to the Catholic Church. Moreover, the Thirty Years War began in 1618 when the Protestants of Bohemia revolted against the policies of the Holy Roman Empire, setting off a lengthy series of sporadic wars in which the German Protestants were supported in turn by the English, Dutch, Danes and eventually the Swedes. And while France waited until 1635 before directly intervening in an attempt to contain the power of Spain and the Empire, this contagion across Europe provided the backcloth to Louis's attempt to control the situation in France. He still had to contend with Marie, who escaped from Blois in 1619 and lent her name to a new nobles' revolt led by the king's own brother the Duc d'Orléans. Louis suppressed this and brought back Marie's former adviser Richelieu to effect a temporary reconciliation. When Luynes died in 1621, he became increasingly reliant upon this ambitious cleric, for whom he now obtained a cardinal's hat, and who shrewdly worked his way up to become his chief minister in 1624.

Cardinal Richelieu is one of the outstanding figures in French history, if a controversial one. His image as popularized by Alexandre Dumas's novel *Les Trois Mousquetaires* (*The Three Musketeers*) is that of a ruthless, secretive, hypocritical schemer – the 'Red Eminence', with his shadowy collaborator and original 'Grey Eminence', Friar Joseph, in his grey homespun Capucin habit. He was widely hated in his own time and Louis XIII himself resented his dependency upon him, to the point that he found it hard to conceal his delight when Richelieu died.[1] As a man of power who kept his cards close to his chest, Richelieu's personality was rather chilly and he was not endowed with the common touch, but he was obviously a person of exceptional gifts – clever and rigorous in his thinking while being pragmatic in practice. He was seen by his contemporaries as a statesman and even as a military man rather than as a cardinal – Cardinal de Retz said dismissively that 'he had enough religion for this world', implying that he might not have quite enough for the next.[2] However, he was not without principle and, as for his other qualities, they were well suited to the demanding situation in which he found himself. At all events, a fellow statesman, Louis XIV's finance minister Colbert, regarded him as the model to be followed and the fundamental importance of his contribution over the next eighteen years is widely recognized today.

While Richelieu had his own very clear ideas, he was in the tricky position of being in the middle of the dysfunctional relationship between royal mother and son, neither of whom liked or quite trusted him but each of whom needed him. He was also in a tricky position in a more general respect. There was a strong Counter-Reformation in the Catholic Church at this time, led by the Jesuits along with various new religious orders, and associated with such prominent figures as the future saints François de Sales and Vincent de Paul. But, if this assertion of Catholic orthodoxy was successful in religious terms, it might nevertheless conflict with the self-interest of individual states. Whatever their religious loyalties, both Cardinal Richelieu and his successor Cardinal Mazarin were obliged to pursue *la raison d'État* .

So, whereas Marie had thought of him as her protégé, he disappointed her by not adhering to her strong pro-Catholic, pro-Spanish line and, feeling betrayed, she tried to get rid of him. In 1630, on what became known as the *Journée des Dupes*, or Day of Dupes, she and the king's brother the Duc d'Orléans succeeded in persuading Louis to dismiss

Richelieu – or thought they had. For at that point the Cardinal, who knew exactly what was going on from his network of spies, strolled coolly into the room, inquired smilingly whether Their Majesties were talking about him – and proceeded to reverse the whole situation. Louis was won over, gave him a dukedom and from then on his position was secure. What Marie had not grasped was that Richelieu, cardinal or not, was more bent on advancing the national interests of France than those of Spain and the broader European ambitions of the Roman Church.

Richelieu was in fact pursuing a coherent plan designed to contain the religious disunity that had been reignited and to centralize power by strengthening the throne. On the one hand, he had to deal with a sequence of pro-Habsburg, pro-Catholic plots by the king's brother and the princes of the blood in alliance with the old feudal nobility. This he did in uncompromising fashion, by destroying their fortified castles, forbidding duels and executing as traitors such figures as the Duc de Montmorency and even the king's lover Cinq-Mars. On the other hand, he had to cope with pockets of rebellion among the Protestants and he dealt spectacularly with a Huguenot rising supported by the English by himself leading the siege of La Rochelle in 1627. While he deprived the Protestants of certain political protections, he was wise enough to ignore Catholic demands for the abrogation of Henri IV's Edict of Nantes and to maintain their freedom of worship. However, it was not enough to tread a delicate line between Catholic conservatism and Protestantism at the national level, he had to perform the same trick in relation to the Thirty Years War. Whereas France had previously only secretly supported the Protestant forces, their defeat at Nordlingen in 1635 drew him into the conflict in order to ensure that France would never be swallowed up in the universal Catholic monarchy dreamt of by the Spanish Habsburgs. And this war with Spain would drag on beyond Richelieu's death in 1642.

By that time, however, Richelieu had largely set up the central State machinery required to subordinate local and religious interests to the national interest as represented by the king. He had subordinated provincial officials to state commissioners, forbidden the *parlements* to discuss State affairs and gained control of opinion by censoring the press. He had both maintained the independence of the country and enhanced its prestige through his sponsorship of the arts, having founded the Académie Française, built the present Palais Royal and created a distinguished art collection. In short, he had established the general framework for the glory days of the absolute monarchy of Louis XIV. Except, of course, that with another damaging regency looming when Louis became that absolute monarch in 1643 as a small boy not yet five, it looked like being '*déjà vu* all over again'.

In the eighteen years before he took personal control in 1661 following the death of Richelieu's successor Cardinal Mazarin, the young Louis had a ringside view of the problem of running his country. Anne of Austria, the neglected wife of Louis XIII, unexpectedly took well to the role of regent and, devout Spanish Catholic though she was, pursued the independent line of Richelieu, helped by his hand-picked successor Mazarin – who had comparable diplomatic skills, even if he had a greedy eye for the perks of office. They may or may not have had an intimate relationship, as rumour had it, but they certainly had a close working one – and they needed it. For one thing, they were still engaged in the costly business of the Thirty Years War, which had to be financed by unpopular taxes. Fortunately, France won a decisive victory in 1643 at Rocroi, in the Ardennes, and in 1648 Mazarin was able to sign the advantageous Treaty of Westphalia.

This ended the supremacy of the Holy Roman Empire by recognizing the independence of the German states and the Netherlands and, in consequence, marked the beginning of

Spain's decline, even if a separate Franco-Spanish conflict dragged on. France, in contrast, emerged very well, with the gain of most of Alsace as well as the bishoprics of Metz, Toul and Verdun. At home, however, the country was in a state of near anarchy, Mazarin was deeply unpopular because of the tax burden and the Parlement de Paris – a State tribunal rather than a representative parliament – led a rebellion which forced the frightened young king and his mother to steal out of Paris in the middle of an icy January night in 1649.

This rising was put down by the royal prince and hero of the victory of Rocroi, the Prince de Condé, but this was only the first stage of the rebellion known as the Fronde – a name actually taken from a children's game, the word *fronde* meaning sling. For in the following year Condé not only turned his coat and led an aristocratic rebellion but even sought support from Spain. After a confused series of engagements, he was defeated outside Paris, which enabled Louis and his mother to make a triumphant return to the city in 1652, while Mazarin bought off the remaining rebels in the time-honoured fashion. It had been a trying time for the throne, but what the whole confused episode had revealed was that there was no unity among the various disaffected groups, that the country quickly became intolerant of marauding bands and that, in the end, there was no serious opposition to the increasingly centralized state. By the time Mazarin had put an end to the war with Spain by arranging a marriage between the young king and his first cousin the infanta Maria-Teresa of Spain, France was ready for Louis XIV.

What was it like to be this Louis XIV of the Hyacinthe Rigaud portrait? To the twenty-first century visitor to Versailles, he may seem quaint and even ridiculous. With his elaborate regalia of wig, white hose and red high heels – which he designed himself – he might almost suggest the

inveterate cross-dresser or the ageing call-girl. Yet Louis
particularly admired this painting, to the point that, when he
was unavoidably absent for a council meeting, it was carried
into the room to represent the royal presence. Of course this
was only one of many hundreds of portraits of Louis that
were reproduced throughout the kingdom, often showing
the same knightly leg and going to the farthest reaches of
allegory. There was Louis as Apollo, as the Good Shepherd,
as Defender of the Faith, as Protector of the Arts, as the
Conqueror of Heresy, as the Miracle-worker curing scrofula, as St Louis or as the Roman Emperor straddling a horse
as elaborately accoutred as himself – not to mention the
World Paying Homage to Louis. There seemed to be no past
hero, from Augustus or Constantine to Charlemagne or
Clovis, who could escape identification with this Sun King,
presiding over a glittering residence reminiscent of the Palace
of the Sun in Ovid's *Metamorphoses*.

And then there was the minutely regulated etiquette of the
court, the royal liturgy well described by the biographer
Petitfils.[3] The king's *petit lever*, or initial rising ceremony,
took place at 7.30 a.m., when he was examined by the royal
doctors in the presence of close family members and a few
specially honoured courtiers. These were then joined by a
group of court officials to whom the king gave instructions
while he performed his natural functions on the commode
and had his wig and beard treated. There followed the *grand
lever*, to which were admitted ambassadors, cardinals and
other leading figures of the kingdom. He ate a light breakfast
in his dressing-gown and then dressed, the garments being
handed to him by the dauphin or other family member, after
which he prayed.

Having given orders for the day in the council chamber,
he proceeded to the chapel for mass, trooping with his
retinue through a Great Gallery thronged with courtiers and
important visitors eager to be noticed by him or even, if they
had previously obtained permission, to have a word with

him. He ate dinner at noon watched by a restricted group of standing courtiers, though often joined at table by his next-in-line brother, known as 'Monsieur', who would hand him his serviette and then be invited to sit down. The evening meal would be an elaborately ceremonial public affair, with the family members eating off gold plate watched by a select group of invited guests, the ladies sitting and the men standing throughout. The arrangements for bedtime were a mirror image of those for the morning, with men of high rank vying for the honour of holding the twin-sconce gilt candlestick. From morning to night, Louis XIV's life, even the normally private part, was a public performance.

This tightly choreographed ballet mirrored the etiquette of the court, which combined order, precedence and elaborate conventions. To survive at Versailles you had to know a plethora of unwritten rules – that you removed your hat if the king passed by, that only the princes and princesses could sit in his presence, and so on – and you also had to know mysterious exceptions to those rules. And these hierarchical differences operated in minute detail right down the social scale. At one level it was reassuring to live in an ordered society that defined your exact social rank and told you what to wear or say on what occasion. So enveloping was this prestigious centre of power that many grandees felt that there was no salvation away from the king, that they could neither afford nor bear to be absent from the networking, the lavish entertainments, the amorous encounters and the possibility of a retainer or a rewarding position. At another level, there was the frustration of failing to get noticed, the discomfort of living in cramped and smelly conditions under the spying eyes of servants, the jealousy, the bitchiness and the fear of perpetrating some terminal faux pas. Like the rich young officer mentioned by the Comtesse de Boigne, who innocently attended the wrong ball, was brusquely ejected, never survived the ridicule and committed suicide – or the gentleman who came regularly

over ten years to solicit the king and never got selected for
an audience.[4] Versailles, as Patrice Leconte illustrates in his
stylish film *Ridicule*, was an ongoing fancy dress party where
vices were tolerated but where the slightest gaffe could
resonate and kill.[5] For everyone was on show in this grand
performance theatre, not only the king.

The difference, of course, was that the king was also the
master of ceremonies controlling this masked ball – or, as
one historian puts it, the director, star and designer of his
own self-glorifying theatre.[6] Inevitably, this whole 'fabrication of Louis XIV', as another writer calls it, invites
comparison with the personality cults of the totalitarian
states of the twentieth century, though he recognizes that it
was not simply megalomania but 'to some extent at least a
response to demand, even if the public were not completely
aware of what they wanted'.[7] Certainly, even if it was to the
king as the embodiment of the State, that response was a
strong one, for Louis had in effect become the object of a
quasi-religious cult. In his bedroom, where he regularly
received ambassadors and other great personages, the bed
was separated off by a gilded balustrade just like the altar in
a church and officials passing through in his absence duly
bowed to the empty bed. Louis, by seeing himself as second
only to God, had, in effect, nationalized the religion and
become his own pope. So it may be a little surprising to find
him in his *Mémoires* – the more reliable in that they were
never intended for publication – showing himself to be sober
and shrewd within the limits of the value system of the time
and telling his son that 'the job of the king is basically to see
that common sense prevails'.[8]

When he took over at Mazarin's death in 1661, Louis,
whether as a hunter, actor, dancer, musician or lover, was a
successful young man – and one who had a strong enough
constitution to survive the innocent medical practices of the
time, which consisted largely of bleeding and advising
against washing. He also had an old head on young

shoulders. Having understudied Mazarin, experienced the disorder in the kingdom and heard from his mother about the grand formality of the Spanish court, he had a firm view of his role. At the fundamental level, he did indeed believe that the king derived his authority directly from God. So 'kings are absolute rulers who can naturally dispose of all property, secular or ecclesiastical' and the ruled are bound to absolute obedience because of 'the sacred knot which binds the subjects to their sovereign'.[9] Since he is answerable to God for his discharge of his role, however, the king must be a father to his people and treat all conditions, rich and poor, fairly. Also, he is not entitled to divest himself of his sacred responsibility by passing it to another, but must assume it directly – so Louis became his own prime minister. He also stresses to his son the constant hard work that this will entail. What Louis was doing, with the blessing of the prominent theologian Bishop Bossuet – who also believed firmly in gallicanism, the independence of the national Church from Rome – was taking Christian monarchy with its divine right of kings about as far as it could go.

Of course this fundamentalist view of kingship corresponded closely in his mind with practical imperatives: if he started building Versailles as soon as he took over – though it would take years to complete – it was also because it was at a safe distance from that factious Paris he had fled from as a child. To avoid domestic disorders like those of the Fronde he needed a strong State, and to keep control he would work with small groups of advisers who would be entirely dependent on him – every decision would go through him. He had seen the problem of controlling the nobles, so he would keep them under his eye at court and direct their energies into harmless foppish pursuits and amorous intrigue. He recognized that people craved excitement, that they were vain and status-conscious, so he would provide a prestigious royal theme park that would keep them occupied. He had also observed that people could be bought, so he kept the princes and certain great nobles on a string with retainers, which could be dropped if they misbehaved. Such a court would outshine the Spanish and English courts as well as answering the needs of France. In all this he was aware of the difficulty, if you are being flattered all day long, of knowing whom, if anybody, you can trust. But this was just one aspect of the more profound problem that, since he both believed in himself as absolute monarch and was constantly watching himself construct the role, he was creating for himself an ongoing identity crisis.

He started with a bang by dispossessing and imprisoning for life the rich and brilliant finance minister Fouquet on the charge, not too clearly established, of fraudulent self-enrichment. This at once told the shocked nobles who was in charge, especially since Louis now brought in as Fouquet's replacement the man who had accused him, the ambitious and energetic Colbert. With Colbert he pushed forward the centralization that would become the hallmark of the French state, imposing on the provinces more state commissioners, directly appointing the mayors of larger towns and cleaning up local finances.

Colbert shared the dream of making France the most powerful and brilliant country in the world, at once a new Rome and a new Athens. To that end he encouraged industry and trade, created state-owned factories, reorganized state finances and the court system, built up the navy, founded East and West Indies Companies and promoted the arts. As a 'mercantilist', he believed that national wealth depended on accumulating gold by exporting goods while imposing tariffs on imports. The disadvantage of this protectionist approach, obviously, was that other countries would retaliate and that, at a time when Britain and the Netherlands were expanding through free trade – Amsterdam had the biggest bank in Europe – France's approach might be too inward-looking. And this is the point at which Louis's foreign policy began to conflict with the country's domestic needs.

In 1667 he attacked the Spanish Netherlands, the present-day Belgium, as representing the inheritance of his wife Maria-Teresa, whose dowry had never been paid. When this provoked a Dutch–English–Swedish alliance he withdrew, having gained some fortified towns including Lille, but five years later he invaded Holland, only to find himself facing a European coalition. The war dragged on for years, but he finally emerged triumphant through the Treaty of Nijmegen of 1678, by which he secured his frontiers with the gain of Lorraine and the Franche-Comté. This enhanced his prestige to the point that he now saw himself as the foremost monarch in Europe and even the world. He still considered himself to be untouchable when he blithely annexed Strasbourg in 1681. But, if at the end of his life he saw that he had been too fond of war, it is because he had not sufficiently recognized the cost of these glorious exploits, which had in fact undone much of what Colbert, who died in 1683, had achieved. The country was still large and rich, with a strong army and navy, but it was now in deficit and, even with increased taxes, would be living on credit from now on. Most of the State-owned factories were in decline, the Canadian colonists neglected, the East and West Indies Companies virtually disbanded. In an expanding world France was not quite reading the signs. For the moment, however, Louis was at the height of his fame and fêted by the glittering collection of writers and artists at his court.

Yet the writers and thinkers began to drift towards Paris when, after a scandal involving a recent mistress in an affair of sorcery and murder, Louis imposed stricter behaviour at court and, on the death of the Queen in 1683, married secretly the pious Madame de Maintenon. However, it was not simply because absolutism called for conformity, but because he needed the support of the Catholic clergy in facing up to Spain that he acted harshly against the Protestants and, in 1685, revoked the Edict of Nantes. This impoverished the country by driving into exile up to 200,000 economically useful people such as merchants and artisans. It also antagonized the Protestant countries and, once William of Orange became its king in 1689, turned England – already a rival on the high seas – into a powerful enemy. So followed another prolonged war against the Habsburgs, the Dutch and the English, including a failed attempt to invade England and the spread of fighting to the colonies, which lasted until 1697. The Treaty of Rijswijk was unfavourable to France, but it at least provided an interval before the outcome of the vexed question of the Spanish succession, following the lingering death in 1700 of Charles II. And it was in that interval, in 1701, that Rigaud painted his portrait of the king in majesty.

The longstanding idea of the 'French exception', a special national destiny and a commitment to *grandeur*, is based historically on the combination of two ideas which are spectacularly enshrined in the monarchical society of the *grand siècle*: the notion that France embodies not just national but universal values and the belief in the central and encompassing role of the State in enforcing those values. This was a society which self-consciously measured itself against antiquity, which was setting itself up in noble terms to surpass Rome and to establish an advanced civilization of grandeur, order and harmony. It was proclaimed in its architecture, as in the grandiose châteaux of Versailles or Vaux-le-Vicomte, which set new standards for magnificence in Europe. The ideal construction was seen as combining symmetry with the perfect integration of building, setting and decoration, while the gardens subordinated unruly nature to a geometric order emphasizing rational human control. And the same search for a universal order was to be seen in the field of culture.

The first step was to order the language itself. At the beginning of the century the poet Malherbe and the grammarian Vaugelas had worked on refining French usage on the basis of the language of the court. Richelieu, acutely aware of the unifying effect of a purified language, carried the process further with his creation in 1635 of the Académie Française, which undertook an authoritative dictionary. Stabilizing the language went hand in hand with the attempt to codify the composition of literary works and establish the theory of a new art. Of course, under Louis XIV artists and writers were supported financially to the extent that they glorified the monarchy and added lustre to the court. At a time when copyright did not exist, writers were heavily dependent on patronage, whether by direct subsidy or by appointment – as in the case of Molière and Racine – to some undemanding position at court. Yet it is interesting that this cultural concentration and absolutism should have produced the great period of French classicism without stifling individual differences.

A striking example of this is the contrast between Descartes and Pascal. Descartes, whose skull ended up oddly in a glass case in the Musée de l'Homme in Paris, is of course a great name in Western philosophy. He largely demolished traditional scholasticism – a risky undertaking which led him to migrate to the freer climate of Amsterdam – and went back to first principles by asking how we know and what we can know. Even if his own conclusions are not widely shared today, this new epistemological method opened up the fundamental question of the relation between body and mind, and made possible the development of a philosophical framework for the developing natural sciences. The French still see themselves as 'Cartesian' in the popular sense of being more rigorous and theoretically based in their thinking than the empirical British.

Unlike the optimistic rationalist Descartes, Pascal, it is tempting to say, was one who saw the skull beneath the face – though his outlook may have been coloured by the fact that he suffered from a painful nervous illness. A very considerable mathematician and physicist – he contributed to the development of probability theory and his inventions included the digital calculator, the hydraulic press and the syringe – he was also a master of French prose. But after a near-fatal accident he underwent a conversion and joined the austere Jansenist sect that believed in predestination. In his fragmentary *Pensées* he presents a vision of man lost in the 'frightening infinite spaces' of an unknowable universe, unable to achieve truth or justice or happiness, and dependent solely on the grace of an unknowable God. By his famous and in some eyes less than spiritual 'wager', however, he argues that it is a rational two-way bet to believe in God, since if you are right you have so much to gain and if you are wrong you have nothing to lose.

It is significant that, of the great classical dramatists of this period, it is the writer of comedies Molière who travels most easily. He has to glide over a certain contradiction in that, while advocating naturalness of behaviour, he still has to align his characters with the orthodoxy of a monarchical society, but in poking fun at misers or hypochondriacs or bigots he is portraying foibles familiar to audiences every-where. If the tragedies of Corneille and Racine do not transfer easily into English, however, it is not just because of the alexandrine verse form. The Cornelian hero's pursuit of *gloire*, meaning the obligation to maintain his own and his family's reputation at whatever sacrifice to himself, may seem artificial. The subtle work of Racine is much more true to life, but the lack of plot and the fact that it is as much poem as drama make it highly dependent on an audience's sensitivity to the language. Yet the high level of stylization of this type of tragedy was essential to what was seen as the noblest literary form, in that it sought to express what was permanent and universal in human nature rather than to depict people as differentiated by their particular historical circumstances. And it was the will of this monarchical culture to conceive of itself in terms of the eternal and the fundamental that led to the situation – which may seem curious given that Shakespeare had already in the previous century been presenting historical British figures – whereby the French in this period found their self-image in plays about the ancient world.

Of course there was something of a grand illusion about all this. Louis le Grand might have echoed the words of the emperor Augustus in Corneille's *Cinna* – 'I am master of myself just as I am master of the universe' – but he was living in a quite different world. While French scholars of the period knew the Greek and Latin texts, they had little understanding of the specific cultures of Greece and Rome as subsequently revealed by anthropologists and historians. Their assumption that they were the same as Greeks and Romans depended ironically on the Christian idea of an unchanging God-given human nature. The sense of fate in Racine's tragedies related to the Christian idea of original sin rather than to the gods of a polytheistic society, while Corneille's *gloire* derived obviously from the aristocratic society of his own time. All this reflected an innocent appropriation of the ancient world, which lent the absolute monarchy of Louis XIV a false sense of permanence – as indeed was prefigured in Racine's great tragedy *Phèdre*, in which civilization itself in the face of destructive human passions seems to be no more than a clearing surrounded by a dark and threatening forest.

The commanding Louis XIV of the Rigaud portrait also knew something about the gap between illusion and reality, between himself and his royal projection. He had lost his top teeth, the heroic stance disguised his gout, the red high heels masked his shortness and he was in between damaging wars. He too doubtless sensed what Racine called the 'majestic sadness' of tragedy.

5

THE ENLIGHTENMENT AND THE FALL OF THE MONARCHY

Eighteenth-century France is a paradox. On the one hand, it was a rich and powerful country which, with its Enlightenment philosophers and its sophisticated literary *salons* was the envy of Europe, to the point that French became the international language of culture and diplomacy. On the other hand, it had underlying structural and financial problems which, together with social and religious tensions, would lead it towards a shattering revolution which would have a dramatic impact not only on itself, but on Europe and beyond.

The final years of the reign of Louis XIV, up to his death in 1715, were overshadowed in a number of ways. First, since the incipient modern nations of Europe were still caught in a web of dynastic royal relationships, there was the War of the Spanish Succession, which began in 1702 and dragged on until the Treaty of Utrecht in 1713. While France's claim to the Spanish throne for Louis's grandson was based on the fear that it might otherwise go to the Austrian claimant and thus revive the Holy Roman Empire, there was also the incentive to create a bloc of two Bourbon monarchies. But this meant fighting a coalition war against most of the German states, the Dutch and the English – who would not welcome a union of French and Spanish overseas territories and more competition on the high seas. So France found itself having to put around a quarter of a million men under arms to fight on all sides, only to be heavily defeated by Marlborough at Blenheim and Ramillies and fail in an attempt to invade Scotland in 1708. Louis was finally let off the hook by the fact that the rival claimant to the Spanish throne, the Archduke Charles, became emperor and, since neither side wanted a return to the Germano-Spanish Empire of Charles V, the dispute faded away. But France had lost Nova Scotia and Newfoundland, leaving the way free for the great period of English imperial power.

A lengthy foreign war was never likely to be popular at home, nor the tax burden required to pay for it, which had to be supplemented by loans, as by the issue of rapidly devalued government bonds. Opposition became sectarian in the south-east when frustrated Protestants of the Cévennes region started a guerrilla campaign against Catholics in 1702 which ran for three years before the army put it down. But, if that was the last skirmish in the Wars of Religion, it was not the end of the matter, partly because the ageing Louis, in atonement for his highly adulterous past, as it emerges from Madame de Maintenon's absorbing memoirs, had become increasingly devout.[1] He tried to bring into line those other unorthodox Christians, the fundamentalist Catholics of the Jansenist movement. He razed their convent of Port-Royal and even went against his own Gallican principles – and an important section of the French church – by getting the Pope to issue the bull *Unigenitus* condemning Jansenist teachings. To these strains were added the terrible famine of the 'great winter' of 1709 and the shock of the death of three of his heirs from measles in one week, leaving only his great-grandson to become Louis XV at the age of five. Concerned that his free-thinking nephew the Duc d'Orléans should not influence the child, he specified in his will that the role of regent should fall to the Duc de Maine, his favourite among his illegitimate children. But the power died when he died and within two days the the Duc d'Orléans had got the parlement to declare his will null and void.

The country relaxed in relief under the regency of the Duc d'Orléans, with a little boy with blond curls on the throne but the power in the hands of an intelligent, open-minded libertine. In this suddenly permissive, get-rich-quick society there was a new sense of freedom in fashion, in the arts and in religion – a magical interlude dreamily rendered in the paintings of Antoine Watteau. However, the regent relaxed a little too much in relation to the Parlement de Paris, the judicial body which formally registered royal edicts and, if it thought one not in conformity with law or established custom, could send it back for reconsideration with a 'remonstrance' – though the king could force an edict through by order or by simply attending the parlement. Since its members held purchased hereditary offices, it was in fact a branch of the nobility that was anxious to exercise political influence and maintain its own privileges. Louis XIV had given it short shrift, but in order formally to be granted full powers as regent, powers not specified in the will, the Duc d'Orléans recognized officially once more the parlement's right to present remonstrances – which provided a platform for opposition to the throne. Also, whereas Louis had deliberately worked closely with advisers from middle-class backgrounds such as Colbert, the regent replaced them with eight councils consisting of the princes and the old nobility. The grandees, at a time when the commercial and professional middle classes were increasing in importance, were back in the saddle.

Louis XIV's extensive wars had left an enormous national debt and to deal with it the regent called in the Scottish economic theorist and adventurer John Law. Law proceeded to set up a government-backed central bank, like those already operating successfully in London and Amsterdam, which would not only move France beyond the cumbersome use of metal money, but would stimulate trade by increasing the money supply. The bank boomed after he set up an associated trading company which was granted a monopoly of trade with the West Indies and North America. Within a few years Law controlled not only the lucrative slave and tobacco trade, but also the printing of money and the collection of taxes – in effect monopolizing both France's foreign trade and its finances.

This was a bold venture in a traditionalist country which still saw wealth as residing in the possession of land and gold, but it succeeded only too well: the price of the shares soared in a classic market bubble, doubts crept in about the adequacy of the returns, the nobles sabotaged it effectively by suddenly demanding the restitution of their investments in gold, there was a classic market crash and Law had to flee the country. The nobles, of course, preferred the old system under which they had used their official positions to take a cut out of the hard currency transactions involved in tax collecting, army supplies and loans to government. The outcome of all this was unfortunate, not just because the bank's debt had to be taken over by the government and repaid through yet more taxes, but because the hostility to paper money which it engendered was such that it was not until the nineteenth century that France established a modern banking system.

Louis XV (1715–74), who took over on the death of the regent in 1723, was to provide France with another long reign. And, since he does not have a high reputation, it is only fair to say that a political system which takes a child, orphaned at the age of two, and drops the whole panoply of absolute monarchy upon him at the age of five without knowing whether he will have any aptitude for that role, is taking a very great gamble.

Louis XV was elegant and cultivated, but his traumatic childhood left him emotionally vulnerable and dependent on senior figures – his governess, the regent and then the elderly, upright Cardinal de Fleury, who served for seventeen years as his first minister. Partly because of this dependency no doubt, as well as by temperament, he only worked at kingship by fits and starts, though he could act energetically on occasion. He hid his shyness beneath a certain formal coldness, lacked self-confidence, did not readily trust his ministers and was prone to bouts of depression. To relieve the strain or the boredom, he hunted a lot and, though he was fond of the Polish princess Marie Leszczynska he had been married off to – who was older than him – he went through a succession of mistresses, often frowned upon as commoners or prostitutes, and also had a busy lover's nest in the park at Versailles. While he was well liked initially, these leanings played a part in his later unpopularity, particularly after he took a mistress with him to war in 1744. This led to a non-military ambush when he seemed to be at death's door with a fever and the clerics refused to give him the last rites until he had repented his licentious ways before witnesses. He recovered, only to find that his abject repentance was being read out in every church in the country.

It has to be said, however, that there was a notable increase in prosperity over the course of his reign, an obvious indication being the rise in population to around 26 million. It helped, of course, that the plague did not return after a strike on Marseille in 1720 and that the wars would once again be fought outside the country, but it was largely due to economic progress over most of the country. There were marked advances in coal-mining, metalworking and in the increasingly mechanized textile industry, while there was a trebling of external trade, with colonies such as Martinique and Guadeloupe providing rich pickings from slaves and sugar. In the countryside also there was an increased standard of living, although the landlords, larger farmers and clerics benefited markedly more than the ordinary peasants.

Moreover, the reign made significant and lasting contributions to the economic life of the country. A highly ambitious network of roads was begun with the use of requisitioned labour and the École des Ponts et Chaussées (College of Bridges and Highways) was set up – the first of the Grandes Écoles, or specialized higher institutions, which were to become the driving force of French education. Two veterinary schools were created as part of a campaign to improve agriculture, the École Militaire was established in Paris and the country's natural resources were taken into Crown ownership. It was in other areas that the throne ran into problems.

The first of these problems was political opposition. There was as yet no serious threat from the freethinkers in the *salons* and the cafes. Dissident publications were routinely burnt by the censorship police, while offending authors were parked in the Bastille for a month or two – Voltaire had spent eleven months there during the regency and now saw his reflections on England, *Lettres philosophiques*, impounded. The main opposition came not from the rising middle class but from the hereditary aristocracy in the form of the parlement, which made doubly sure of excluding commoners by gradually restricting membership to those with four noble grandparents. Exploiting the political space granted to it by the regent, it seized on the religious tension created by the papal bull *Unigenitus* and, in the name of the Gallican principle of the independence of the French Church, defended Jansenist priests banned by the Archbishop of Paris. The Crown forced through recognition of the bull, but this was only the first of many skirmishes – which were not lessened by the indecisive, unpredictable behaviour of the king himself after he decided, following his adviser Fleury's death in 1743, to act as his own first minister.

Indeed, the confusion at court became such that the main stabilizing factor was the arrival, as mistress, of Madame de Pompadour. A commoner in origin, with the unfortunate name of Mademoiselle Poisson, or Miss Fish, which inevitably led to cruel gibes or *poissonades*, she was nevertheless stylish, beautiful and talented. She became Louis's 'immaculate marvel', acting not only as a political collaborator but as a kind of minister of pleasure, devising all sorts of entertainment to keep the shy and moody monarch amused. A great patron of the arts, she was involved in such building projects as the École Militaire, the Petit Trianon at Versailles and the Place Louis XV – the present Place de la Concorde. She was a lover of the decorative arts in particular, sponsored the creation of the Sèvres porcelain factory and was an admirer – unlike Louis – of the new writers known as *philosophes*. She managed her delicate situation with great skill, even after she ceased being Louis's mistress for health reasons. But it was a hard world and when she died at the age of forty-two, while Voltaire mourned her as one who 'had righteousness in her soul and justice in her heart', the king's cooler comment was that she 'had bad weather for her funeral'. She has of course given her name to a rococo style in the decorative arts, as to a big hair fashion and, inevitably, she lives on in many films and biographies.[2]

The main problem, however, was the old one of waging wars and finding the money to pay for them. For the complex dynastic relationships of the monarchies across Europe made it difficult for a large country like France to keep out of the conflicts over succession that regularly arose. So, when the King of Poland died in 1733, Louis supported the claim of the queen's father, Stanislas, but was defeated by the Russians who backed a different claimant, whereupon the fighting spread to a French attempt to drive Russia's ally Austria out of Italy. In the end, Stanislas was granted the new principality of Lorraine, which would eventually revert to France, but the episode increased the national debt considerably.

The next such war was over the infernally complicated matter of the Austrian succession, with France dragged in by its ally Spain on the side of Prussia against the Austrians supported by Britain. Significantly, this extended into a naval and colonial war with the British, in which the French fleet set out in 1744 to invade England in support of the intended Jacobite rising, but turned tail on seeing a superior British force. The French navy, due to neglect and the bankrupt state of the treasury, was indeed no match for the British and regularly lost out in frequent skirmishes in the Atlantic, in which each was trying to block the colonial trade of the other. As far as the Atlantic was concerned, the British – who also captured the French fortress of Louisbourg in Canada – already ruled the seas.

However, the French had not only captured Madras (now Chennai), the main British trading post in India, but had won a splendid victory over the British at Fontenoy, in present-day Belgium. It is of this battle that the famous anecdote is told of the two armies arriving within thirty metres of each other, of the officers doffing their hats in salute and the British officer chivalrously inviting his French counterpart to shoot first. 'Non, Messieurs les Anglais' replies the gallant French offer proudly, '*you* shoot first' – an offer which the British graciously accept and proceed to mow down the French front line. Louis was suddenly very popular after this victory – at least until he signed the peace treaty of Aix-la-Chapelle of 1748, which returned all gains on all sides, and wiped out the war as though it had never happened, leaving the French asking angrily what this politely murderous and extravagantly expensive business had been all about. And they were also beginning to ask about the fairness of the system of tax collection in regard to these wars. For an attempt in 1749 to make the clergy contribute was vigorously attacked by both the clergy and the nobility, who were outraged at the suggestion that the two superior orders should be asked to pay tax like commoners – and the king gave in.

All this strengthened the hand of the parlement, which refused to register new taxes and which stoked up opposition to Church and throne after the Archbishop of Paris refused to permit the dying to be given the last rites unless the priest had a certificate proving that he adhered to the papal bull *Unigenitus*. And it created the climate in which a disturbed individual named Damiens attacked and wounded the king. His treatment, as described by the philosopher and historian Michel Foucault, provides an ironic contrast with the gallant niceties of Fontenoy, for he was tortured, had the flesh torn from his bones, had a mixture of molten lead, boiling oil and burning resin poured on to his wounds, and was then torn apart by six horses, while being asked earnestly if he had anything to say.[3]

As if this was not enough to send Louis into a decline, there was worse to come once France got drawn into the Seven Years War (1756–63), a war fought on four continents which has been called the first world war. At the European level it centred around a struggle between Austria and Prussia for the domination of Germany, while at the broader level it featured a conflict between France and Britain for imperial supremacy which was part of what is often called the second Hundred Years War. France gained nothing from the continental war and lost enormously in the maritime war with Britain, which was ruthlesssly driven by its prime minister, William Pitt the Elder. Tied to the old perspective of supremacy in Europe and short of money, France had neglected to develop its colonies, treating them essentially as a source of quick profits. And it was now to pay the price.

Even before the war began, the British – no gentlemen at sea – regularly pounced piratically on French ships to prevent them from supplying their colonies and in 1759, partly to prevent any further attempt at invasion, they struck a devastating blow by destroying the main French line fleet at Quiberon Bay. In India, after Clive's victory at Plassey and the capture of Pondicherry, the French were left by the Treaty of Paris in 1763 with only unfortified trading stations. They were similarly wiped out of North America, losing Canada and leaving Britain with the whole eastern side of that continent. They lost several of the West Indies, though they were allowed to keep Guadaloupe and Martinique, while in Africa they lost Senegal. Initially, these heavy losses aroused little interest among the French – they were more concerned about the cost – and even Voltaire, though admittedly in a comic fable, dismissed Canada in *Candide* as 'a few acres of snow'.[4] However, as it dawned on the French that they were being left behind by this suddenly predominant world power, the idea of Britain as the 'hereditary enemy' gained strength and Anglophobia, like its counterpart Francophobia, began to grow apace.

This did not significantly affect sophisticated intellectual circles, where there was rather an opposite tendency towards Anglophilia or Francophilia – major figures such as Hume and Gibbon could hold court in French *salons*, while Montesquieu and Voltaire made regular visits to England. But in the Hundred Years War the marauding British had been popularly known as *godons*, a corruption of 'goddam' – which, even according to Beaumarchais in *Le Mariage de Figaro* of 1784, the English still used on every occasion – and even as *godons coués*, or having tails like devils. And there were now much clearer differences between the two countries to feed this stereotyping. While France had an absolute monarchy, the British had a parliamentary system after killing their king. France was Catholic while the English were Protestant. Also Britain, as an island, had for long been more in favour of free trade than France with its protectionist tradition as laid down by Colbert.

What with these differences and with each country having recently made plans to invade the other, there was enough fear to lead each to turn the other into a *bête noire* and to begin to define itself as the opposite of the other. So the Goddams are seen as ruthlessly commercial and greedy, having a public life lacking clear social hierarchies which is coarse and full of drunken horseplay – they know nothing about food or fashion, their women are horse-faced and mannish, and they actually think that vulgar Shakespeare is a writer. The Frogs, in turn, are absurdly pretentious and preening, there is a clockwork artificiality to their *salon* formalities, the men are effeminate fops carrying little parasols, the women are all dolled up and shameless, and who with British blood in his veins could sit through anything as anaemic and affected as a plotless play by Racine? And this is just the eighteenth-century version of a set of prejudices which is still alive today.[5]

Yet Louis XV had increasing internal opposition to worry about, since the parlement now felt strong enough to defend the independence of the French Church by having the Jesuits closed down and expelled from France – a decision which both the king and the Pope were forced to accept. Finally driven to react, Louis went before the parlement to assert his royal prerogative and in 1770, with a triumvirate of competent ministers, began a determined campaign to break it. This was risky and he hardly enhanced the royal image by taking as his mistress Madame Du Barry, a former prostitute whom he made a countess. Nevertheless, his Chancellor Maupeou boldly abolished the hereditary rights and perks of the parlement, replaced it with a new court staffed by judges directly appointed by the State and made justice free. The finance minister, Terray, for his part, began a sustained effort to deal with the enormous national debt and was about to institute a tax on wealth when the whole reform programme collapsed with the sudden death of Louis, swept away in a smallpox epidemic. Leaving his shocked twenty-year-old grandson, now Louis XVI, and his wife Marie-Antoinette, as described affectingly by Madame Campan, dropping weeping to their knees and passionately praying, 'Oh God, guide us, protect us, we are too young to reign'.[6]

Meanwhile, in this France of the Enlightenment there was now a whole new intellectual climate, fostered by greater literacy, an increase in the publication of books and newspapers, and of course the exchange of ideas through such famous literary *salons* as those of Madame du Deffand or the passionate Julie de Lespinasse. The serious discussion of ideas had also moved from the old university orthodoxies to a score of new *académies*, or provincial societies set up on the model of the Académie Française – it was for a competition of the Académie de Dijon that Rousseau wrote his famous essay on the origin of inequality among men, 'Discours sur l'origine et les fondements de l'inégalité parmi les hommes'. Libraries were also being set up by rich individuals, while booksellers were renting out books by the day. And it was in this situation that an intelligentsia was arising, writers of often humble origin who were no longer dependent on noble protectors but could actually live by their work – Diderot was the son of a cutler, while both Rousseau and Beaumarchais were watchmakers' sons. As such they were the voices of the new educated community which was excluded from political representation and which would ultimately provide a more profound challenge to the monarchy than the privileged parlement.

Much of this activity was stimulated by the political tensions within the society, such as the religious intolerance dramatized by the execution of Jean Calas, a Protestant merchant of Toulouse in 1762. Wrongly accused of killing his own son who, it was said, wanted to convert to

Catholicism, he was condemned in a farcical trial and broken on the wheel while proclaiming his innocence. In protest, Voltaire opened up a famous debate on tolerance and had Calas rehabilitated posthumously. Another stimulus was the increasing awareness of the outside world and of the challengingly different customs of non-European peoples – the cultural relativism exemplified by Montesquieu's satirical portrait of French society in his *Lettres persanes* (*Persian Letters*, 1721) as in Bougainville's *Voyage autour du monde* (*A Voyage Around the World*, 1771), which nourished the idea of the 'noble savage'.

However, the catalyst for much of this intellectual ferment was doubtless the sense of a new scientific outlook, influenced by the empiricism of the English philosopher John Locke and by the inductive method and mechanics of Isaac Newton, offering the prospect of a new conceptual model of the world. In the monumental twenty-eight-volume *Encyclopédie* (1751–72), intended as a 'collection of all human knowledge', Diderot and his fellow *philosophes* sought to bring together all these strands into a coherent structure – in effect a fusion of Cartesian rationalism and English empiricism in the service of a new view of the world and society.

Not that French culture at this time consisted solely of heavy philosophical speculation. There was painting, from the delicately sensuous scenes of Boucher or Fragonard to the neoclassical history paintings of David. In the theatre, there were the subtle comedies of Marivaux about the inner confusions of love, and the satirical comedies of Beaumarchais, whose hero Figaro memorably lectures his noble master about the falsity of the class system. There was much variety in fiction, ranging from the novel of sensibility as with Rousseau's *Julie: ou la nouvelle Héloïse* (*Julie: or the New Eloise*) to the libertine novel with its tragic feminist heroine *Les Liaisons dangereuses* (*Dangerous Liaisons*) by Laclos.

The *philosophes* themselves were more than philosophers in the narrow sense of the word. Voltaire wrote histories, tragedies, comic fables, essays and poetry. The versatile Diderot turned his richly original mind in all directions, from philosophy and drama to fiction and art criticism. The troubled genius that was Rousseau produced social and political criticism, fiction, writings on the theatre and on education – ranging from prophetic statements about society to his unusually frank *Confessions*. And of course the *philosophes* were not identical in their beliefs. It is true that the Church was generally scandalized by these thinkers, whether by Montesquieu treating religion as a social phenomenon, Fontenelle's work on comparative religion, the naturalist Buffon's work on geological history, or the direct attacks of Voltaire or La Mettrie. But if Diderot and d'Holbach were materialists, Voltaire was a deist believing in a non-personal God, and Rousseau a Catholic turned Protestant who then renounced revealed religion in favour of natural religion. There was in fact a wide range of views on different issues among the *philosophes*.

There has inevitably been a tendency, with the illusion of hindsight, to see these thinkers as having been the direct cause of the Revolution, but that ignores the whole social and political background, let alone the variety of their views and the fact that their work was only known to a limited section of the population. They were nevertheless influential and, since they were responding to the society in which they all lived, there was broad agreement on certain basic ideas, the first being the need to re-examine everything starting from first principles. They therefore believed in human reason rather than faith – though Voltaire and Diderot, while discarding traditional faith, never made a god of reason – and in the capacity of reason to improve society. This led naturally to the idea of progress, which becomes very explicit towards the end of the century with Condorcet's *Esquisse d'un tableau historique des progrès de l'esprit humain* (*Historical Outline of the Progress of the Human Mind*). And it accordingly led to the beginnings of critical history as opposed to chronicles, to cultural relativism and a comparative approach to different societies – though there was as yet no organized opposition to the slave trade.

This relativist approach could only lead to a rejection of absolute monarchy by divine right, but the general preference, as expressed in Montesquieu's *De l'Esprit des lois* (*The Spirit of Laws*), was for the separation of powers as in a constitutional monarchy on the British model. Inevitably, there was also a rejection, not only of the political role of the Church, but of the idea of original sin – a belief in the fundamental innocence of people at birth and in their equal right to freedom. So there was a shift from seeking salvation in the next life to finding happiness in this one – an idea expressed with startling simplicity by the young radical Saint-Just during the Revolution itself when he said 'happiness is a new idea in Europe'.[7] And a shift from thinking that the wars and cruelty in the world are due to inherent human evil to the belief that they arise out of badly organized societies.

The problem was that the thinking of the *philosophes* in this transitional historical period was in a sense preparatory and that, while they broadly agreed that a rational reorganization would ultimately lead to the good society, they could not visualize that society clearly. And the ambiguity and self-contradictions of Rousseau, the wild card in the pack, came to exemplify this confusion. He opens his work on the social contract, *Du Contrat social*, with the famous declaration 'Man is born free, but is everywhere in chains', yet he ends up by imprisoning him in a different set of chains. For he carries his ideas of freedom and civic virtue to the point of propounding an ill-defined theory of the general will which, where necessary, citizens would be forced to obey – a totalitarian notion later adopted by Robespierre and by thinkers such as Hegel and amounting, as Bertrand Russell memorably described it, to 'the right to obey the police'.[8]

Since the idea of a historical or racial imperative overriding all individual rights was also argued by Lenin and Hitler, Rousseau has the curious distinction of playing an unwanted part in the origins of both fascism and communism. To complicate matters further, there is a quite different side to Rousseau since, through the opposite emphasis in his confessional writings on sensibility and the uniqueness of the individual, he not only anticipated the Revolution but the romanticism which followed it.

In fact, given the nature of this intellectual climate, it would have required both vision and deftness on the part of the monarchy to steer a way through it. So it is almost painful to observe Louis XVI's reign repeating the pattern of the previous sixty years so closely as to demonstrate a systemic weakness sliding increasingly beyond control.

Louis (1774–92) was a well-meaning but limited young man, whose interests were hunting, lock making and geography, but who had no aptitude for kingship and who, if only because he rarely got out of Versailles, knew little about the country he was ruling. Being timid, short-sighted and plump, he was rather awkward in manner. That he was unable to consummate his marriage until he had a small operation after five years hardly enhanced his status with two ambitious brothers or with his spoilt and innocently frivolous wife Marie-Antoinette, whose wild extravagance made her deeply unpopular. He saw the need for some reform, but was too indecisive and easily influenced to follow through.

He began with an irretrievable blunder by dismissing the chancellor Maupeou and Terray, the finance minister, which allowed the reform of the parlement to lapse and, although under the guidance of Maurepas he appointed some competent ministers, he had neither the confidence nor the personal authority to back them against the predictable opposition from nobles and clergy, so that it was largely they, ironically, who would bring the regime down. Initially, his popularity was boosted by the outbreak in 1775 of the American War of Independence, which fired Lafayette and other volunteers with idealistic enthusiasm and offered the chance of revenge against the British. France gave decisive help to the colonies in both ships and troops, and recouped several territorial losses including Senegal, thereby enhancing its international standing. But the downside was first that the Declaration of Independence – with its talk of men being created equal and 'governments deriving their just powers from the consent of the governed' – presented an obvious challenge to absolute monarchy in the medium term. And, more immediately, it added enormously to the already unmanageable national debt.

The first finance minister to attempt reform was the bluff liberal economist Turgot who, after establishing free trade in cereals and opening the closed guilds to free competition, attempted to institute a land tax, which would have hit noble and clerical landlords. The outrage from both the parlement and the court made Louis dismiss him – at which point Turgot warned him bluntly that 'it was weakness that put Charles I's head on the block'.[9] Next to try his hand with the finances was the plump Protestant Necker, a wealthy Swiss banker and philanthropist who performed the magic trick of financing the war in America without increasing taxes – except that he did so with ever more loans, which forced him in turn to put forward a taxation scheme. When he hit the same wall of resistance, he cheekily published a report in which he revealed the vast retainers paid to courtiers – which saw him fired.

His successor Calonne, after getting by on yet more loans, produced a repeat of the tax plans of his predecessors in 1786 and, in an attempt to circumvent resistance from the parlement, called an Assembly of Notables – a body which had lain dormant for 160 years. Flouted by the Assembly, he too was fired and the baton passed to Brienne, who had opposed reform but who now, with trouble brewing in the country, had to try to implement it. He dismissed the Assembly and then the parlement before being driven in 1788, following rejection of his reforms by the Assembly of Clergy, to the last resort of proposing the convening of the Estates-General. Since this body had not met for 174 years and had only increased conflict among the three orders even then, it did look like a desperate gamble.

Why did the clergy and the nobility – representing respectively 0.05 per cent and 1.3 per cent of the population – behave in what might seem to have been a suicidal fashion? It is true that they were not homogeneous groups and that they had their own internal hierarchy. There was a difference of interest between the high clergy and the parish priests living close to the people, as there was between the royal princes and court nobility on the one hand and the lesser nobility living on their lands on the other. And of course there had been cardinals and nobles serving as ministers. It was rather through their class institutions, the Assembly of Clergy and the parlement, that they acted against the throne. Was it merely blindness, or greed, as has so often been assumed? Did they see the writing on the wall and try to wipe it off? Or, if they felt insulted by the suggestion that they should be taxed like commoners, was it because they perceived that this would destroy the whole nature of a kingdom structured as three orders in which the clergy was meant to serve by the spirit and the nobles by the sword and through high office? At all events, what they clearly did not perceive was that they were destroying the system from within.

For from then on neither they nor the king were in control. With disturbances in Grenoble and elsewhere and a bad harvest creating food shortages, the king had to agree to convene the Estates-General at Versailles for 5 May 1789 and to double the representation of the Third Estate to 600, leaving the nobility and clergy at 300 each. The elections released an avalanche of *cahiers de doléances*, or written statements of grievances, with demands for equality and the abolition of privileges. It was therefore hardly surprising that the commoners of the Third Estate, with support from a number of ordinary parish priests, should insist that the voting be by head rather than by separate vote of the three orders and that they should all sit together as a National Assembly – in effect transferring sovereignty from the king to the people. When the king locked them out on 20 June, many of them took over a covered tennis court and swore an oath not to disperse until a constitution was established.

After hesitating for three days, Louis ordered them again with veiled threats to return to their separate orders, declaring 'I alone shall be responsible for the happiness of my peoples', only to give in a few days later, leaving them free to set themselves up as the Constituent Assembly on 9 July. But when it became known that he was trying to bring in 20,000 troops, there was panic in Paris, a militia was set up, a crowd raided the Invalides for arms and then went to find powder from the arsenal at the Bastille. Though long a symbol of the arbitrary power to imprison people without trial, the Bastille was 'the prison of the rich', which enabled aristocratic families to lock away black sheep such as the notorious Marquis de Sade while protecting them from the courts. But the Bastille, ironically, was now a largely empty shell with only a handful of elderly prisoners and a token force of non-combatant troops. So it fell; the governor's head was cut off by a butcher's boy and paraded around on a pike, the common people had entered the game – and the Revolution had begun.

Perhaps the most telling indication of the disconnection between the monarchy and the national energies that were about to engulf it is the king's diary for this month of July. It is primarily a hunting diary which also, in its one-line or simply one-word daily entries, records attendance at vespers or political events. Thus the entry for 1 July reads 'Nothing.

Separation of the Estates'. He hunts and records his kill on three days, three days have no entry at all and three others have the one word *Rien*, for nothing. And whether he did not know what was happening, or whether it was more important to record that he had no luck on the hunt that day, the entry for 14 July, the day the Bastille fell, is *Rien*.[10]

6

FROM THE REVOLUTION TO NAPOLEON

When asked what he thought of the French Revolution Zhou Enlai, the Chinese Premier under Mao Zedong, said that he thought it was too early to say. The remark was doubtless a quip, but it reminds us of the longstanding division of opinion over this spectacular political explosion that affected much of Europe and left its aftershocks not only in the revolutions of 1830 and 1848 but in the Bolshevik revolution in Russia – where we find Lenin using it as a template and even as a timetable in managing the Red Terror in the summer of 1918. In the space of twenty-five years, France turned a historical somersault by moving in succession from absolute monarchy to constitutional monarchy, then to various versions of a republic and then to an empire under Napoleon before bringing back the Bourbon monarchy in 1814. But this was not at all a return to the situation as before, for the pattern of constitutional instability would continue through the nineteenth century and indeed right up to the present time, reflecting a struggle between traditional Catholicism and republican secularism and, in general, the cleavage in political opinion which is still evident today – the very terms Left and Right derive from the Constituent Assembly of 1789. The Revolution was a watershed in French and European history and, even more than 200 years later, the echoes of the voices of Danton or Robespierre have not yet died away.

So it is hardly surprising to find vigorous disagreements among historians about the nature and the significance of the Revolution. Up to the Cold War period of the last century, when Marxism was a strong influence in France, the dominant tendency of historians such as Georges Lefebvre and Albert Soboul was to explain the events in socio-economic terms as a revolution of the new progressive middle class against a feudal aristocracy.[1] This was regarded as simplistic by François Furet and other revisionist histor-ians, who laid the emphasis on the role of political ideology.[2] Of course the argument need not be polarized in these terms, since it was precisely the interaction of economics and politics that was involved. And the same applies to the argument between those who see the Revolution as an essentially French phenomenon and those, such as Jacques Godechot, who see it as part of a series of revolutionary disturbances taking place in America, Britain and various other countries across Europe.[3] Both views are correct in that, while the English and American revolutions took place in protected, insular countries, the French Revolution was different to the extent that it took place in the most powerful country on the Continent and that, since it threatened the political traditions of the whole of Europe, it had to maintain itself against external opposition, as would the Russian and Chinese revolutions later on.

It is fair to say that the army of books inspired by the bicentenary of the Revolution in 1989 has shown a trend away from unitary explanations towards the study of neglected areas, such as the cultural, religious or military aspects, or the role of women. Nevertheless, the basic questions are obvious enough. Why did absolute monarchy as practised by the Bourbons fail? Why did the attempt at constitutional monarchy fail in its turn? Why was the Republic unable to maintain itself? Was the Terror due to immediate circumstances or was it inherent in the Revolution? Was Napoleon the saviour or the destroyer of the Revolution? And what, finally, was the legacy of the Revolution?

So was the *Ancien Régime* bound to fail? The answer would rather obviously seem to be yes. It is true that short-term factors played a part in the upheaval of 1789. There was Louis XVI's lack of grasp – though that pointed to the long-term weakness of a dynastic system which could hand absolute executive power over 20 million people to an inadequate figure and even a child of five. There was the fact that the aristocracy, through the Parlement and the Assembly of Clergy, had helped to dig its own grave. There were also food shortages and unemployment caused by drought and bad harvests from 1785 onwards, creating anxiety in Paris and disturbances in a number of provinces. But these were symptoms of a long-term failure of the monarchy to respond adequately either to external challenges from a world enlarged by imperialism or to internal challenges from a changing society.

The Revolution of 1789, as is well argued by Godechot, was in fact the point of convergence at the political level of a series of 'revolutions' not entirely specific to France: an agricultural revolution brought about by improved techniques, a related demographic revolution, an economic revolution due to the rise of capitalism, a social revolution with the rise of a commercial and professional middle class excluded from power, an intellectual revolution with the Enlightenment and, indeed, the beginnings of the industrial revolution.[4] The medieval formula of absolute monarchy by divine right no longer corresponded to the reality of a nation obliged to change in response to a changing world. The more relevant question is whether the move to a constitutional monarchy was also bound to fail.

Who were these men who met in the Constituent Assembly of 1789–91? They tended – to mention only those who became household names – to be either aristocrats like Lafayette or Mirabeau, scientists like the astronomer Bailly or the physician turned journalist Marat or, inevitably, lawyers like Danton or Robespierre. They were often quite young – in 1789 Lafayette, for all his legendary American involvement, was only thirty-two, Danton thirty-one and Robespierre thirty. But a number had written on political and constitutional matters or – like Mirabeau or Marat – had observed the British parliamentary system at first hand so that, if they had no experience of wielding national power, they were a well qualified group by the standards of the time. While there was a minority of supporters of the king on one side and a small minority of radicals or 'patriots' like Danton or Robespierre on the other, the moderate majority in the centre was intent on setting up a constitutional monarchy.

The outlook was favourable in that the other European countries were as yet showing only rhetorical opposition to the Revolution, but the moderates were operating in a febrile new atmosphere of uncertainty, hope and fear in which rumours of conspiracy were rife. The common people had made its presence felt in spectacular fashion at the Bastille and with the lapse of royal censorship there had been an astonishing explosion of newspapers in Paris and in the provinces. One of these was the *Ami du Peuple* of Marat, who was later immortalized by David's painting of him following his murder in the bath. A widely travelled court physician with philosophical, scientific and political works to his name, Marat now turned to journalism with a vengeance, chiding the moderates for not cutting off the heads of those he began to term the 'enemies of the people'. The constitutionalists were sharply aware that public opinion was now a factor in the country for the first time ever – with the proliferation of political clubs to channel and polarize it. And they were attempting to steer a middle course between the royalist loyalists on the one hand and the populist demagogues on the other.

Prominent among the majority leaders was Lafayette who, having returned showered with honours from his military successes against the British in the American Revolution, presented the Constituent Assembly with a draft for the Declaration of the Rights of Man and the Citizen that he had worked on with American Secretary of State Thomas Jefferson. In addition to playing a prominent part in the debates he also became commander of the new National Guard. However the dominant orator in the Assembly and a striking figure because of his heavily pockmarked face, was Mirabeau. A man with a colourful career as soldier, gambler, libertine, secret agent and highly undiplomatic diplomat, his hatred of absolutism was fed by his own experience of being imprisoned without trial on several occasions – indeed, he was once condemned to death for abducting and eloping with the love of his life, 'Sophie'. This experience, as well as his admiration for the British parliamentary system, also fed the various writings in which he attacked over-centralization of government, the taxation system or the absolute rule of Frederick the Great of Prussia.

Mirabeau's pragmatic approach as well as his commanding speeches won him great popularity and, when he died in April 1791 at the age of fifty-one, he was the first to be honoured by having his remains placed in the newly adapted Panthéon in Paris. In the event, they were promptly removed when it was discovered from his private papers that he had secretly been advising the king. He was not alone in this, since his highly respected colleague Barnave, a trained lawyer from a wealthy Protestant family, was also communicating discreetly with Marie-Antoinette. This was of course seen by many as treachery but, while there may have been an element of personal ambition involved, they were essentially trying to coax the king into accepting a constitutional settlement.

Running parallel to the discussion in the Assembly was the often intense activity of the new political clubs. The largest of these was the Jacobin club, so called because it rented a hall in a Dominican monastery and the Dominicans were familiarly called Jacobins since their first house had been in the rue St-Jacques. This club expanded until it had thousands of chapters and hundreds of thousands of members all over France. Initially dominated by Mirabeau and other moderates, it also included radicals like Maximilien de Robespierre, whose name would become synonymous with the last stage of the Revolution. A young lawyer who had attended the famous Louis-le-Grand school in Paris, he was schooled in the classics – which gave him a Roman sense of virtue – and had been inspired by the Enlightenment philosophers, especially Rousseau. Modest in manner and frugal in his way of life, though always carefully turned out, he had initially some difficulty in imposing himself as a speaker because of his light voice, a certain shyness and the almost naive earnestness with which he expressed his views. His emphasis on universal suffrage and equal rights – ideas hardly surprising today – soon made him a particular hate figure for the royalist press. Famously incorruptible and a believer in the Supreme Being, he was the idealistic, inflexible young purist in the harsh world of politics.

A contrasting figure was Georges Danton, then president of the more radical Cordeliers club, which tended to advocate direct action rather than the parliamentary path. Unlike Robespierre, Danton was a giant of a man with a thunderous voice and a more open, generous personality who was a natural leader of men. He was also more corruptible in that he acted as a paid informer for the court, but though he remains a flawed and controversial figure there is little doubt of his belief in the Revolution, even if he became more moderate as Robespierre became more unbending. In the end, as the Revolution began to eat its own children – as revolutions under extreme historical pressures tend to do – it would come down to a final struggle between these two.

In just over two years the Constituent Assembly of 1789–91 achieved an extraordinary amount. Its Declaration of the Rights of Man and the Citizen – which would later provide the basis of the United Nations' Universal Declaration of Human Rights – recast completely the relationship between the individual and the State. While it recognized the existence of a Supreme Being – a definition of God sufficiently wide to give freedom of conscience to Jews and other minorities – the king no longer ruled by divine right but by the will of the sovereign nation. The three Estates and inherited privileges were abolished and the separation of the executive, the legislative and the judiciary established. The subject had become a citizen, with the right to freedom, equality before the law, security and an 'inviolable and sacred right to property'. In short, it was a constitutional monarchy, in which the legislative assembly devised the laws while the king chose his ministers and could at least delay the implementation of legislation of which he disapproved.

The franchise was limited to property owners, just over half of the male population – far more than the figure of less than 3 per cent in Britain at that time. Women, of course, although they were very active in the Revolution, as a valuable study demonstrates, were still regarded as belonging to the private domain of the family, and were entirely excluded from voting rights.[5] But this was a quite historic settlement to which were added many other measures such as the institution of civil marriage, the recognition of divorce, the rational division of the country into eighty-three *départements*, the introduction of the metric system and the suppression of internal customs barriers in order to create a truly national market.

So why did this new bourgeois regime, which might have effected a peaceful transition to modernity, fail to take root? One reason was that the Assembly made a tactical error in relation to the Church. Many ordinary parish priests were supportive of change and, since there had long been an independent Gallican strain in the country, there was no marked resistance to cutting off funds to the papacy or to selling off part of the Church's extensive land holdings covering about 8 per cent of the national territory. Nor indeed was there any real resistance to the democratic reorganization of the Church, with a bishop for each *département* and archbishops to oversee them, now treated as salaried public officials whose appointment was subject to election by the wealthier members of their flock.

Yet if all this gave the Church a full place within the new national structures, a sticking point came in November 1790 with the requirement that priests swear an oath of loyalty to the new Constitution. Assembly members from the towns tended to be more aware of the often scandalous behaviour of high members of the clergy than of the valued role in peasant communities of the ordinary parish priest and it was tactically naive to insist on this aspect. In the event, if around half of the priests took the oath, the bishops and the other half refused, leading the Pope to reinforce his opposition to the Revolution with a stinging denunciation of this civil constitution of the clergy in March 1791 – which not only fed internal division but raised the issue to the European level.

Another very obvious problem was the lack of vision or trustworthiness of the king, who only went along with these developments under pressure, while constantly looking for a way out. When he initially refused to sanction the new rights, thousands of hungry women, angered by the severe food shortages and afraid that he might bring in troops, marched to Versailles and brought him back to Paris to stay in the Tuileries. And when he tried to flee secretly in June 1791, in order to muster foreign and émigré French troops on the border, his credibility as head of a constitutional monarchy evaporated. The moderates in the Assembly, afraid of popular agitation in favour of a republic and anxious to get the new Constitution voted in, pretended officially that Louis had been kidnapped. But when Lafayette and the National Guard dispersed a public protest against the monarchy in July by firing into the crowd, there was no room left for pretence.

It was clear that there was now an ominous opposition between the radicals and the moderates, many of whom now left the Jacobin club, just as there was an opposition between the Assembly and the *sans culottes*, the common people who wore cotton trousers rather than the upper-class knee breeches. The tension was not eased by the decision of the Constituent Assembly, before it disbanded after completing its work, that its members would not be eligible for the Legislative Assembly which replaced it in October 1791. This was a self-denying ordinance designed to give the new Assembly a fresh democratic mandate, but the unfortunate unintended consequence was not only that the new body was inexperienced, but that the activism moved towards the more volatile atmosphere of the political clubs.

In the end, however, the main reason for the failure to set up a constitutional monarchy, already suggested by the Pope's intervention and the émigré troops on the borders, was that this Revolution in the largest country on the Continent was bound to provoke hostility from the other monarchies of Europe; so that it can only really be understood as a combined international and domestic phenomenon.[6] Implicit in the Revolution was the broad European conflict which it increasingly became and, while there was initially some sympathy from Britain and while the other powers waited before committing themselves, Austria and Prussia called in August 1791 for a European coalition against the Revolution.

This threat combined with fear of royalist treason and revolts due to the developing religious conflict to create an atmosphere of paranoia, which led France by the following April to start a preventive war – with the agreement of the king himself, who of course was banking on defeat. This sharpened the split in the Assembly between the remaining Jacobins – also called the Montagnards because they sat in the higher tiers – and the Girondins, moderates mostly from the provinces. The difference between them is historically significant in that the Girondins, dubbed 'federalists' by the Jacobins, opposed the Paris-based centralism which has become the defining characteristic of French political life. Ironically enough, it was the moderate Girondins who supported the war in the idealistic hope of exporting the principles of revolution and the 'bloodthirsty' Robespierre who opposed it, saying presciently that war would only lead to despotism.

In the event, it would also lead to over twenty years of war with the other European powers. In the meantime, it brought about disastrous defeats and increased the paranoia, which intensified with the desertion of Lafayette, the king's veto of a call-up of provincial guards to defend Paris and, above all, with the provocative threat from the invading émigré army commander to execute anyone resisting it or not accepting the restoration of absolute monarchy. This inevitably rebounded against Louis, who had to seek refuge in the Assembly from an attack on the Tuileries by a popular uprising whipped up by Danton and Marat.

Shortly afterwards, in the panic that arose when the fall of Verdun on 2 September left Paris wide open to the enemy, the mob ran amok for several days, 'executing' some 1,100 prisoners, including aristocrats, priests and women. The Assembly failed to contain the hysteria and the situation was only relieved by an unexpected victory over the invading forces two weeks later at Valmy, which the German writer Goethe saw as a turning point in world history in that a patriotic citizens' army had defeated a professional one – opening up an age of popular nationalism and conscription. But by this time Louis was imprisoned, the constitutional monarchy was dead and the Assembly was setting up a constitutional Convention to introduce a republic.

So, if a constitutional monarchy could not survive in this Franco-European situation, was there any chance for a republic? Probably not, given its more profound challenge to the idea of monarchy and since war has its own destructive logic, but then the triumphalism of the Convention after Valmy was certainly provocative. Buoyed up by further military victories over the next six months, it proclaimed a mission to help all peoples seeking freedom and took a leap in the dark by putting the king on trial in December 1792 on a charge of treason. While Robespierre accused him of 'crimes against humanity' and Marat declared that he 'would only believe in the Republic when Louis's head was no longer on his shoulders', others were cautious. Though he was judged guilty by a vast majority of conspiring against the Republic, it was only after a tortuous debate and voting procedure lasting thirty-six hours that he was finally condemned to death by 380 votes to 310. So, on a cold misty January morning, he was driven in a carriage to the guillotine, where this kind, but weak and indecisive man, placed by an accident of birth in an untenable position, impressed all with his calm and died with dignity. When his head was held up for the crowd, as the priest accompanying him reported, there was an 'awful silence' until 'Vive la République became the universal shout of the multitude and every hat was in the air'.[7]

If the Republic had rather shocked itself by guillotining the king, it had certainly shocked Europe. It now found itself not only facing invasion from a coalition of England, Russia, Spain, Austria, Prussia, Sardinia and Naples, but having to contend with violent rebellions in different parts of the country, notably in Vendée and Brittany. If, on the one hand, it was abolishing slavery, introducing a post-Christian calendar and officializing the cult of the Supreme Being – a politically implausible ambition in a peasant Catholic country – it was, on the other hand, putting down provincial revolts and political opponents with extreme severity. It was in the desperate position of fighting for survival against a superior external enemy while at the same time fighting a fierce civil war. And it was the stresses of this situation, especially the food shortages and the conspiracy theories causing panic among the common people in Paris, that led to the Terror.

The Terror, in fact, came out of terror – the fear of retribution following defeat and the fear of hunger. It led to the effective transfer of power in April 1793 to a Committee of Public Safety, increasingly dominated by the Montagnards under Danton and Robespierre, who brought in harsh emergency measures against food profiteers in particular. As the situation worsened dramatically that autumn, the Committee's attitude hardened correspondingly into a ruthless do-or-die approach. In October, not only did it send the Girondin leaders to the guillotine, but it burnt its boats in the grand manner by mounting a crude show trial of Marie-Antoinette. The Widow Capet, as she was now officially called, was taken to the guillotine, where she apologized nervously for accidentally stepping on the executioner's foot, before going under the blade and being quickly buried in an unmarked grave. By which time the Republic had become a dictatorship with the overriding purpose of winning this desperate internal-cum-external war.

And in the short term the Terror was successful. With the ruthless repression in Vendée and elsewhere leaving up to 200,000 victims and the guillotine accounting for some 2,000 over fifteen months in Paris alone, the internal situation was largely stabilized by the end of 1793. More than that, with the rigorous control of resources, the ruthless imposition of mass conscription to create a numerically superior army of some 600,000 men and, it should be said, the patriotic ardour of troops led by new young officers, the tide of the war against the attacking European powers was beginning to turn. But the Terror had its own internal dynamic and, in this tense wartime climate of class enmity, suspicion, denunciation and food shortages, the split between Girondins and Montagnards inevitably reproduced itself among the Montagnards themselves. The leadership, increasingly dominated by Robespierre, now found itself steering between newly defined extremes.

First it had to deal with a threat from the *Enragés*, or wild men of the populist extreme left, who wanted to increase the Terror – and who were dispatched by the guillotine in March 1794. It then turned on Danton and his followers on the opposite wing, the so-called *Indulgents*, increasingly concerned at the totalitarian police state that was emerging, who argued for a relaxation of the Terror now that the situation had improved – and who were executed in April. This powerful strike at both wings purified the Revolution in the eyes of Robespierre, who believed earnestly that it must be defended at all costs, even if it required despotism to protect liberty from tyranny. But his victory over Danton left him increasingly exposed, made those around him afraid for themselves and appeared fanatical and gratuitous as the Republican armies began their successful counter-offensive with the striking victory of Fleurus on 26 June.[8] It took only a month for the Convention to send Robespierre to the guillotine in his turn, on 27 July, bringing to a symbolic end this phase of the Revolution.

It is possible to say coldly that the Revolution got rid of Robespierre as soon as he had served his purpose, as it is possible to argue in the structuralist style of one comparative study that what mattered were the objective pressures on France to reconstruct itself to play its part in a new Europe of competing modern nations, and that therefore ideological difference were secondary.[9] But beyond the fate of those individuals who were ground up in the process there is the larger tragedy of a revolution which, at the critical point of that pressure, is driven to turn itself inside out. And there is a tragic irony about the fate of Robespierre himself. A high puritan, a deist who attacked atheism, a believer in access to individual property and to work and education for all, he had not the breadth of experience of the more flawed Danton and could not recognize the limits of political possibility at that time. He was not personally ferocious like some Simon de Montfort, nor indeed did the Revolution dispatch anything like the number of Cathars slaughtered by the Inquisition, but there was a chillingly ceremonial aspect to the public parading of victims towards their death under the knife of the kindly faced Dr Guillotin's 'humane and democratic' killing-machine. There was also a chilling necessity about the fact that, with his jaw already smashed from a failed attempt to kill the only man left to kill, himself, Robespierre ended up under it in his turn. The irony is that, in attempting to combat absolutism, he was driven to reproduce it in mirror image form.

The end of the Terror brought back to prominence the middle-class moderates, who set up a new constitution giving executive power to a five-man Directoire, with two legislative bodies to provide checks and balances. The sense of relief was enhanced by the success of the armies which were advancing into the Netherlands, Germany, Switzerland and Italy, where they were setting up sister republics – though they would recklessly begin to antagonize these by engaging in pillage. At home it was a time of extravagance and opportunism, exemplified by the leading figure among the directors, the loose-living and corrupt Paul Barras.

Though the regime was weak, it managed to suppress, on the one hand, a neo-Jacobin threat mounted by the extreme egalitarian Babeuf and, on the other, a serious royalist revolt in Paris in favour of Louis's short-lived heir, the notional Louis XVII (1792–5) – which was briskly put down by a young general of twenty-six called Bonaparte. And when this young Napoleon Bonaparte fell passionately in love with a former mistress of Barras, Joséphine de Beauharnais, Barras gave him almost as a wedding present command of the French army in Italy.

Napoleon and Joséphine are best seen in the context of this disturbed and dangerous transitional period – Joséphine's husband, a general, had been guillotined and she had herself been arrested at one point, as indeed had Napoleon. Six years older and with two children, she came from a family which owned a sugar plantation in Martinique. She had been married off to the notorious libertine Beauharnais and in this permissive milieu had been the mistress of several notable figures. She was one of the fashionable women of the time, slim, good-looking and, while her teeth were not good, possessed of a beautiful voice. If she was extravagant and rather frivolous, she was also gracious, likeable and kind. And it is perhaps because she was an experienced lover – which her romantic young idealist of a husband was not – that she attached less importance to fidelity than he did.

Napoleon, from minor Corsican nobility and with French as his second language, was also something of an outsider. In good Corsican fashion, he retained a close tie to his mother even though she called Joséphine a whore and constantly predicted disaster, felt himself responsible for the whole family and, despite being an agnostic, crossed himself superstitiously before going into battle. But, away from home at the military academy at Brienne and then Paris, he developed independence and displayed not only his high intelligence, but his ambition and his formidable capacity for work. It was fortunate for him that he did not qualify for the aristocratic cavalry and therefore joined the more modern branch of the army, the artillery, since it was through his decisive use of artillery that he had first come to be noticed at the siege of Toulon. And he was more than ready, within hours of his wedding – having told the registrar to get on with it – to seize his big chance in Italy.

The Italian front was initially seen as a sideshow in the battle against Austria, but in his 1796–7 campaign Napoleon, with a succession of victories including Mantua and Milan, made it central to the point of reversing a dire military situation. Though the soldiers at first looked askance at this slight, youthful commander, he quickly won them over by leading boldly from the front, displaying flair and focus, and never talking down to them. He ended up by invading Austria and negotiating the peace treaty of Campo Formio, all of which – together with the fact that he helped to build up his own legend through regular army bulletins – made him extremely popular at home.

Napoleon soon became a little too popular for Barras, who was aware that the Directoire was far from popular due to its failure to create order or unity – and who was therefore happy to see off a potential rival by granting Napoleon command of an expedition to Egypt. The strategic aim here was to weaken Britain's imperial control of Egypt and then India, but with his considerable intellectual curiosity Napoleon also took with him a team of scholars – who with their inventory of treasures and the discovery of the Rosetta stone founded Egyptology. As a military operation, however, it was a disaster. He did gain Cairo by his famous victory at the Battle of the Pyramids, but when Nelson destroyed his fleet at Aboukir Bay in August 1798 he found himself isolated with an army suffering from the plague and, on hearing of the threat from a fresh coalition, he handed over command and returned quietly to France.

Meanwhile, the iron had begun to enter his soul, not just with the knowledge that Joséphine had been unfaithful to him while he had been away, but with the humiliation of having seen letters concerning the affair intercepted by Nelson and unsportingly spread across the London *Morning Chronicle*. Though he would never cease to love her, even after the need for an heir led him to divorce her in 1810, the power balance shifted and it was he who would periodically be unfaithful. The wounded idealist was becoming harder and, with little respect for the weak and corrupt politicians he found on his return, he readily lent himself to a *coup d'état* led by the old Jacobin Sieyès, who intended to use him and Ducos in a three-man consulate led by himself.

In fact, though the plot only just succeeded, it was Napoleon who came out as First Consul and who would gradually centralize power in his own hands as he faced the enormous task of bringing order, unity and prosperity to this radically divided and near bankrupt post-revolutionary state. And this had to be carried out in the face of the foreign hostility that would require him to defend the country against six further coalitions of European powers from 1799 to 1815. There was the related internal threat of assassination attempts sponsored by the British, notably the spectacular attempt in 1800 to blow him up as he left the opening night of Haydn's *Creation*, and it was in the context of further such attacks that he became a hereditary emperor in 1804 in the attempt to give the regime permanence beyond himself.

In dealing with this internal-cum-external opposition, Napoleon came to depend in particular on two perpetual survivors in the dangerous politics of the time, neither of whom he liked or trusted but neither of whom he could do without. The first was his minister of police, Fouché, a former teacher, an ambassador under the Directoire and a radical Jacobin whose ruthlessness in repressing a rising against the Convention in Lyon had shocked Robespierre. Uncouth, unkempt and unwashed – though he was also a loyal family man and the perfect father – he was a master of intrigue who kept order internally by means of a tight spy network.

A contrasting refined, very *Ancien Régime* figure was the foreign minister Talleyrand, an ex-aristocrat, ex-bishop, ex-exile, who has become a byword for diplomatic deviousness and inscrutability. A sensualist, a womanizer, a gourmet, a wine connoisseur with his own Bordeaux vintage, his apparent idleness baffled Napoleon, but he had lived in both England and America and appeared to have contacts everywhere. He may seem today to have been as corrupt as an old camembert, but in taking bribes for his services he was following a custom of the time and his attitudes owe much to his background. An aristocrat who had lost his rights as the oldest son because of a club foot and had to make do, though an atheist, with being made bishop of Autun at the age of thirty-five – which entailed the inconvenience of a three-day visit to the place – he had espoused the Enlightenment and supported the Revolution. But, while Napoleon was conditioned to the idea of military glory, Talleyrand saw war as a tiresomely noisy affair which killed people. His value, which to his credit Napoleon recognized, was that, at a time when France was at war with the traditional powers over the political future of Europe and with Britain in particular over imperial hegemony, Talleyrand was a man of peace.

Having secured peace with the Austrians after defeating them at Marengo in June 1801 and forcing the now isolated British to accept peace a year later, Napoleon set about transforming the country. He allowed émigrés to return and came to an agreement with the rebel Chouans in Brittany, who had resisted the Revolution. He made a concordat with the Pope which brought the Church back into the national community under State supervision – and in appointing bishops insisted that, even if he did not, they should actually believe in God. He created a new national administration system based on appointed prefects and set up the Conseil

d'État, or Council of State. He established a properly unified
legal system with his Code Civil or Code Napoléon – later
adopted by a number of other countries – and reorganized
the judicial wing with twenty-nine courts of appeal and a
high court.

Beyond that, he set up the Banque de France and
stabilized the currency so firmly that the franc remained
steady up to the outbreak of the First World War in 1914.
He created a rather regimented State secondary education
with his *lycées* and a higher education system dominated by
the highly selective colleges known as the Grandes Écoles.
He also created the Légion d'honneur to reward service and
encourage loyalty to the Republican State. In short, on these
'granite blocks' as foundations, he created the enduring
legislative, administrative, judicial and educational features
of the modern French state. And he rounded off this
comprehensive undertaking by taking steps to improve
agriculture, extend industry and promote public works,
including several familiar Paris bridges and the Bourse, or
stock exchange.

And then, with the resumption of war in 1805, it gradually
became more difficult. Firstly, he was fighting almost
constant war on two sides, with both the major continental
powers and imperial Britain. Secondly, he was a victim of his
own temperament, for Napoleon was very much a transitional figure, a blend of opposites. On the one hand, he was
the exceptionally gifted Enlightenment rationalist, the statesman with an eye for the realistic compromise; on the other
hand, he was the romantic idealist, the believer in military
glory, the visionary who dreamt of a united Europe, the
outsider intrigued by his own 'destiny' and tempted to see
how far he could go. And thirdly, of course, he was caught
in the turmoil of events which led him, with the British
financing assassination attempts, to try to ensure permanence for the regime by having himself crowned hereditary
emperor in the presence of the Pope.

And indeed this empire of 1804–14, with its authoritarian liberalism, its fusion of revolutionary ideas and monarchical forms, achieved military dominance in Europe in the next few years with such famous victories as that over Austria and Russia at Austerlitz (1805) or that over Prussia at Eylau (1807). But things went wrong. His plans to invade England fell apart when the British destroyed his fleet at Trafalgar and his continental embargo on trade with Britain turned his neighbours against him. If he had his reasons for creating a hereditary empire, it was overdoing it to create a new hereditary nobility. He set up one brother on the throne of Holland, another on the throne of Westphalia and made his son-in-law Viceroy of Italy. Also, in the words of Lefebvre – who at the end of his vast Marxist analysis is driven to conclude that the decisive factor was indeed Napoleon's temperament – 'the best way to defend the natural frontiers of the country might have been not to advance provocatively in conquering fashion beyond them'.[10]

The turning point came in 1808, when he decided to force the King of Spain to abdicate and replaced him with another of his brothers, Joseph. This provoked a running rebellion which he never quite succeeded in quelling, so that his army was weakened and Austria was tempted to declare war again. Napoleon responded in the grand manner by defeating it at Wagram, divorcing Joséphine since she had not produced the necessary heir, and by marrying the Austrian emperor's eighteen-year-old daughter Marie-Louise, who did. By 1810 therefore, even if Fouché and Talleyrand were by now conspiring secretly with his enemies, he seemed to be at the pinnacle of his power, with an empire stretching from Holland to Italy.

But when the Tsar broke the terms of the embargo by reopening trade with Britain, he gambled on an invasion of Russia in 1812, only to be defeated by a scorched earth policy and be forced to trail back with the loss of half a million men. The whole of Europe now turned against him and he was forced to abdicate in 1814 – only to return like a jack-in-the-box from exile in Elba and had to be defeated all over again at Waterloo in the following year. He was exiled to the remote island of St Helena in the South Atlantic, where he died at the age of fifty-two in 1821. While he was inconsiderately treated by his British captors, and while his medical care was poor, he was hardly murdered, as a whole array of conspiracy theorists have suggested. He had ongoing gastric problems and apparently died of stomach cancer.

Napoleon was not the ogre of British propaganda. Nor was he the gravedigger of the Revolution – he probably consolidated the middle-class revolution as far as it was possible to do so in the French and European circumstances of the time. But, as Martyn Lyons points out, he was not the 'passive instrument of any class or social group', but rather a unique and dominant individual.[11] And it was in fact when his 'destiny' led him beyond the terms of the consolidation of that revolution that he ran into trouble. He lost all French gains in Europe and lost the imperial struggle with Britain, but he had exported revolutionary ideas with his armies, he had opened up great questions about forms of government and he had created the modern secular state. When the Bourbon monarchy returned in 1815 – having, in the words attributed to Talleyrand, 'learnt nothing and forgotten nothing' – it was to a different world.

Yet Napoleon lingered on in that world. For his life, as he himself recognized, had been the stuff of legend. And the legend was maintained in the nineteenth century by his own memoirs and by such prominent writers as Byron, Stendhal and Victor Hugo, to the extent that it prompted King Louis-Philippe in 1840 to bring back the emperor's ashes to be interred with great ceremony in Paris. But that naive attempt to unite the country by incorporating the legend simply prepared the way for Napoleon's nephew to become Emperor Napoleon III in 1852. And this underlines the permanent political legacy of Napoleon, which is that his attempt to bridge the gap between left and right initiated a Bonapartist strain in French politics running through Napoleon III up to de Gaulle and Sarkozy.

But what, since history is not all about battles, of the abandoned Joséphine? She made her own real contribution to the softer side of civilization by turning herself into a serious horticultural expert and developing a famous collection of roses at the Château de Malmaison, where she also built up a fine art collection before her death in 1814.

7

REVOLUTIONARY AFTERSHOCKS
AND ANOTHER NAPOLEON

The end of the Napoleonic drama brought the restoration of the Bourbon monarchy, yet there could be no restoration of either France or Europe as they had been before the Revolution. The preceding quarter of a century seemed to many to have devalued the old unifying values not only of Christendom but of the Enlightenment itself. Europe, if only because Napoleon's wars had stirred up resistance across the continent, was turning into a hotbed of competing national-isms – this would be the century of German and Italian unification, as of Greek and Belgian independence. In France itself, as it moved rather belatedly towards the industrial society, there would be increasing polarization between secular ideologies such as democracy and socialism and a royalist-inclined Catholicism. In this situation, since the revolutionary period had thrown all the constitutional cards up in the air, the country would once again zigzag through different regimes before finally achieving stability towards the end of the century. All of which was a recipe for a lively period in which France would be the centre of significant revolutions and would make key contributions to social thought, the Romantic movement, literary realism and, of course, modern art – particularly in the form of the iconic Impressionist paintings which have imprinted a certain image of France on the mind of the world.

Louis XVIII (1814–24) became king in a deal negotiated by the ubiquitous Talleyrand, having been brought back 'in the baggage train of the enemy'. He was almost sixty, out of touch and lacking in energy due to the long years of exile in Italy and England, and to the obesity combined with gout that would gradually confine him to a wheelchair. He declared himself to be in the nineteenth year of his reign, as though the Revolution and the empire had never existed, but was forced by the allied powers to accept a limited version of constitutional government – the main limitation being that out of a population of almost 30 million only 100,000 were entitled to vote. But even this was too much for his ultra-royalist émigré entourage, whose arrogant behaviour helped to provoke the sudden return from Elba of Napoleon which sent them rushing back into exile. When they returned after the Battle of Waterloo (1815), the thirst for revenge led to a White Terror answering the previous Red Terror, in which supporters of Napoleon and Protestants were attacked and several hundred people killed. The government itself followed this up by purging the administration and the army, executing several of Napoleon's generals, and by passing laws not only against seditious writings but against 'seditious shouts'. Louis himself became so concerned by these excesses that in 1816 he accepted the advice of his more liberal young minister Decazes – for whom he also had a sentimental attachment – to dissolve this ultra-royalist chamber and look for a more moderate one.

With a little gerrymandering, a more moderate chamber

was engineered and for the next four years, under the guidance of Decazes, more liberal policies were pursued. There was some relaxation of the censorship and an electoral law rather more favourable to the middle classes, along with sound financial management enabling France to pay back its reparation costs to the victorious foreign powers. But the conservative Austrian minister Metternich was concerned at this new liberal direction by Decazes, as of course were the ultra-royalists, who had strong support from the press and from influential societies such as the Chevaliers de la Foi, or Knights of the Faith. They had an idealized view of absolute monarchy – which chimed with a return to the simpler medieval world by the Romantics – and, since they saw it as the only way of preserving the Church and the Catholic worldview, they accepted nothing less than its restoration along with that of the three Estates and the concomitant privileges of nobility and clergy. So when a disturbed Bonapartist saddler assassinated the king's nephew the Duc de Berry in 1820, they seized the chance to blame Decazes, forced his resignation and ran the country for the next ten years. They came completely into their own when their leader, the Duc d'Artois, succeeded Louis XVIII as Charles X (1824–30), since Charles, as devout and authoritarian at sixty-seven as he had been scandalous and womanizing in his youth, insisted on a return to the full medieval coronation ceremony, down to exercising on thousands of sufferers – with no noticeable success – his new God-given power to heal scrofula with a touch of his hand.

Over the next few years his missionary alliance of throne and Church set about returning education to the Church, imposing the death penalty for any act of sacrilege and – a measure which the middle classes found especially threatening – passing a law to compensate émigré nobles. All this inspired opposition from both left and right, and even from some members of the Church. When Prime Minister Villèle tried to outmanoeuvre this opposition by calling an election in 1827, he found himself in a minority and was forced to resign. After a lengthy interval, Charles appointed the ultimate ultra-royalist, the mystical Catholic nobleman the Prince de Polignac, whose mother had been a favourite of Marie-Antoinette and who looked down a particularly long nose upon anything subsequent to the *Ancien Régime*.

When Polignac's appointment was taken as a provocation, Charles dissolved the chamber in May 1830, only to see the opposition return in greater numbers in July. Blind to the lessons of 1789, as to ominous signs of dissent arising out of an economic crisis following bad harvests, Charles attempted a top-down coup, declared that he would rule alone – and blundered straight into the bottom-up revolt known as the 1830 Revolution. It was started by the printers, soon joined by other workers, students and army veterans, who mounted barricades and fought off heavy attacks from the army before occupying the Louvre and the Tuileries. Within three days a startled Charles X was fleeing towards the standard bolt-hole for French kings and aristocrats at the time, England.

Meanwhile the middle-class leaders, who had wanted a properly functioning constitutional monarchy, were alarmed at the republican tone that the insurrection had assumed. But they had a plan up their sleeves for just such an eventuality and, with the inevitable Talleyrand oiling the wheels as go-between, they produced out of the hat Duc Louis-Philippe of the junior and more liberal Orléanist branch of the dynasty. The ageing Lafayette presented him, draped patriotically in the tricolour flag, at the Hôtel de Ville in Paris and the July monarchy of 1830–48 was born. It is often referred to as the 'bourgeois monarchy' since it marked the passage of power from the aristocracy to the upper middle class and, accordingly, the country's new monarch – who would also be its last monarch – was proclaimed King of the French, rather than King of France, in order to emphasize that his sovereignty came from the people.

Louis-Philippe was of course hardly a bourgeois himself – as well as being of royal blood he was the wealthiest man in the kingdom – but he had the modest lifestyle of a family man with eight children. In his youth he had fought with the revolutionary armies before going into exile in 1793, but he was now a mature fifty-seven-year-old marked by long years of residence in England, in quiet Twickenham. Apparently easy-going, less confrontational and more intelligent than Charles X, he looked to his backers like a reasonable compromise. But he did not look like that to the republicans, who thought they had been robbed, or to the legitimists, the old royalists who thought him a usurper, or indeed to the Bonapartists, whose opposition would only be increased by the return of Napoleon's ashes to the Invalides in 1836.

The first sign of trouble was the strike of the Lyon silk workers in 1831, famous as the first working-class insurrection in France, which led to an occupation of the town that was then brutally repressed by the army using cannon, leaving many dead and wounded on both sides. This was followed by a republican rising in Paris, put down by the army under the command of Louis-Philippe himself, and then by a comically inept legitimist attempt at a rising by Charles X's daughter-in-law, the Duchesse de Berry, who happened to be pregnant with an illegitimate child at the time. A failed attempt in 1835 to assassinate the king by the Corsican republican Fieschi – the first of seven such attempts during the reign – led to a series of repressive measures which maintained order sufficiently to enable the regime to cope comfortably with another unsuccessful rising, this time by Louis Napoleon, Napoleon's nephew and the future Napoleon III, who was promptly clapped in prison.

The leading minister at this time was the stiffly conservative François Guizot, a historian who encountered history at the age of seven when his father was guillotined by the Convention. This experience doubtless conditioned his fear of popular insurrection and his admiration for the British constitutional monarchy with its limited franchise. He is celebrated today both for telling the French to get rich by working and saving – '*enrichissez-vous*' – and for establishing a system of State primary schools throughout the country, not compulsory or free, but cheap and increasingly frequented as education was seen to be useful in a changing economy. Not that change, in what was still an *Ancien Régime* type of agricultural society, was as rapid as in Britain. While an ambitious law to create a railway network was passed in 1842, the plan was only partly implemented, industry remained a poor second to agriculture and the banking system remained slow to see the advantages of investing its considerable funds in new ventures or major public works. What with that and with the onset of the falling birth rate that would seriously weaken the country's relative strength by the end of the century, France was already beginning to fall behind.

While Louis-Philippe managed usefully to avoid war with other European powers, it was at the expense of a certain amount of humiliation at the hands of the British, who prevented the newly independent Belgium from choosing a French king and kept France out of the settlement of an Egyptian–Turkish dispute. For this reason his success in establishing a friendly connection with the British throne was not much welcomed at home. He also became bogged down in Algeria, where a young Islamic leader started a holy war which took seven years to bring to an end, but he managed to make some minor additions to the diminished French colonial empire in the Ivory Coast and in Polynesia. However, the reign was hit from 1846 onwards by an economic downturn due to bad harvests and a fall in demand, leading to unemployment, sabotage in factories and the looting of bakers' shops. All this, plus juicy aristocratic scandals like that of a duke murdering his wife, fed inevitably into political opposition from all sides. The republicans in particular – now called 'radicals' since the throne had banned the term 'republican'– had long been campaigning, with the eloquent voices of the poet Lamartine and the historian Michelet, for the extension of the right to vote. And it was the short-sighted banning of one of their traditional banquets on 22 April 1848 that triggered the French revolution of 1848.

For this brought about a student protest in front of the Panthéon, which was soon swollen by workers, and the evening ended in scuffles in the streets. Next day, as barricades were being thrown up, the army moved in to restore order, only to find that the National Guard had swung over to the insurgents and was also demanding reforms. Louis-Philippe dismissed Guizot, but failed to find another prime minister, while that night the army fired on insurgents trying to besiege the Ministry of Foreign Affairs, leaving fifty-two dead and causing hundreds more barricades to be thrown up across Paris. Louis-Philippe drew the obvious conclusion and took the well-trodden path back to England. It had taken only three days to put a final end to the French monarchy.

Naturally, the political change over the previous thirty years reflected profound underlying changes in France's culture. This was the era of Romanticism, a complex European phenomenon arising out of the widespread sense among intellectuals and artists that their civilization was in crisis. As the certainties of the Middle Ages had been undone by the Enlightenment, so the assumptions about reason and fraternity had been undermined by the violence of the Revolution and the Napoleonic Wars. The continuum that had been Christendom was replaced by a new Europe of competing nations, each trying to define its identity in specific terms – in Germany, where the term originated, the Romantics reacted against French neoclassical culture and attempted to establish a separate Germanic tradition going back to the Middle Ages. There was a widely shared sense among these essentially middle-class intellectuals that in the absence of a universal order – social, moral or philosophical – individuals were thrown back upon themselves. The sense of being a misfit in a leftover world, where the orthodox went sleepwalking on as though nothing had happened, could lead to a vague longing for completeness (the German *Sehnsucht*), to a return to nature as with Wordsworth, to an imaginative flight into medievalism or fantasy, or to a search, following Rousseau, for the truth within the mysterious recesses of the self. There was of course the flatteringly tragic idea that if the poet was condemned to live on the margins of society it was because he was a genius. But, if it is understandable that Arnold Hauser should see all this as a 'flight from reality' based on 'fear of the present and of the end of the world', it is fair to agree with Jacques Barzun that 'the problem was to create a new world on the ruins of the old'.[1] And many writers did involve themselves actively in public affairs.

Chateaubriand, for example, may have been a melodious voice for the *mal du siècle*, the discontent felt by the genius marginalized by a philistine society, in prose works such as *René* (1802), but he became foreign minister during the Restoration. Lamartine, in his *Méditations* of 1820, brought a more intimately personal tone to this elegiac search for meaning in nature and for a faith. That his preoccupation with death and destiny was inspired by the recent death from consumption of his lover Julie Charles reminds us that the Romantic angst derived not only from social and political upheaval but from the conditions of life at that time – a whole book could be written about the ravages of tuberculosis and venereal disease among French writers in the nineteenth century. Yet none of this prevented Lamartine from pursuing a diplomatic career or from becoming briefly the head of the provisional government after the revolution of 1848.

However, the most striking example of the engaged Romantic writer is Victor Hugo, a giant talent fed by the giant ego that inspired Jean Cocteau's wicked joke that

Victor Hugo was a madman who seemed to think he was Victor Hugo. Enormously productive, with a rich imagination and an empathy that enabled him to universalize profound private emotions, he was not only a virtuoso in literary forms but an accomplished artist. In his play *Hernani* of 1830, an improbable Spanish imbroglio saved by lyricism, he famously smashed the rigid neoclassical rules and established the Romantic hero as the ill-fated plaything of a dark unknowable destiny, driven onward by some deadly inner force towards he knows not what. Yet he became celebrated as a republican opponent of Napoleon III and his funeral in 1885 brought Paris to a standstill. The major Romantics did engage in their world.

Even so, it is the novelists, as might be expected, who provide a fuller description of their society and it is here that Romanticism begins to merge into realism. Hugo himself marks the transition with his political novel *Les Misérables*. Stendhal, the pseudonym of the diplomat and art critic Henri Beyle, offers a coolly satirical picture of Restoration society in his famous *Le Rouge et le noir* (*The Red and the Black*), but his hero Julien is a romantic outsider from a modest background, whose ambition is blocked now that Napoleon's 'opening to all the talents' has ended. In this frozen society in which only class privilege and wealth count, the sole choice is between the red uniform of an army which has no longer any glorious battles to fight and the black uniform of a now all-powerful conservative Church – in the end Julien rejects both and chooses an indirect form of suicide.

However, the most significant novelist of the period – and the French Dickens in some sense – is the prodigiously prolific Honoré de Balzac. Constantly in debt, working night and day, he produced a whole parallel world in the vast series of novels he finally grouped together under the title *La Comédie humaine*. He had a powerful Romantic imagination, but he was fascinated and sometimes horrified by the world around him as it underwent dislocating social and moral change. As a provincial from Tours, and a perpetual innocent in some ways, he was particularly fascinated by the life of Paris – at the start of his novel about the old martyr to paternal love, *Le Père Goriot*, he warns that the reader who does not know the city may not understand the story. He can create an intense sense of reality not only through observational detail, but through a powerful magnifying effect in his presentation of characters such as Goriot or the villain Vautrin which elevates them to the status of great literary types. And he was halfway to the forthcoming realism in seeing the extent to which character may be determined by milieu and circumstance.

Yet the difficulty of practical engagement with a changing world is perhaps best seen in the work of the French Utopian Socialists, as Karl Marx dubbed them – Saint-Simon, Fourier and Proudhon. They were fundamentalists, less interested in surface politics than in trying, as a major study of utopias describes it, 'to discover the core of human nature and to build a new social structure with the hard blocks of reality – man's reason, instincts, desires, needs, capacities'.[2] Of course they were different people with competing systems. Saint-Simon was a colourful charmer who had travelled widely, made a fortune, lost it all and become a pawnbroker's clerk; Fourier was a dour obsessional loner who waited every day at the hour of noon for the millionaire who was about to turn up to back his plans, which included the nice idea of putting citric acid into the sea to turn it into lemonade; Proudhon was an independent, engaging anarchist, famous for saying that 'property is theft'.

While they all believed that people were unable to achieve their full humanity in a false society, their solutions varied. Saint-Simon imagined a rational, collaborative industrial order living according to a 'new Christianity' – though his followers later caused scandal with free love colonies not unlike some American examples of the 1960s. Fourier wanted ideal communities grouped according to the members' passions. Proudhon retained the monogamous family, but dreamt of a mature society of equals in which the State would be redundant. If their ideas seem a little comical today, it should be said that followers of Saint-Simon became influential in areas from banking to engineering, while Fourier's ideas also bore fruit, notably in the development of the co-operative movement – even if such visions were not immediately applicable to the 1848 revolution.

The year 1848 saw a series of revolutions in various parts of Europe – though not in Britain, where the extension of the franchise through the Reform Act of 1832 helped to contain discontent. The immediate circumstances varied from country to country – in Prussia and in the Austrian Empire the demand was for a constituent assembly, while in the Italian states the constitutional aims were combined with a reaction against the Austrian presence. But while the events were triggered by an economic crisis, and while a desire for national unification was part of the motivation in the German and Italian states, the events across the continent broadly reflected a struggle by the liberal middle classes to defend and advance their interests against aristocratic forces bent on retaining power. Populations were increasing, cities had doubled in size, there was some access to education and, with the rise in journalism, people were better informed about the forces governing their lives.

If France was the symbolic centre of this continental movement, it was because of its revolutionary tradition and because it was ahead of other continental countries in terms of social and constitutional development. In practice, of course, the middle-class revolution had to be carried out with the support of the rising working class, but the alliance was not an easy one. And indeed 1848 – though it remained important as a test case – was a replay of 1830 in that those who made the revolution were not necessarily those who enjoyed its fruits.

Yet the triumphant republicans certainly got off to a quick start, for no sooner had Louis-Philippe left the scene than they proclaimed the Second Republic at the Place de la Bastille and set up a provisional government – including not only their own leading figures such as Lamartine, but the socialist Louis Blanc and even a worker known as Albert. They then did some great things and learnt some hard lessons. They not only abolished censorship, but introduced universal suffrage which, though restricted to men – since women were still regarded in law as appendages – nevertheless raised the franchise in a giant step from under 250,000 to 9 million. The snag, from their point of view, was that the majority of voters still lived in the conservative countryside, with the result that in the April election a third of the chamber turned out to be royalists and the rest the more moderate republicans. Nevertheless, the new government reduced the working day to ten hours, abolished slavery in the colonies – soon reversed by its successors – and set up Louis Blanc's novel workshops to provide work for the unemployed. Unfortunately, these did not work well, and became a bone of contention between socialists and the government, which closed them down and provoked the workers' rebellion in Paris known as the 'June Days'.

This uprising and its memorably bloody repression caused the deaths of around 1,000 soldiers and 5,000 insurgents. Some 15,000 were arrested, of whom 5,000 were deported to Algeria, censorship was brought back and the early innocence of the Republic was lost. Or not quite, for the law of unintended consequences struck again when, in the constitution it set up in November, the government decided to follow the American model and have a president elected by universal suffrage. Democratic as this seemed, it left the way open – as the deputy Jules Grévy pointed out – for some populist figure to turn up and take over.

Which is exactly what happened when Louis Napoleon Bonaparte stood and romped home with 75 per cent of the votes. The republicans were again routed in the legislative elections of 1849, by monarchists and other conservatives, who once again reduced the franchise and financed Church schools. And Louis Napoleon, having failed to reform the constitution to enable him to serve longer than his four-year term, carried out his predictable *coup d'état* in 1852, with the result that 26,000 republicans were arrested, close to 10,000 were deported, universal suffrage was brought back for a plebiscite – and France once again had an emperor.

Meanwhile, the revolutions elsewhere had long since been easily put down, especially in Germany. And it is telling to find Karl Marx, who saw the June Days as the first battle in the class war, speculating on the outcome at the end of 1848. If he found the Utopian Socialists romantic, the circularity of his argument leaves him looking equally romantic – he too had after all written romantic poetry and he was still only thirty. Deciding that a revolution in Germany was not possible, since it lacked a proper proletariat, he thought there might just be a chance if it could be attached to a French revolution. Except that the British would immediately invade and crush that. Which would require the British themselves to be defeated in a wider conflict. So 'the agenda for 1849', he writes, 'is revolution by the French working class, world war'.[3] But if you are unable to start a revolution in Germany, how on earth do you start a world war? The notion of a discrete international proletariat defeating an equally coherent international bourgeoisie would remain a period fantasy. Progress would be gradual and it would not be by world war.

Napoleon III (1852–70) has had a bad press and it is possible, as is suggested in one of the reappraisals published in 2008 for the bicentenary of his birth, that his achievements have been unduly obscured by the shock of defeat by the Prussians in 1870 and by the loss of Alsace-Lorraine – not to mention by Victor Hugo's scathing dismissal of him as a mini-Napoleon: '*Napoléon le Petit*'.[4] Certainly, you will not find many streets in French towns named after Napoleon III. Yet a contemporary like Louis Pasteur viewed him quite favourably, while for others – including Bismarck, who called him 'the sphinx' – he was more of a mystery. He was indeed something of a walking contradiction – with a strong sense of destiny but unsure of himself, humane but outwardly cold and secretive, cautious but with a streak of romantic recklessness, intelligent but often seeming to lack concentration. But then these inner conflicts mirrored the ambiguity in the political approach of this man who, as another reassessment illustrates at length, adhered to the Utopian Socialist views of Saint-Simon while yet acting the imperial autocrat.[5]

Of course, this was an ambiguity that he shared with Napoleon himself. For his political project broadly followed that of his uncle, in that his aim was to maintain the country's standing abroad and promote progress at home while reconciling left and right within a climate combining order with liberty. This implied a single executive figure directly elected by the people and therefore representing the national interest better than parliamentary parties, seen as representing local and sectional interests. This Bonapartist synthesis – reminiscent in some ways of the Gaullist approach since the Second World War – sought therefore to protect both the leftist values of liberty and social progress and the rightist values of order and the religious tradition. At a time when France's divided society was undergoing industrialization and urbanization, this was hardly an easy task.[6]

It is perhaps ironic that the first, autocratic phase of the emperor's tenure was more successful than the second, more liberalizing one. For, while in its first decade this plebiscitary, would-be democratic empire was more or less a police state, the dirigiste modernizing approach of Napoleon III achieved considerable results. The railway network would increase fivefold over the next twenty years, opening up the country, giving a great impulsion to iron and steel production and to the building industy through the construction of bridges and stations – and of course leading to the creation of seaside resorts such as Deauville or Biarritz. A notable beneficiary of rapid mechanization was the textile industry, well developed in centres such as Lille, Roubaix and Rouen. As a believer in free trade – he signed a treaty with Britain to promote it in 1860 – Napoleon also encouraged economic liberalism in what had traditionally been a protectionist country. Several large maritime trading companies were created, as was a new port at Saint-Nazaire. Major French banks such as the Crédit Lyonnais and the Société Générale were established and the interaction of industry and finance produced a new and influential moneyed class, able to support projects such as the construction by Ferdinand de Lesseps of the Suez Canal. With the gross domestic product almost doubling within twenty years, the Paris stock exchange was busy.

It was at this time also that, under the direction of the formidable Prefect of the Seine, Baron Haussmann, Paris was being systematically transformed. The principal aim was to demolish slums, provide modern drainage and create a properly planned capital with major through roads to facilitate commerce. So the old medieval streets were giving way to broad, straight boulevards – which answered the secondary aim of enabling the use of cavalry and artillery against possible uprisings. But there was also a real attempt to beautify Paris, with the Bois de Boulogne and the Bois de Vincennes being laid out, new parks like the Parc Montsouris being created, and the opera house and a host of public buildings being built. With all this, and with the rigorous limitation of apartment houses to six storeys, the handsome, well-ordered Paris that we know today was emerging. Of course the industrial revolution in the country still lagged behind that of Britain, there was considerable inequality and the rising proletariat was being pushed to the outskirts, but the great trade fairs of 1855 and 1867 proclaimed to the world that France was successful and that Paris was its shining face.

Paris was indeed beginning once again to look like the intellectual and cultural capital of Europe, reflecting the fact that France's combination of political tensions and economic and social change made it a particularly representative society for that time. The culture was increasingly marked by 'scientism', the desire to move beyond traditional metaphysical speculation and establish philosophy, history and the arts themselves on a scientific basis. A leading figure was Auguste Comte, widely seen as the founder of sociology, who argued that history was subject to general laws which could be discerned by the application of the scientific method. We may smile today at his attempt to found a 'religion of Humanity', with secular saints like the political economist Adam Smith, but his Positivist method strongly influenced important figures like the physiologist Claude Bernard and the biologist Louis Pasteur.

Comte's approach was mirrored in the work of influential historians and cultural critics. Alexis de Toqueville, in his studies of France and of American democracy, took history beyond the routine narration of events into the domain of the philosophy of history. Jules Michelet's history of France conditioned generations of schoolchildren to a sense of their own country, not only through his attempt at a total resurrection of the past but through his highly colourful language. Ernest Renan, through his work on the future of science and the origins of Christianity, like Hippolyte Taine, in his attempt – as in his history of English literature – to situate writers in relation to their ethnic, historical and social context, also helped to dictate the new intellectual temper of the time.

Although there was inevitably an idealist reaction against scientism – in the art for art's sake Parnassian poetry of Leconte de Lisle or the hauntingly personal verse of Charles

Baudelaire – the new watchword in art and literature was Realism. Gustave Courbet led a revolt against the old Romantic heroics and idealized historical painting with canvases such as his *Burial at Ornans*, which not only depicted ordinary people, but did so in a boldly monumental fresco style. Jean-François Millet recorded the back-breaking work of peasants in such pictures as *The Gleaners*, while Honoré Daumier – best known today for his brilliant satirical lithographs – showed the reality of urban poverty in works such as *The Third-Class Carriage*. Interestingly, it was not just because of their depiction of 'low life' that such paintings were felt to be morally and politically sub-versive but, more subtly, because they undermined the old romanticized higher reality that art was supposed to be about – there were outraged letters to the press when Renoir put a folded newspaper in a painting.

Needless to say, there was a certain innocence about the enthusiastic scientism of certain writers, particularly in the case of the proclaimed leader of the Naturalist group of writers, Émile Zola – who was also a great supporter of the painters Manet and Cézanne, an old school friend. Zola conceived his *Les Rougon-Macquart* cycle of novels (1871–93) as a vast, controlled, 'scientific' experiment plotting the combined effect of heredity and environment. Inevitably, his depiction of degradation among the working class and the peasantry was deemed to be shocking, but a characteristic-ally powerful novel like *Germinal*, about a mining disaster, benefits not only from the thousands of pages of notes he took on a visit to a mine, but from his epic imagination.

For writers such as Champfleury or Maupassant, how-ever, Realism was based more simply on the idea that character was the function, not of a God-given and therefore unchanging human nature, but of the individual's particular family background, social milieu and historical situation. And it was the pressure of this demand for objectivity that led Gustave Flaubert, often seen as the 'father of the modern novel', to bring about a mutation in the form. For up to that point fiction had been something of a bastard literary form in which the writer tended to present himself – rather like a dramatist wandering among his own characters on stage – not only as narrator but as commentator, historian, psychologist and philosopher, everywhere showing his hand. It was Flaubert in *Madame Bovary* who devised the technique of getting the writer off the page so as to let the story work by itself. And by giving the novel the apparent separate existence or autonomy that characterizes high art, he revolutionized the form.

That Flaubert had to face an absurd charge of immorality for his pains is some indication of the gap between the intellectuals and this imperial regime. It was partly in recognition of this that Napoleon III began to liberalize his government from 1859 onwards – though it was also partly because he had lost the support of the increasingly influential Catholics, since the struggle for the reunification of Italy in which he had involved himself was thought to have damaged the interests of the Vatican. He allowed political exiles to return, granted a limited right to strike, and gradually gave more powers to the legislature, until by 1869 the regime had become a 'liberal empire' not unlike a constitutional monarchy. While this enlarged the space for parliamentary opposition and while there were violent strikes in that same year, he obtained overwhelming support for the change in the plebiscite of April 1870 and could happily declare that France was facing a sunlit future. So why did the regime collapse like a house of cards less than four months later?

It was because Napoleon was tempted, out of hubris, to play at being the greater Napoleon; he reserved foreign affairs to himself as emperor, and listened too much to his pious but politically naive Spanish wife Eugénie. He had already weakened the army through costly victories in Italy and in the less than glorious Crimean War of 1853–6 – where at least the losses were from cholera rather than from spectacular follies like the British Charge of the Light Brigade. He weakened it further through his ill-considered foray into Mexico in 1862, to enforce the repayment of loans repudiated by a new government there. He got bogged down in fighting and tried to turn the country into a client state by imposing his own candidate on the Mexican throne, only to be forced into a humiliating withdrawal in 1867.

Finally, in 1870, he walked into an elephant trap laid by the formidable Prussian minister Bismarck after France, afraid of encirclement, opposed the nomination of a relative of the Prussian king Wilhelm I for the vacant throne of Spain. In fact, the king withdrew the nomination, sent Bismarck a telegram to that effect and authorized him to make it public, but Bismarck craftily doctored it to imply that the king had refused to see the French ambassador, thus making this famous 'Ems telegram' look like a blatant insult to France. So Napoleon was led by the empress and by public outrage to declare war on Prussia and, though he was visibly ageing and suffering from a painful gallstone at the time, to take to horseback himself.

The lesson was brutal. The army had not been reorganized after the Mexican expedition, mobilization was slow, the general staff was divided, the Krupp steel artillery was far superior to the French copper cannon, the French were outnumbered almost two to one and the enemy tactics were more sophisticated. The erratic Marshal Bazaine became encircled at Metz and Napoleon, trying to relieve him, became encircled in his turn at Sedan and, to avoid heavy losses, surrendered alongside his troops. This ignominious lightning defeat stunned Europe by its revelation that the major power on the continent was no longer France but Germany. It also, inevitably, set in motion the old constitutional see-saw, for no sooner had the news from Sedan reached Paris than the republican deputies proclaimed a new republic. But its beginnings, equally inevitably perhaps in this divided society, would be bloody.

8

THE THIRD REPUBLIC: *SEMAINE SANGLANTE* TO THE FIRST WORLD WAR

Paris, as the French will remind you, *n'est pas la France*. Even today there tends to be a certain political tension between Paris and the provinces – the real France or *la France profonde* as some still see it. It was Paris which led the way in the successive revolutions from 1789 onwards, only to discover – as when the republicans were routed in 1849 – that the Catholic, conservative countryside was not behind it. And a defining moment in the relationship between Paris and the rest of the country was to present itself with a vengeance in 1871, in the months following the humiliating surrender of Napoleon III at Sedan.

Within two weeks of the declaration on 4 September of this new Third Republic the Prussian army was at the gates of Paris and had the city under siege. But the government decided to fight on and, in a colourful episode, the minister of the interior Gambetta escaped from the city by balloon and went to Tours, where he raised a new, if ill-trained army of 600,000 men. However, Marshal Bazaine, largely out of opposition to the republican government, surrendered with his 180,000 men at Metz and, when attempts to break the stranglehold on Paris failed, initial peace overtures were made. These were rejected by Bismarck and during the cold winter months, without coal or wood, Parisians were not only bombarded but reduced to eating everything from cats, dogs and rats to the two well-loved elephants, Castor and Pollux, in the Jardin des Plantes. A succession of military defeats in December and January forced the government to withdraw to Bordeaux and the ultimate humiliation came when the Prussians, ensconced by now in Versailles, consecrated the unification of the Germanic peoples with the proclamation of the new German Empire in Louis XIV's Hall of Mirrors on 18 January 1871. By this time much of Paris lay in ruins.

Yet the nightmare was only beginning. For as a condition of the inevitable surrender Bismarck insisted on elections for a new government, ostensibly to give legitimacy to the agreement but no doubt also because he anticipated the result, which was a sweeping victory for the royalists over the republicans. This added to the sense of betrayal of the Parisians, who had been running their own city during the siege and who resented the terms of an armistice involving not only the loss of Alsace and much of Lorraine plus an indemnity of 5,000 million francs, but the disarmament of the troops in the capital who had withstood the long siege. This anti-Prussian, anti-government feeling was reinforced by the installation of the newly elected assembly at Versailles, which raised fears of a restoration of the monarchy, and by the withdrawal of the pay of the National Guard, which had been the only income of many families during the siege. So, when the army was sent in on 18 March to remove the cannons at Montmartre used for defence during the siege, it met armed resistance which forced it to withdraw, leaving the triumphant Prussians with a ringside seat over the next ten weeks for the fratricidal stand-off between the French government in Versailles and the city government set up in its own capital, the Paris Commune.

The Commune was largely a spontaneous reaction to these highly exceptional circumstances. But while there was no deep-laid plan involved, its driving ideas – a will to continue the war, social justice, anti-royalism and anti-clericalism – had been hardened by the siege and the government's surrender. Republicans, socialists and anarchists rubbed shoulders with National Guard members and ordinary lower middle-class and working-class Parisians in an extraordinary experiment in democratic self-government, conducted by leaders who on the whole – Varlin, Jourde and Vaillant, if not, for example, the famous Louise Michel – were cautious, moderate and respectful of property. They set up representative structures, declared the separation of Church and State, established a system of workers' control in factories abandoned by their owners, and imagined a federal France consisting of self-governing communes like their own. And indeed there were similar communes set up in several other towns, but these were rapidly suppressed and it was doubtless only a matter of time before the heavily royalist new republic put an end to this humiliating defiance from its capital city.

It did so with 100,000 troops in the *Semaine Sanglante*, or 'bloody week', towards the end of May and with a vengeance inflamed by the desire to stamp out once and for all these neverending 'revolutionary troublemakers' in Paris. While the Communards, facing defeat after pitched battles in the streets, executed some 500 hostages and set fire to the Tuileries and the Hôtel de Ville, what shocked the correspondent of *The Times* was rather 'the inhuman laws of revenge under which the Versailles troops have been shooting, bayoneting, ripping open prisoners, women and children during the last six days. So far as we can recollect there has been nothing like it in history'.[1]

The final tally of this systematic killing and mass summary executions, as drawn up by the historian Jacques Rougerie, was 20,000 to 25,000 Communards as against less than 1,000 government troops. In addition, over 43,000 prisoners were taken, of whom more than 10,000, in military tribunals extending over the next five years, received sentences ranging from execution or hard labour for life to deportation to New Caledonia in the Pacific or a fixed term of imprisonment.[2] The new Republic had certainly shown its teeth, to the extent that it weakened the socialist movement in France for a generation.

For long, the Commune was rather like an embarrassing family secret for the French – as illustrated by the controversy in 2001 over finally naming a small square in Paris after it.[3] The bitterness it caused was not simply due to the number killed, but to the fact that this civil war was a feast for the Prussians and that it involved the Republic killing republicans. The Mur des Fédérés, or Wall of the Confederates, in Père-Lachaise Cemetery, where the Communards made their last stand, is still a place of pilgrimage for the left, which has always detested the triumphalism of building the great white basilica of the Sacré-Coeur to overlook the site of this urban battlefield – 'in order to expiate the crimes of the Communards' according to the government decree of 1873. More significantly perhaps, beyond the bitterness, the wild rumours and the taboos surrounding the Commune, there are questions to be asked about its real political significance. If the Commune was hardly the bloodthirsty 'red spectre' presented in the conservative newspapers of the time, was it, as Marx described it after the event, 'the glorious harbinger of a new society' or the very image, as Engels put it in 1891, of 'the Dictatorship of the Proletariat'?[4] And why did it fail?

In fact, Marx would later change his mind about the value of the Commune as a model. As well he might, for the circumstances in which the event had occurred were so exceptional as to be unlikely to recur. More fundamentally, the Utopian Socialist 'communalism' of the Commune, with its democratic republican forms, its respect for private property and its federal ideas, was some way from what would emerge as communism. If it was later annexed by the French communists – who still organize a pilgrimage to the Mur des Fédérés on May Day each year – this was more for sentimental and propaganda reasons, to situate the party in a national revolutionary tradition going back to 1789, than because it conformed to ideological orthodoxy. It was a national tragedy which may have produced the revolutionary hymn the 'Internationale' or the moving 'Le Temps des cerises' ('Cherry time'), but it is significant that French Socialists such as the future party leader Jean Jaurès did not see it as the model of a Socialist republic.

The Commune was less the harbinger of the Russian Revolution than the last of the series of revolutions opened up in 1789, the last throw of the Jacobin tradition. For, as one historian argues shrewdly, 'the physical power of the State had been greatly increased by economic modernization and its political authority strengthened by universal male suffrage'.[5] The Commune failed because the utopian city state could not prevail against the unitary national state – even one that had suffered a humiliating defeat in war – in the Europe of nations of that time.

Having got off to a terrible start, the Third Republic now had to establish itself. But it still had no constitution and the chamber was dominated by royalists and Bonapartists. Adolphe Thiers, who had handled affairs so far, raised enough money in loans to pay off the indemnity and get rid of the German occupiers, but when he proposed a republican constitution he was forced out and Marshal Mac-Mahon, the nobleman of Irish ancestry who had put down the Commune, was installed as president with the support of the monarchists. However, there was the little problem, as

Thiers had pointed out, that there was only one throne but two claimants – the Comte de Chambord of the senior branch of the Bourbons and the Comte de Paris of the junior branch. There now ensued a lengthy, comical royal ballet in which they worked out that the former, since he had no children, could go first, then hand over the throne on his death. Except that Chambord insisted on the Bourbon white flag while his Orléanist rival insisted on the tricolour and, symbolism being of the essence, the whole plan fizzled out. So that in 1875, even if the new constitution with its strong president left room for conversion to a monarchy, France became a republic by default.

It was soon to strengthen its position, for in the legislative elections of the following year the republicans gained two-thirds of the seats. Yet Mac-Mahon defiantly appointed as prime minister a hardline royalist and advocate of a clerical conservative 'moral order' movement, the Duc de Broglie, who suppressed even the word 'Republic' from official documents. But in the rancorous elections that followed the republicans won again and in 1879 the Senate went the same way. Mac-Mahon had to give way to the moderate republican Jules Grévy, while the prime minister was now the pragmatic lawyer Léon Gambetta – who, though he had disapproved of the violence of the Commune, brought in an amnesty for deportees. With the seat of government being brought back from Versailles to Paris, and with the 'Marseillaise' being declared the national anthem, it appeared that, ninety years after the Revolution of 1789, the Republic had won its long battle with royalty.

The next ten years up to the lavish Exposition Universelle, or world fair, of 1889 was indeed a period of consolidation. In honour of the Republic, street names were changed and statues of its female image Marianne erected, while the statue of Liberty was donated to the Americans – a little belatedly – to celebrate the centenary of their own revolution. More significantly, there were legislative changes which would largely shape French society up to the present time. The 'republican liberties' of freedom of the press and of assembly were introduced, along with the right to divorce. The election of mayors was brought in, as was the right to form trade unions, though on condition that they remained non-political.

Above all, there were the changes in education associated with the most prominent republican of the time, Jules Ferry. These were especially important in the distinctive French context, given the bitter struggle for power between the secular republican tradition and the Catholic monarchist tradition. The introduction of free, compulsory primary education and the setting up of teacher-training Écoles Normales for both sexes, together with the later hard-fought removal of all religious teaching on grounds of freedom of conscience, was a fundamental change. For by taking from the Church its control of the basic education of children, and above all of girls, the government was replacing religious conditioning with the republican conditioning that would provide it with a lasting basis in public opinion.

France having been accepted back into the concert of nations at the Congress of Berlin of 1878, Ferry set out to enhance its power and prestige through colonial expansion. This took place not only in Africa – in French West Africa, French Equatorial Africa, Tunisia and Madagascar – but in Asia, with the conquest of Indochina. Also, Paris was beginning once again to look like the cultural centre of Europe, particularly with the new wave of Impressionist painters – who produced what is still the most popular body of artwork in the world. If only through calendars or chocolate boxes or even T-shirts, most of us are aware of Monet's *Water Lilies* or *La Gare St-Lazare*; Renoir's opulent nudes or happy outdoor dancing scenes such as *Le Moulin de la Galette*; Manet's provocative *Le Déjeuner sur l'herbe*, with the nude woman sitting among fashionably clothed men, or his intriguing *Le Bar aux Folies-Bergère*; Degas's ballet dancers or his keyhole views of nudes bathing; Cézanne's still lives of fruit or his muscular renderings of the Mont Sainte-Victoire or Lake Annecy. And also the English Sisley's *Snow at Louveciennes*, Pissarro's *Boulevard Montmartre* or the exotic studies of Tahitian women in the post-impressionist phase by Paul Gauguin. These are some of the pictures that have imprinted an abiding image of Paris and the French countryside upon the imagination of the world.

So how did these artists come together and what was distinctive about their approach? In the 1860s, when many of them were starting out, they found that their work cut no ice with the official establishment as represented by the Académie des Beaux Arts. The Académie was the guardian of traditional standards in painting and, in its annual exhibition of new work, the selection panel looked essentially for historical subjects or portraits of known figures, as well as for classical perspective and a highly precise finish. When the younger painters saw most of their work turned down at this annual Salon – which after all offered the chance to become known and to get commissions – they banded together to display their work independently. Their first such joint exhibition took place in 1874 and there would be seven more – not always with quite the same artists – in the years up to 1886. While Manet and Degas were independently wealthy, most of these artists were not and it was only in the 1880s, by which time the art market was opening up to American buyers in particular, that they really tasted success.

So what was new about this new style? Like Gothic, Impressionism arose as a satirical term of abuse, inspired in this case by Renoir's painting of a sunrise, *Impression, Soleil Levant*. And indeed these painters did aim to provide an impression or momentary effect of a scene – often involving movement – rather than a completely worked out treatment. They chose immediately contemporary subjects – either city scenes or landscapes – and, even if they finished in the studio, chose to work outdoors since their interest was in the play of natural light on objects. This approach dictated their technique: quick, thick strokes of paint, bold colours applied with little mixing from the newly available commercial tubes of paint, and perspective often created by the juxtaposition of colours. That they were interested in the movement of light in time leads the prominent art historian Bernard Dorival to equate their activity with a methodical scientific analysis of reality.[6] And it is true that, exposed as they were to the popular 'scientism' of the time, they defended their approach in terms of current theories of perception, the need to 'de-intellectualize the eye' in order to get away from false perspective, and the colour theories of the German physicist Helmholtz.

Yet there is a glaring paradox here. Science implies objectivity, whereas their approach was obviously highly subjective. But does that justify the opposing charge that their work is an expression of bourgeois individualism, that these paintings are popular because they are pretty-pretty and that Impressionism, as the Marxist critic T. J. Clark puts it, was 'the house style of the bourgeoisie'?[7] Here again it is true that these painters ignored the 1870 war and the Commune, that the only reference to class tends to be through the ironic juxtaposition of fashionable men and prostitutes, and that there are few scenes of poverty outside the work of Pissarro – simply in terms of subject matter, Impressionism offers an often dreamy view of the good life of the middle class. To say this, however, tends to miss the larger consideration that, with photography starting to take over the traditional function of recording reality, painting was beginning to change in character, to become precisely the expression of individual subjectivity – a response to the real rather than an objective reproduction of the real. Impressionism leads directly, through Cézanne and the Post-Impressionists, towards Fauvism and Cubism. What these painters were doing, whether they realized it or not, was ushering in a shift towards the most stylized art that Europe had seen for centuries, one that would ultimately lead to a notion of abstract art in which painting would become its own subject.

Not that as yet any of this concerned the almost 30 million visitors who turned up for the Exposition Universelle of 1889, the centenary celebration of this well-established and culturally vibrant French republic. They trooped in under the arch of this astonishing new Eiffel Tower – the tallest structure in the world and not even meant to be permanent. They marvelled at the inventions in the Galerie des Machines and they enjoyed the Wild West Show and the 'Negro Village' with its encampments of imported colonial people, including the Javanese musicians and dancers who so enchanted Debussy. They doubtless also admired Haussmann's fine boulevards, sampled the music halls and other delights of the city, and may well have left with the sense that France had not only recovered its poise and its prestige but had great days ahead of it.

It was not to be so easy. For France had not only to protect its interests within an increasingly nationalistic Europe, but to maintain its own unity by overcoming its endemic internal divisions. And indeed the Republic had just managed to withstand the challenge of a populist movement, of a Bonapartist or pre-fascist type, led by the dreaded 'general on a white horse' – though in this case the general had the uninspiring name of Boulanger and the horse happened to be black. A handsome, ambitious demagogue and a former minister of war, Boulanger had made himself popular with the public by improving conditions in the army and by his jingoistic threats when a French frontier guard was seized and imprisoned in Germany as a spy. When this led to his being nicknamed Général Revanche, or General Revenge, and to Germany calling up reservists, however, he was sacked as minister and posted out of harm's way to Clermont-Ferrand in 1887.

However, he had become enormously popular in the country – helped by the scandal surrounding the sale of decorations by the son-in-law of President Jules Grévy, who was forced to resign – and he now developed a political programme based on his own 'three Rs': Revenge for the defeat of 1870, Revision of the constitution and Restoration of the monarchy. Acclaimed as a man of destiny, he was elected as a deputy for Paris in January 1889 and was being pushed towards a *coup d'état* when he got cold feet, fled when the government issued a warrant, and ended up in Brussels, where he shot himself on the grave of his mistress two years later. What was disconcerting was that this loose cannon, a hollow figure and no orator, should have been able to muster support across the board from monarchists and Bonapartists to the extreme left.

And a new dimension was to enter this volatile mix of public opinion with the Panama scandal of 1892. De Lesseps, who had built the Suez Canal, had for thirteen years been president of a company set up to join the Atlantic to the Pacific by means of a canal. The project had enthused some 800,000 French investors, but the conditions were difficult and heavy losses were incurred. In 1892 a number of ministers were accused of taking bribes from de Lesseps at the inception of the project, while hundreds of deputies, including several ministers, were accused of taking bribes from the Panama Canal Company to conceal from the public the extent of the losses – which meant that people continued innocently to invest.

This was a truly major scandal in that it not only lost the investors over a billion francs, but involved so many prominent figures – including the leader of the Radical party Georges Clemenceau, as well as Eiffel and de Lesseps himself. Commissioned by parliament to lead an inquiry, the Socialist leader Jean Jaurès denounced this business state-within-a-state, a conclusion later vindicated by so many cynical acquittals of those accused. So, while the scandal did not threaten the survival of the Republic, it was in its way more damaging in that it showed the State to be corrupt. All this, especially since the two men who had distributed the bribes on behalf of the company were both Jewish with suggestive Germanic names, was meat and drink to the ferociously anti-Semitic journalist Édouard Drumont, who had already published *La France juive* in 1886. France was gearing itself up for the even more resounding scandal of the Dreyfus Case.

When it was discovered in 1894 that military secrets were being passed to the German embassy, suspicion fell on a captain on the general staff with a wealthy Alsatian Jewish background, Afred Dreyfus. Condemned at a court martial, where key documents were kept from the defence and the handwriting experts disagreed over others, he was deported to Devil's Island, off Guyana – to solitary confinement and to a hut 4 metres square. Two years later Colonel Picquart, a courageous but rather naive head of counter-intelligence, discovered that the real culprit was the spendthrift officer Major Esterhazy. The War Office packed Picquart off to Tunisia to hush up the affair and, when the truth leaked out and it was forced to put Esterhazy on trial, acquitted him within two days.

As the truth threatened to emerge, the lies to protect the honour of the army and the War Office got bigger. When Émile Zola produced his famous set of charges in the newspaper *L'Aurore*, under the headline *J'accuse*, the government prosecuted him for libel, driving him into exile to escape a year's imprisonment. For good measure it then put Picquart himself on trial – only to have it revealed that documents incriminating Dreyfus had been forged by a Major Henry, who confessed and committed suicide. Even when Dreyfus was eventually brought back in 1899 for retrial, he was again found guilty but given a pardon – to save face while getting this humiliating fiasco out of the world's press before the next Paris world fair of 1900. It was a further six years before he was acknowledged to be innocent – and left free to serve with distinction alongside his anti-Semitic brother officers in the First World War. Unlike Esterhazy, who was discreetly given his pension, which he continued to receive in England, where he had exiled himself, until his death in 1923.

A non-French person may well be surprised at the virulent hatred aroused by this shameful affair – which may indeed even lie behind the mysterious death of Émile Zola. Of course it is true that French opinion had been traumatized by the defeat of 1870 and that this was a fractious society – only months before the Dreyfus affair hit the headlines the President of the Republic, Sadi Carnot, had been assassinated by an anarchist. The fragmentation of opinion was shown by the election of 1898, which produced 254 moderate Republicans, 80 Royalists, 74 Radical Socialists, 57 Socialists, 15 Nationalists and 4 well-known anti-Semites, including Drumont – even the Socialists being split into two factions. But beneath this surface confusion there was the broad and bitter division of opinion specific to the French situation. Whereas in Britain, a Protestant country which had killed its king much earlier, the broad political division had a fairly straightforward class basis, here it was overlaid by religious or anti-clerical beliefs inflamed and polarized by a troubled century of post-revolutionary history. At a time when the Church was under severe challenge from agnostic social theories and Darwinism, the Dreyfus affair was part of a continuing conflict over the national identity – a conflict which would re-emerge in the 1930s and during the German Occupation.

In fact the Church itself took no official position on the dispute, and indeed Pope Leo XIII, more aware of a changing world than his predecessor, had advised the French Church in 1892 to accept the Republic in order to try to preserve the religion. But Catholic opinion, urged on by the recently created newspaper of the Assumptionist order, *La Croix*, took little notice and lined up with the royalists and the army – most of whose senior officers had been educated by the Jesuits – against the anti-clerical republicans, socialists and other defenders of Dreyfus. And this brought about two lasting changes. One was that the involvement of intellectuals – following the part played, particularly on the Dreyfusard side, by prominent figures from Zola to Marcel Proust – would become a distinctive feature of French political life. The other was that the idea of the nation, a universalist republican notion based on all of the people as representing humanity, now shifted towards a particularist notion of the country or 'race' in opposition to outsiders, so that nationalism became a right-wing value. And this was exemplified by the creation in 1899 of Charles Maurras's anti-republican, nationalist and royalist movement Action Française.

In reaction to that and to other provocations in that same year – an attempted *coup d'état* by the jingoistic author and politician Paul Déroulède, a physical attack on President Loubet and the failed assassination of one of Dreyfus's lawyers – the republicans struck back. They clarified their aims with the creation of a separate Radical Socialist party and a separate French Socialist Party – which Jean Jaurès began to lead away from Marxism towards a reformist, humanist approach – and formed a leftist Bloc government to defend the Republic. It closed down the Assumptionist order and its newspaper, and went on to complete the separation of Church and State.

The State would no longer pay Church salaries, whether for Catholics, Protestants or Jews. The Church would lose its control of education and religious education would no longer be permitted in publicly owned areas, but religious belief was a right and freedom of worship was guaranteed. The new and highly conservative Pope Pius X regarded the separation as 'gravely insulting to God' but by 1905, as though to bring the Revolution of 1789 to its logical conclusion, France had become a secular republic.

It was only in retrospect, after the catastrophe, that the years leading up to the First World War came to be seen nostalgically as the 'good times' – *la Belle Époque*, enshrined in French memory through Proust's depiction of a vanishing upper class in *À La Récherche du temps perdu* (*In Search of Lost Times*). And on the surface they were indeed good times. France was, after all, one of the world's two great imperial powers and the march of progress was evident in Louis Blériot's pioneering flight across the Channel, the Paris–Madrid automobile races, the increasing use of the telephone and the invention of cinematography. The country was entering, if belatedly, the later phase of the industrial revolution and, even if it was being outdistanced by competitors in other areas of science, Pierre and Marie Curie could still win the Nobel Prize.

Above all, France could still see itself as epitomizing civilization, with Paris as the recognized cultural and, indeed, with its operettas, cabarets and flourishing fashion houses, pleasure capital of the world, attracting artists such as the Russian Chagall or the Italian Modigliani from all over Europe. If the decorative Art Nouveau style did not last, the seeds of a less obvious but major cultural change were being sown. As though in tune with the revolutionary new ideas, such as those of Einstein and Freud that were creeping in, Picasso and Braque – like climbers roped together on a rock face, as Picasso saw it – were trying to take art into the unknown territory beyond the illusion of reality with their adventure of cubism.

Naturally this affected only a small elite. Since compulsory primary education had only been introduced in 1881, and had not been completely implemented in the provinces, around 90 per cent of adults were illiterate and many still only spoke their local patois. More significantly, France had a demographic problem. From having a quarter of Europe's population in 1789 it now had just under 10 per cent and, in particular, it had just under 40 million in 1911 as opposed to almost 65 million for Germany. This was an obvious concern, since defeat in 1870 had left a heavy shadow and replaced Britain with Germany as the new 'hereditary enemy'. And of course Europe remained an unstable, edgy place.

Germany, led by the vain and erratic Kaiser Wilhelm II, wanted to get into the colonial race, while in the Balkans there was pressure towards independence from the different peoples making up the Austro-Hungarian and Ottoman empires. The colonial problem was patched up after the first Moroccan crisis of 1905 – when the Germans supported the Moroccans against the French – and in the second crisis of 1911 by France giving Germany a piece of the Congo. But by then the prevailing insecurity had led Britain and France to form their Entente Cordiale of 1904 and to join an alliance with Russia, ranged against a triple alliance of Germany, Austria and Italy. With that line-up and the seething situation in the Balkans, where the underlying conflict between Slav and Germanic peoples caused tension between Russia and Germany, anything could happen.

And it did. A Bosnian nationalist student assassinated the heir to the Austro-Hungarian throne, Archduke Franz Ferdinand and, on 28 July 1914, Austria–Hungary with German support, declared war on Serbia. A week later, Russia had mobilized to support Serbia, Germany had declared war on Russia and France, which it proceeded to attack via neutral Belgium, and a reluctant Britain had entered the war on the side of France. The chain reaction of alliances took over, 20 million men were called up and all of a sudden Europe was at war. The French for their part, despite all the talk of revenge against Germany and even if war had long seemed a possibility, did not in their vast majority want this war and the sheer speed of events took them by surprise. There were of course propaganda stories – that the men were laughing their way to the front with rifles bedecked with flowers, that they were dying to get their own back on the brutal Boches, that the Germans were cowards who could not shoot straight or that, in the words of one bishop, the war was a purifying experience.[8] But most felt simply that, since the Germans were the attackers, they had no choice. Nor did the assassination by a young nationalist of the Socialist leader Jean Jaurès prevent the left from sharing in this reflex of national unity. And at least they knew it would be short.

It was not short. For the course of the war was determined essentially within the first two months by the failure of the Schlieffen plan, devised by the Germans in 1905. This had been dictated by the fear of being encircled and of having to fight on two fronts, so the idea was to attack France through Belgium, reach Picardy within a month and take Paris from the west – thus quickly knocking out France before having to deal with the Russians. It worked to the extent that by early September the German troops were directly threatening Paris, but General Joffre mounted a heroic defence in the famous Battle of the Marne – in which everything from buses to taxis was commandeered to take troops to the front – so the chance of a quick victory was lost.

And that was the end of the heroics, of the idea of war as colourful display – and incidentally of the dashing red trousers of the French infantry, which left them like sitting ducks for the German machine-guns. Death was becoming inglorious and anonymous, meted out by some unseen gunner who would never even know what he had done. For while the action continued at sea and in Africa, where the Germans were ousted from their colonies, the next three years saw the Western Front become a strange struggle in a blasted landscape in which men led a semi-underground life in trenches, enduring regular bombardments in the company of corpses and rats. Ironically, for all the signs of mechanical progress – the trucks, the spotter aeroplanes, the tanks that lumbered on in 1916 – the war had settled into a static struggle in the mud.

Of course there were attempts to break the deadlock. The British and French tried twice in 1915, but failed to break through. The Germans fired 60 million shells over ten months in 1916 during the Battle of Verdun, in the course of which the Allies tried to divert them with the equally unsuccessful and costly attack at the Battle of the Somme. Then there was the disastrous attack mounted by General Nivelle at the Chemin des Dames in the Aisne in 1917, which led to mutiny in the French army, to 4,000 soldiers appearing before military tribunals, to 49 executions and, indeed, to the withdrawal of the left parties from the government.

General Pétain, the 'hero of Verdun', settled things down by putting an end to pointless attacks and by improving the rations, but it was time for something to turn up. And what turned up was the Americans, whom the Germans had foolishly outraged by interfering with the free movement of ships in the Atlantic and by sinking the unarmed British liner the *Lusitania*, with 128 Americans on board. Their entry was not immediately so significant in military terms – although they would still lose 120,000 men – especially since it was balanced by the withdrawal of the Russians following the 1917 revolution. But the Germans realized that this would load the scales against them in the medium term and there were also now revolutionary stirrings in Berlin. They made a last massive effort to break through in 1918 and, when that was contained, sued for peace.

It is an ironic fact that nature itself mocked the losses in this world war when no sooner had the fighting abated than an influenza epidemic killed 20 million people. Even so, the casualty figures for the Western powers alone are sobering. Those listed as killed in action on each side were 898,100

French, 485,000 British and 1,483,000 Germans, giving a broad balance for each side. But the real losses, if we include those missing in action or who died of wounds or disease, amount to 1,327,000 French, 717,000 British and 2,037,000 German. Yet this takes no account of the French war injured who were unable to contribute to the life of the nation, of the inevitable fall in the birth rate of a country already at a demographic disadvantage – France had needed to call up more men per thousand and had proportionately lost more – or of the physical destruction wrought in France in contrast to Britain and Germany. Add the suffering of widows and families and the devastating effect of this war – visible on the war monument of every village in France – becomes evident. And it was to cast a long shadow. In his study of the nation's attitude to the war, Jean-Jacques Becker concludes that by 1918 the French were at the end of their tether and that, if they endured this war to the end, they might not endure another: that 'the France still holding out in 1918 foretold the defeated France of 1940'.[9]

9

1919–1940: DEFEAT OUT OF VICTORY

The Hall of Mirrors, where illusion had merged with reality in the heady days of Louis XIV, was the highly symbolic venue for the signing of the peace Treaty of Versailles on 28 June 1919. For this was where the new united German Empire had been proclaimed on 18 January 1871 after the devastating defeat suffered by France in the Franco-Prussian War. And this is where, by ironic reflection, Germany was now to be humiliated in its turn – a humiliation the more crushing in that it had been all but excluded from the peace negotiations and that no delegate from the defeated nations was present among the diplomatic guests in the crowded hall. The sunlight fell on the gushing fountains outside, for the delectation of the huge throng that had gathered in the hope of glimpsing American President Woodrow Wilson or British Prime Minister David Lloyd George, or their own 'father of victory', the 'Tiger', Georges Clemenceau – and of course the chastened German delegates. But it was all over almost as soon as it had begun. The delegates arrived, were led upstairs between resplendent troopers in plumed helmets and breast-plates, were directed to one end of the table and, after a telling minute or two of cold, contemptuous silence, invited to sign. They were then escorted out as the guns announced in their own warlike language that Europe had achieved a lasting peace. Meanwhile, Clemenceau was receiving the congratulations of delegates with a wry smile.

The peace negotiations that he had been chairing for the previous six months had themselves been something of a battle. While the 'Big Four' included Orlando of Italy, the basic debate was between Wilson, Lloyd George and Clemenceau, the only one who spoke both English and French. And the essential clash of perspectives was that between Wilson and Clemenceau, with Lloyd George mediating to some extent between them. Wilson, whose very presence represented a turning point in Europe's history, brought a broad transatlantic approach which tended to see the war from without in world terms, whereas Clemenceau and Lloyd George, who had both been energetic wartime leaders and had seen more directly the effects of the carnage, tended naturally to see the problem from within the tangled European situation. All three had of course to be mindful of the mood of their electorates. Clemenceau and Lloyd George were very aware of the hatred of the Germans which the war had unleashed, while Wilson had the opposite problem in that he was going beyond his country's isolationism – and would be disavowed by his own Senate in the end. To a degree, of course, the outcome of the negotiations also depended on the chemistry between the three major participants.

A former academic who had been president of Princeton, Wilson was a distinguished Democratic president with a record of promoting significant legislation such as the right to vote for women. Of Scots-Irish ancestry and from a Presbyterian background, he was an idealist and an internationalist who wanted the establishment of a League of Nations that would guarantee collective security and promote international law and self-determination for all peoples. It was to implement this vision that he came to Paris to argue his Fourteen Points for the resolution of the conflict, including disarmament, free trade, freedom of the seas and self-determination for colonial peoples.

Tall and stiffly formal, Wilson contrasted strongly with the short, plump, elderly but worldly wise and commanding Clemenceau, with his slightly countrified elegance and his constantly worn grey suede gloves, and whose quite different viewpoint came directly out of his own life. A doctor, a fervent Republican and the journalist who had published Zola's 'J'acccuse', he was a tough realist known for his barbed wit – at the expense of the French, the British, the Americans and all and sundry. As mayor of Montmartre in 1870 he had experienced the Franco-Prussian War, as the Radical Republican leader he became known as 'the destroyer of governments', and now he had seen the German invasion of neutral Belgium, the bombardment of civilians and then, in his visits to the front as wartime leader, the human cost of the carnage. Clemenceau wanted to make Germany pay and prevent it from causing a third war. He found Wilson's approach naive and sentimental.

These radically different perspectives were clearly irreconcilable and there was little that the clever, intuitive Lloyd George – who, like Clemenceau, was much quicker in argument than Wilson – could do to bridge the gap, if only because he was himself divided. He was happy to see Germany pay, as British opinion wanted, but did not want to see France become too powerful and, as the leader of an imperial power, he was not enthusiastic about Wilson's idea of self-determination. He was in favour of the destruction of the German navy, but not of sharing the freedom of the seas. In these circumstances, the outcome could only be delay and compromise. In broad terms, Wilson got his League of

Nations and self-determination for the peoples of the Austro-Hungarian Empire while, if the Allies took over Germany's colonies, they were now put under League of Nations mandates. France got Alsace-Lorraine, Allied occupation for fifteen years of the Rhineland, and international control of the Saar basin. Germany's navy was to be reduced and the manufacture of tanks, submarines and poison gas forbidden. Above all, it was declared responsible for the war and required to pay reparations for the civilian damage incurred – a down payment of $5 billion and the rest over thirty years.

The many studies of the Treaty of Versailles have tended to give it harsh treatment. Already in 1919, the economist John Maynard Keynes, the representative of the British Treasury who resigned in dismay, was particularly critical of Clemenceau for trying to 'set the clock back and restore the situation of 1870' with his reparations plan.[1] Jacques Bainville, in that same year, thought that Keynes had understated French losses and argued that the real problem was Germany, which had been left the most populated and homogeneous country in Europe, with the weak states arising out of Wilson's self-determination for nationalities policy unable to provide balance.[2] He might have added that Germany had become a potentially explosive force due to its combination of historical factors: late acculturation – when France was having its *grand siècle*, the Germanic lands were being overrun by the Thirty Years War – followed by late industrialization, late unification and late entry into the colonial race, with the Prussian military tradition to boot. And now, since the German civilians had not seen the destruction wrought by the war, the myth could be fostered that the country had been betrayed rather than defeated – a myth which, together with the economic slump at the end of the decade, would feed the mystique of Nazism.

The failure to synthesize the two opposing perspectives in the treaty was such that, as one historian pointed out, 'the

sole guarantee for the maintenance of peace was the
maintenance of solidarity by the victors'.[3] But Britain drifted
away while America went Republican, did not ratify the
Treaty and did not even join the League of Nations, so that
France was left with the contradictions and the consequent
failure of its efforts. Yet it would be unrealistic to blame
individuals. Clemenceau may have been too tied to the past
and Wilson too far ahead of his time, but they tried. The
treaty embodied the contradictions of a traumatized Europe
still sunk in old fears and hatreds after this first, shocking
world war. Indeed the outcome was perhaps predictable
from the start in the choice of the Hall of Mirrors in
Versailles for the ritual humiliation of the defeated Germans
at the signing of the treaty. The mirrors of Versailles,
ironically, reflected not only the previous war, but the next.

With the war over and France entering its '*années folles*', the
mad years, Paris reverted to its dual role as cultural capital
and Gay Paris. The writers and artists moved from Montmartre to Montparnasse, Coco Chanel displayed her
fashions, the Moulin Rouge and the Folies Bergères featured
Mistinguett or the American Josephine Baker and, with the
increasing availability of radios and gramophone records, the
whole country could now hum the latest jazz tune or listen
to Lucienne Boyer singing 'Parlez-moi d'amour'. People
tried to forget.

But there were those who could not forget. And in 1919
alone, the year of the Treaty, there were several events worth
noting. Paul Valéry published his article on the European
crisis, suggesting even from the striking first sentence – 'We
civilizations now know that we are mortal' – that the
continent had committed moral and intellectual suicide.[4]
Oswald Spengler published *The Decline of the West*, a book
that was to lead the young André Malraux to develop, in
relation to the 'death of Man', the new idea of the Absurd.[5]
Also in 1919, if we are to believe André Breton, the leader

of the Surrealist movement, the young writer Philippe Soupault made a practice of visiting apartment blocks and asking the concierge whether Philippe Soupault lived there. If the concierge replied that Philippe Soupault did indeed live there, Breton tells us, 'Soupault would not have been surprised, but would have gone and knocked on his door'.[6] In short, he was actualizing precisely the sense of the lack of identity and meaning implied by Malraux's idea of the Absurd.

As the Romantic movement had largely been a response to the turmoil of the Revolutionary period, so a new cultural landscape was emerging in answer to the shock of the war and to a new world of hectic movement and technological advances. A major upheaval was under way: in philosophy with the appearance in French of Hegel and then Heidegger, in music from Stravinsky to Messiaen, and in the plastic arts from Cubism to abstract art. The new driving forces in thought that emerged were figures who had been known before the war, but who only came into their own – as though on to a prepared stage – after 1918. The most influential were Einstein with his theory of relativity, Freud with his emphasis on the unconscious, and Bergson, with his elevation of intuition over intelligence.

These influences coloured the literature of the time. The plays of Pirandello, with their fluctuating characters, suggested that there was no continuity to the individual personality and therefore no coherent self. Proust, often ill and writing in his cork-lined room, tried to establish the psychic continuity of the self on the basis of involuntary memory: something as simple as the taste of a small cake – the famous *madeleine* – can bring back a flood of memories, so that we can transcend time by living in a fusion of past and present. It is as though Proust, at a time of growing agnosticism, was trying to find a secular equivalent of the Christian soul. At another level, André Gide was disturbing some readers with his insistence on 'following one's own bent' and his provocative idea of demonstrating one's freedom from convention by engaging in some 'gratuitous act'. All of these writers and thinkers played their part in undermining rationalism and in demolishing the old order. The instability of the world was being elevated into a system.

The most visible expression of this new *mal du siècle* was the Surrealist movement. It succeeded Dada, the name of which was chosen because it did not mean anything – thus implying a rejection of conceptual definition – and which did not get far beyond self-contradiction. The more systematically anarchist Surrealism saw itself as attacking the whole moral, political, social and intellectual order. Its aim was to liberate the unconscious – mainly by automatic writing – and thus free the 'real self' from the prison of the cardboard 'rational man' assumed by bourgeois society. That of course depends on two questionable assumptions: that there is such a 'real self' and that it is possible to have uncontrolled automatic writing. Also, there is something comical about these well-dressed middle-class young men setting out to 'shock the bourgeois', or about André Breton, who became the veritable pope of the movement, self-importantly excommunicating dissenters.

But it was good clean anarchist fun while it lasted, with open letters blasting the vice-chancellors of European universities for pretending to dispense knowledge or the directors of lunatic asylums for not recognizing that only the inmates were sane – not to mention Salvador Dali protesting against the expulsion of a man from the Metro for the 'pure and generous act' of exposing himself to a pretty girl, surreal suggestions for improving public monuments and a host of other stunts. It is fair to add that this was a formative experience for many poets and painters, and that the young writers of the time were as serious about their exploration as were the Romantics – several of them committed suicide. But the Surrealist movement faded as the political situation hardened – and the attack on rationalism was taken over more forcibly by Adolf Hitler among others.

*   *   *

A pointer to the political instability of the time is the turnover not only of governments but of leading personalities. There was the assassination of the Socialist leader Jean Jaurès in 1914 and that of President Doumer in 1932, not to mention the wounding of Clemenceau during the peace conference. There were also disappearances tinged with scandal – to the memory of the terminal heart attack of President Félix Faure in 1899 due to the immoderate ministrations of his mistress was added the curious case of the disturbed man wandering along a railway line in bare feet and pyjamas early one morning in 1920, claiming improbably, if accurately, to be Paul Deschanel, the President of the Republic.

But a more ominous sign of future instability was the splitting into two of the Socialists at their conference in Tours in that same year, following the setting up by Lenin of the Third (Communist) International, or Comintern, in 1919. The larger group hived off to become the Communist Party, taking with it the party newspaper started by Jaurès, *L'Humanité*. The lesser group remained as the Socialist Party, still retaining a broad Marxist analysis but opting for a gradualist, reformist social democratic approach rather than for a revolutionary approach aligned to the fluctuations of policy in Moscow. The split would be replicated within the trade union organization the Confédération Générale du Travail, or CGT, and this division of the left – which at times caused great bitterness, on the principle that the real enemies are those closest to you – would prove to be extremely damaging in the lead-up to the next war in 1939.

Ironically enough, the split took place only months after the whole labour movement was gravely weakened by the harsh repression of widespread strikes by the post-war National Bloc government. Based on the 'sacred national union' which had come together during the war, this was an alliance of parties of the right and the centre which had won power by merging nationalistic rhetoric with warnings about the 'Red Peril' signalled by the Bolshevik Revolution. Having widened the gap between itself and a growing working class industrialized by war production, the government now increased the hostility of the left through its attempt to consolidate the conservative forces by making gestures towards the Church, restoring diplomatic relations with the Vatican and, with a view also to the low national birth rate, stiffening the laws against abortion and contraception. But it inevitably ran into the two basic and related problems of money and Germany. The difficulty of getting the financial reparations from Germany, on top of the costs of reconstruction, drove Raymond Poincaré, prime minister in 1922–4, to occupy the Ruhr in 1923 in order to seize raw materials. However, this caused a general strike there, he received no support from the British and Americans – who thought it might provoke a Communist revolution – and he was forced to withdraw and accept arbitration. This setback brought about a collapse in the value of the franc, which contributed to the fall not only of the National Bloc government but of its successor, the Left Cartel government of 1924–6.

It was at this point that Aristide Briand, a man of unusual vision for the time, came to the fore. A Breton with a background in law and journalism, he had been a strong supporter of the trade union movement and a leading figure in the Socialist party before entering parliament in 1902. Having made his name by piloting through the legislation for the separation of Church and State, he became an almost permanent fixture in the rapidly revolving French cabinet, often as foreign minister, but also as prime minister on no fewer than eleven occasions. A fine orator who knew the machinery of government inside out, his background and early experiences had also given him an understanding of ordinary people and he had the rare quality of common sense. A strong supporter of the new League of Nations, he had a deep dislike of war – sharpened by his experience as wartime prime minister from late 1915 to early 1917 – and he aimed to bring about a reconciliation with Germany through a system of collective security within the framework of the League. Having failed with a first attempt in 1921, he successfully established a rapport with the German Foreign Minister Stresemann, which led to the Locarno Pact of 1925, involving also Britain, Italy and Belgium. This recognized the frontiers defined by the Treaty of Versailles and provided for the demilitarization of the Rhineland and the entry of Germany to the League of Nations. It was then consolidated by the Kellogg-Briand Pact of 1928, which brought the United States into a fifteen-nation pact to outlaw war – and which brought both men the Nobel Peace Prize. By 1930, Briand was putting forward a proposal for a European Union.

By that time, however, the international scene had darkened. The Great Depression following the American stock-market crash in October of the previous year had spread to Europe and was causing unemployment and hardship in Germany in particular. In France itself, as it happened, the situation seemed more favourable. For Poin-caré, who lasted as prime minister for a full three years from 1926, had formed a coalition government of national union to sort out the financial crisis and, indeed, had largely succeeded in doing so. He cut expenditure, raised taxes and devalued the franc to reduce the national debt, as a result of which he was able to modernize with a public housing programme and a social benefits system. And initially France did not suffer as much as Britain or Germany. It had less unemployment, while sectors such as the car industry, chemicals and electricity were still growing strongly in 1930. But, ironically, this was because France was economically less developed and more protectionist than those other countries, so that when it *was* hit in 1931 it was hit all the harder and would take longer to recover. Industrial produc-tion fell heavily, areas of the banking system collapsed, purchasing power came down and unemployment rose rapidly. All of which began to cause serious political instability, mirroring that in Germany and the new Fascist Italy.

Two further governments had tried to deal with the crisis by means of public works and subsidies before the Radical Socialist Édouard Herriot – who would also serve as prime minister on several occasions – took over with a leftist government in 1932. But the hope that he could succeed where others failed evaporated when the radical and socialist wings could not agree on a policy, so that public dissatisfaction became the greater. With anti-parliamentary feeling increasing internally and a looming external threat due to Hitler's rise to the chancellorship and his withdrawal from the League of Nations in 1933, France – with an ageing population and a falling birth rate – was hardly in a position to view the future with confidence. It already seemed to some that the labours of Clemenceau and the recently dead Briand had been in vain – and that the countdown to the next war had begun.

It did not take much to inflame the in-built division in post-Revolutionary French society. And the inability of rapidly changing governments to deal with the economic crisis now combined with growing international tension to sharpen political polarization in the country. Not that there was any great cohesion in either the left or the right. To the left there were the Radicals, republicans who believed in small government and were therefore doctrinally at odds with the Socialists, who in line with Moscow's directives were seen by the Communists as class traitors. On the right, where doctrine mattered less than tradition and sentiment, the running was being made less by political parties than by a scattering of organizations broadly sharing the same militantly anti-republican outlook. There was the Action Française of Charles Maurras, which advocated the violent overthrow of the Republic and the restoration of the monarchy. It had a youth movement, the Camelots du Roi, or street-sellers of its newspaper, as its infantry in the streets and, although the Pope had condemned it in 1926, it still had a strong influence on traditionalist opinion. More explicitly setting out to defend European Christian civilization was the militant Croix de Feu, which took its name from the military cross for valour in the face of enemy fire. This was led by Colonel de la Roque and funded by the perfume manufacturer François Coty, the owner of *Le Figaro*. Other groups with a more or less paramilitary style were the not-so-young Jeunesse Patriotes, funded by the champagne millionaire Pierre Taittinger, the small overtly fascist party called the Parti Franciste, and Solidarité Française. And as enemies they tended to lump together in a vast conspiracy republicans, Socialists, Communists, immigrants and of course Jews – thousands of whom were now coming in as refugees from Hitler's Germany.

The level of mythmaking and loathing between right and left at this period may seem strange today – if not quite as strange as Hitler's own fantasy that the Jews were responsible for both American capitalism and Russian communism. But the fear from which the mutual hatred sprang came from the sense that, with the rise of fascism and Soviet communism, the struggle for the national identity had developed an international dimension. If both sides tended to define the other in terms of its extremist wing, habitually denouncing the other as fascist or communist, it is because they thought that what was at stake was the future of civilization. And it only took a suitably symbolic affair like the Stavisky scandal of 1934 to provoke a level of violence not seen in Paris since 1871. A flashy former nightclub singer and manager, Stavisky was a swindler of Ukrainian Jewish origin who had been sentenced several times for fraud in the past, but who since 1926 – allegedly through connections in government circles – had contrived to have a further trial postponed and himself released on bail no fewer than nineteen times. In his latest scam he had set up a pawnbroking business with fake jewels as security and made a fortune by selling worthless bonds, buying off inquiring reporters or police as he went. Fearing that the game was finally up following the arrest of his confederate, the deputy mayor of Bayonne, he fled and was said to have been tracked down and found dead by the police after a suicide attempt.

This was received with much satirical scepticism from many who assumed that he had been silenced to protect those in high places and, indeed, a minister, prosecutors and radical deputies, as well as journalists, appeared to have some complicity in the scandal. This caused the right wing to declare that the country was being run by a gang of crooks and Jewish foreigners, and to bring its troops on to the streets for a series of violent confrontations during January 1934. Under this pressure Prime Minister Camille Chautemps, who had only been been in office for two months, was forced to resign, to be followed by a quick succession of former – and often future – prime ministers. The first was another radical, Édouard Daladier, who dismissed the Prefect of Police, Jean Chiappe, for favouring the right-wing demonstrators even though he had seen a number of his own officers injured, but this brought the parliament in the Palais Bourbon under attack. During the night of 6/7 February, armed police on foot and on horseback resisted charge after charge by a mob estimated to be at least 20,000 strong attempting to storm the building. By morning, up to 20 people had been killed and possibly 1,500 injured, including many policemen. If this was a failed *coup d'état*, it was an amateurish affair, but it was enough to persuade Daladier, abandoned by a section of his Radical Party, to resign in order to lower the tension – the first time the Third Republic had had to give in to the mob.

So the instability continued – quite apart from the assassination in Marseille later that year of Foreign Minister Louis Barthou and King Alexander of Yugoslavia at the hands of Croatian nationalists. Gaston Doumergue, who took over from Daladier, tried to settle the situation by bringing right-wingers into his cabinet, but the left was hostile and he was gone by November. There followed Pierre-Henri Flandin who lasted seven months, Fernand Buisson who lasted three days before he made way for Pierre Laval, who took over in June 1935 and lasted almost eight months. His attempt to deal with the continuing economic depression through deflationary measures made him unpopular, but it was the belief that he connived at Mussolini's invasion of Ethiopia in 1935 – which in effect killed off the impotent League of Nations – that brought him down in January 1936.

Meanwhile, Stalin had belatedly recognized that the policy of attacking social democracy in Germany had only assisted the rise of Hitler, so that the Communists – who had themselves massed to attack the Palais Bourbon, but thought better of it – had come in from the cold. They were now prepared to work with the Radicals and the Socialists on a broad left-wing front – the more so since their isolationist stance had reduced their membership by around three-quarters. By the familiar dialectical zigzag of French politics, the Stavisky crisis would produce the Popular Front.

This broad left alliance sprang from the conjunction in the spring of 1936 – a quite exceptional event, as a useful study points out – of a powerful workers' movement and an electoral victory by a united left.[7] And it was under pressure from below, as well as from events, that Radicals, Socialists and Communists came together in what, for the party leaders, was a marriage of convenience. The Communists and the Socialists were of course competing for the left-wing vote, but the Socialists were also at odds ideologically with the Radicals – who joined the Front in part because they were losing electoral support. The initial impulse was provided by a cross-party group of anti-fascist intellectuals and the movement was carried forward by a great parade bringing together the parties, the unions and various anti-war and human rights organizations. This led to an electoral pact by which each party agreed to withdraw in favour of the leading left-wing candidate for the second electoral round, the outcome being a clear victory for the Front, with the Socialists having 147 seats, the Radicals 106 and the Communists 72. Of course this new Popular Front government of June 1936 to June 1937, led by the Socialist leader and distinguished intellectual Léon Blum, was never going to find life easy. For a start Blum was Jewish and, however non-practising, was therefore greeted with particular virulence by the anti-Semitic right-wing press – he had already been hauled out of his car and beaten up by young militants of the Camelots du Roi. Also the Communists, for tactical reasons, offered only passive and conditional support. Above all, there was the tricky problem that the workers were already celebrating by holding strikes and occupying the factories.

Blum was determined to use strictly constitutional means and, aware that he had little room for manoeuvre, proceeded to act fast. As it happened, the workers occupying the factories did not, as has often been said, see themselves as starting a revolution. More modestly and pragmatically, as has been well demonstrated, they were trying to pre-empt lock-outs and the bringing in of non-strikers in their place.[8] Blum ended the strikes with the Matignon agreements providing for increased wages, greater trade union rights and collective agreements in the workplace. He brought in the forty-hour working week and the two-week paid holiday, which enabled many workers for the first time to visit the countryside or see the sea. He appointed three women to his cabinet, even though women still did not have the vote. He raised the school-leaving age to fourteen and appointed a minister for sport, who funded playing fields and swimming pools.

The Front also brought in some limited nationalization measures, created a central fund for scientific research and set up a whole set of institutions, including centres for the study of astrophysics and atomic synthesis, the Musée d'Art Moderne and the anthropological museum, the Musée de l'Homme. Its initiatives in regard to the spread of culture combined with the optimism of the moment to influence the theatre, the cinema and even – with Charles Trenet singing at the annual jamboree of the Communist Party – the popular song. It was quite a firework display.

Naturally it could not last. Its economic measures were over-ambitious and in the short term, by limiting production, made things worse. And the international situation became increasingly ominous in July 1936 when General Franco began his rebellion against the Spanish Republic and precipitated a proxy European war, with the Germans and the Italians openly supporting Franco with planes and weapons, while the Soviet Union sent supplies and money to the Republicans. Blum would have liked to help the Republicans – and did so unofficially by helping André Malraux to organize a combat air squadron – but he could not then have held his shaky coalition together. In any event, despite the efforts of Foreign Minister Anthony Eden – who had lost a brother in the previous world war and would lose a son in the next – the British were bent on appeasement and made it clear that they would not support Blum. As a result of the failure to support the Spanish Republicans, the Communists withdrew their support and the coalition fell apart.

For all that, the Popular Front remains a legendary moment for the French left in particular and not just because of 'the massive character of the reforms of the summer of 1936 and the euphoria', as one account puts it.[9] It enlarged the horizons of millions, gave dignity to the workers and imbued people with a sense of the equal ownership of their country. It was a momentary glimpse of a better future and a blueprint for the new republic that would come into being after the Second World War.

The defining moment in the steady progress to war was the Munich Agreement of 1938, which accepted Hitler's claim to the Sudetenland, the German-speaking part of Czecho-slovakia, and opened the way for his invasion of the whole country shortly afterwards. If British Prime Minister Chamberlain was naively delighted to wave Hitler's guarantee of peace, his French counterpart Daladier – head of the government again in 1938–40 – felt ashamedly that the people acclaiming him on his return to Paris were deluded fools. Those industrialists whose motto was 'rather Hitler than Blum' were happy, while Blum himself spoke of a cowardly sense of relief. An opinion poll at this time showed 57 per cent in favour of the agreement and 37 per cent against but, as Europe went on marching open-eyed to disaster, the pessimism increased. A Franco-German non-aggression pact at the end of 1938 merely opened the way for the Reich to annex Bohemia–Moravia, initiate claims against Poland and conclude the Hitler–Stalin pact of August 1939, which opened up further alarming possibilities – quite apart from forcing the Communist Party to perform yet another somersault and decide once again that war against Germany would be a capitalist aberration and not a patriotic act. By this time the larger public could read the writing on the wall and a further poll showed that 76 per cent now believed war to be inevitable. So it was a resigned and dangerously divided country that waited for Hitler to make his move.

The division of opinion is sharply illustrated by the attitudes of intellectuals and artists, a number of whom now believed that the weakness of the democracies left them facing a stark choice between fascism and communism. Picasso's giant mural *Guernica*, inspired by the indiscriminate bombing of civilians in the historic Basque town by German aircraft during the Spanish Civil War, told its own story, while Malraux's novel *L'Espoir*, translated as *Man's Hope*, gave a sympathetic but ultimately pessimistic account of that war, seen as the curtain-raiser to a new world war.

On the other hand, there was a ready audience for right-wing and fascist writers such as Pierre Drieu la Rochelle, whose novel *Gilles* is a counterpart to *L'Espoir*, Louis-Ferdinand Céline and Robert Brasillach – all of whom would side with the German Occupation. Even within Catholic opinion there was division since, while the Church generally favoured Franco's rebellion, the writers François Mauriac and Georges Bernanos finally came out against it. But even the widespread pacifism, fed by memories of the previous war and by films such as Jean Renoir's *La Grande Illusion*, seemed to add to the fatalism about war. This was evident in the theatre, in the frequency of subjects from antiquity, as though the sense of inescapable destiny of Greek tragedy was appropriate to the times – and as early as 1935 in the teasing title of the play *La Guerre de Troie n'aura pas lieu*, or *The Trojan War Will Not Take Place*, by Jean Giraudoux who, as a diplomat, knew that the next war was all too likely to take place.

It is not that France was as ill-prepared for war militarily, as has sometimes been assumed. Except as regards the number of aircraft, its forces were reasonably comparable to those of Germany and, indeed, the country had tended to see itself since Verdun as possessing the 'leading army in the world'. After all, it had throughout the 1930s been constructing the very elaborate defensive Maginot Line on the border with Germany, while Léon Blum had realistically begun an extensive programme of rearmament in 1936. The problems lay elsewhere, the most fundamental being the contradiction between the country's diplomatic approach and its military posture. Its alliances with distant countries such as Poland and Russia – not to mention a wavering offshore Britain – implied that it could come to their aid, whereas the defensive stance rendered this implausible. There was also the problem that the Maginot Line was not only incomplete but, despite the clear lessons of the previous war, stopped at the Belgian border, since it was assumed that Germany could not attack through the heavily wooded hills of the Ardennes. In fact, the generals were geared up to fight the previous war rather than this one and – having ignored the warnings of Charles de Gaulle, then a lieutenant-colonel attached to the National Defence Council – had no answer to the new German blitzkrieg, or lightning war, based on combined air and armoured thrusts that was launched against Poland on 1 September 1939 – a move which finally provoked both Deladier in France and Chamberlain in Britain into a declaration of war two days later. In short, France was diplomatically and strategically in a weak position as it faced this new conflict. Add the internal divisions and the fatalism, which could only be increased by the prolonged inactivity of the *drôle de guerre*, or phoney war, and the outcome is hardly surprising.

When the Germans finally did attack after seven months on 10 May 1940, the effect was stunning. They simply went around the Maginot Line, made an armoured assault through the Ardennes and took the Franco–British forces in the rear. By the end of the month these were in full flight, with a desperate effort being made to evacuate troops to England – almost 250,000 British were saved and over 100,000 French. Gibes about the French soldiers being cowardly are as ignorant as they are unfair – they fought bravely and lost many lives in protecting the humiliating escape of the ill-equipped and poorly performing British expeditionary force. But the strategic position was hopeless, the population was fleeing before the rapid German advance and the government was retreating to Bordeaux. The defeatist faction won over the cabinet and Prime Minister Paul Reynaud was replaced by the disillusioned old warhorse, Marshal Pétain, who asked for an armistice. It had taken less than six weeks.

De Gaulle, now a general and recently appointed under-secretary of state for defence, having failed to sway the cabinet, escaped to London and made his famous BBC broadcast calling upon the French to fight on. Since he was heard by almost nobody in France he was as yet a voice crying in the wilderness, but he was strikingly prescient in his longer-term view of this world war – and his time would come.

10

THE SECOND WORLD WAR: COLLABORATION AND RESISTANCE

'Never were we freer than when under the German Occupation' wrote Jean-Paul Sartre famously, meaning that in that situation people were forced to make significant choices.[1] But Sartre himself did not make any particularly risky choices and his observation would have seemed mere sophistry to a fellow Frenchman with a captured son to worry about or a family to feed. For what do you do when your country is overrun at devastating speed and your everyday life is transformed overnight? When you see well-drilled German troops parading down the Champs-Élysées? When your landmark buildings are commandeered and draped in red banners sporting swastikas? And when you find new signs installed on the Place de la Concorde to direct German vehicles and see German soldiers strolling along the streets or travelling on the Métro?

Nor was it easy to feel free when you were concerned about the food shortage, when you were under an overnight curfew, when you were solemnly warned that sabotage would be punished by death, and when you knew that there were over 1.5 million French soldiers imprisoned in German camps – which in effect held the whole country hostage. So, initially at least, the French did what the British government advised its citizens in the occupied Channel Islands to do – they practised 'passive cooperation'. But the pressure that soon led British police in the Islands to cooperate actively in deporting Jews to concentration camps bore far more heavily upon the French. For this shattering defeat emphasized yet again the fundamental conflict, unresolved since 1789, between the Catholic monarchist tradition and the republican democratic tradition. It was in this situation that ambiguities could arise, that loyalties could be dangerous, and that the wrong choice could one day lead to a firing squad.

And the ambiguity was greatly increased by the terms of the armistice. At one level these were very harsh; the Germans imposed crippling occupation costs, annexed Alsace-Lorraine and took over the more heavily populated and industrialized north, as well as the whole Atlantic seaboard with all its ports down to Bordeaux. France was permitted an unoccupied 'Free Zone' representing about 45 per cent of the national territory and a third of the population in the less economically developed south, though it included Lyon and the port of Marseille. The country was therefore split in two, with a guarded 'demarcation line' between the two parts. This arrangement recognized the fact that the French empire was not directly affected and, in consequence, the country was allowed to keep its navy so long as it was inactive. But it also suited the Germans.

Hitler had famously come and been filmed doing a little victory jig on 23 June 1940 on the esplanade of the Palais de Chaillot. And a German administration had quickly taken over the key official buildings, grand hotels and barracks in central Paris, with the area commander being well ensconced

in the Hotel Meurice in the Rue de Rivoli and the Gestapo
comfortably installed in the Avenue Foch and the Rue de la
Pompe. But Hitler was anxious not to divert resources from
the forthcoming confrontation with Britain and the Soviet
Union in order to garrison and police a large country like
France, nor, since he already had access to its industrial
wealth and held it hostage by not releasing his prisoners, did
he need to. So it was convenient to let the French do much
of the policing themselves and to treat the country as a
rather decadent holiday resort where German soldiers could
come on leave and sample the dubious delights of Paris.
All this obviously raised questions as to how far this lesser
Free Zone could be free and how far it could speak for the
French nation. And the ambiguity was not lessened by the
approach of the two oddly assorted leaders of what was to
become the Vichy regime: Marshal Philippe Pétain and
Pierre Laval.

Pétain was now a grandfatherly, if childless eighty-four-
year-old figure, with a thin fluting voice, a white moustache
and a walking stick, but with famously clear blue eyes. His
later career may have been a surprise even to himself, since
in 1914 he was already a fifty-eight-year-old infantry colonel
on the point of retirement, having had his nomination for
general turned down. But of course the year 1916 had seen
him become 'the hero of Verdun', the key battle in which he
held the fort against sustained attack through a defensive
strategy based on artillery and a maximal deployment of men
and material. Clemenceau and some in the general staff had
viewed him as too defensive, but that in itself had made him
popular with the troops, who found him down-to-earth and
more concerned with their safety than gung-ho generals
dedicated to attack – as he demonstrated after the mutinies
of 1917.

While not a practising Catholic, Pétain had the traditionalist views of his provincial Catholic background and was
fond of saying that – as opposed to urban cosmopolitanism –

'the soil does not lie'. Though no admirer of the Republic, he had not broadcast his political views. But he had been minister for war in 1934 and he had been quite at home as ambassador to Franco's Spain in 1939–40. He was perfectly aware that for several years right-wing elements angered by the Popular Front had been speaking of him as a potential national leader – to the point that, when asked to form a government after the defeat, he could produce a list of ministers from his pocket.

In contrast to the frail but trim old soldier, the fifty-three-year-old Laval looked like an oddly untidy version of the overdressed head waiter – with his swarthy features, dark eyes, dark hair with one lock trailing over his forehead, dark suit, trademark white tie over a cream shirt and his perpetual Balto cigarette. This image hardly helped him since, while the old marshal seemed to invite respect, it was easy to dislike Laval and see him – as indeed he was caricatured in the British press – as a creepy, toad-like careerist who faced both ways just like his name, a palindrome. Certainly, Laval was the more complex figure – he once described himself as having many compartments – but he was also the more intelligent and had behind him a much more substantial political career. A local boy made good from a humble background in the Auvergne, he too declared himself to be a 'lover of the soil' and he had indeed bought a large farm, but he had made his way as a lawyer and become extremely wealthy through extensive property deals and the acquisition of a newspaper.

The village background still left its traces – he was mean with money, was superstitious, could be coarse in speech and manner, and literally blew smoke into the old leader's blue eyes. But he could also be charming and had the self-made man's belief that he could cut through political double-talk and diplomatic niceties and get things done. He had after all, in a career which almost exemplified the instability of the Third Republic, been a government minister in a whole variety of roles and had twice been prime minister – in 1931 and 1935 – before being dispatched to the wilderness by the Popular Front. So in the setting up of the Vichy regime he saw Pétain as the convenient figurehead and himself as the strategist.

Pragmatic fixer though he was, Laval was not without a strongly held guiding idea. Exempted from military service in the First World War because of varicose veins, he had an abiding dislike of war and had been in the pacifist wing of the Socialist party before moving to the right. He had shared with Briand the hope of a unified Europe based on Franco-German reconciliation and he had opposed the war in 1939. But, now that the war was lost, he believed that France would have to accept the reality of a Nazi-dominated Europe and try to maintain its position within it, a view reinforced for this self-made individualist and landowner by his fierce opposition to communism and the Soviet Union. Of course he was assuming that Britain would be defeated and that Germany would win the war. Pétain made the same assumption, but as opposed to Laval's *realpolitik* he had a dreamier view of how France could be restored. For the marshal's idea of France, as expressed by a fervent admirer in 1985, 'came straight from the great Catholic royalist tradition of the Middle Ages: a nation of independent members, joined together not only by spiritual fraternity but by collaboration between the different crafts'.[2] For Laval this was an innocent fantasy and the difference in perspective between the two men would cause tension at intervals.

But there was no disagreement between them about an armistice or about scrapping the Republic. Parliamentarians attempting to leave for French North Africa in order to fight on were blocked at the instigation of Laval, who proceeded to organize the handover to Pétain. The government set itself up on 1 July 1940 in Vichy, a chic little spa town offering tepid, tasteless water from battered pewter cups chained to fountains, and, in the town casino barely more than a week later, the traumatized deputies and senators made Pétain head of government by a huge majority. Whereupon the marshal, despite being charged with producing a new constitution, immediately passed decrees granting to himself all powers as head of a new 'French State'. The two houses of parliament simply lapsed, to be replaced eventually by a merely consultative body of notables, and an authoritarian paternalist regime was suddenly in being by which Pétain, as Laval jokingly told him, acquired more powers than Louis XIV. And indeed, like Louis XIV, he too became the object of a quasi-religious cult. For, as he said in his radio speech of 17 June, he had 'granted France, in order to mitigate its misfortune, the gift of his own person'. He offered himself as the old soldier beyond any personal ambition, the national icon sacrificing himself for his country, the guarantor that the glory that once was France was not entirely lost.

That message would be hammered home over the next few years by a State propaganda effort to rival the glorification of Louis XIV, through speeches on the radio, photographs in the controlled newspapers and visits to towns or schools. The marshal was ever-present: as a bust in public buildings or as an image on everything from wall posters, calendars and coins to postage stamps, paperweights and ashtrays. And he was busily unscrambling the 1789 Revolution in order to establish the 'new moral order' of his 'National Revolution'. The Republic's motto '*Liberté, Egalité, Fraternité*' was now replaced by the Croix de Feu's trio of '*Travail, Famille, Patrie*' – or Work, Family and Fatherland, in that redemptive order. *Travail* implied healthy agricultural toil, in line with a return to the land away from the decadence of the cities – a move also encouraged by scouting and other youth movements. The right to strike was abolished, as were trade unions, to be replaced by corporate unions composed of both management and workforce to discourage any idea of a class struggle. *Famille*, accordingly, implied the traditional peasant unit, now strengthened by family allowances, restrictions on divorce, the criminalization of abortion and the insistence that a woman's place was in the home. All this was further reinforced by the scrapping of free secondary education and State teacher training colleges, and the granting afresh to religious bodies of the right to teach and of subsidies to Catholic schools – which inevitably involved rewriting school textbooks to remove any republican bias.

As for *Patrie*, since it was necessary to 'give France back to the French', that meant taking steps to exclude gypsies, communists, Freemasons and, above all, Jews. So two statutes enacted in October 1940 and June 1941 excluded Jews from public office, State employment and such commercial activities as banking and dealing in property. Those who had obtained French nationality after 1927 saw their citizenship revoked, while Pétain's former protégé General de Gaulle was condemned to death *in absentia* for desertion. The old Anglophobia was also revived by the tragic incident of the sinking of part of the French fleet off the Algerian port of Mers-el-Kébir. Afraid that it might come under German command, the British had requested it to sail to a French colony or some neutral port and, when its commander refused, the Royal Navy sank or disabled most of the ships with the loss of almost 1,300 lives. All this helped to turn France in upon itself and to feed the extraordinary popularity of Pétain in the period following the defeat.

Why was the marshal's bold attempt to reverse the direction of French history so widely accepted? Why this 'regressive dependency' on 'parental leadership from the top', as one writer expresses it?[3] For Pétain's transformative measures were not merely accepted by traditionalists such as the Bishop of Lyon, who saw in the marshal's leadership a manifestation of divine will, but by many disillusioned republicans who felt imprisoned within a national catastrophe in which the only thing left standing seemed to be this frail, self-assured old man – a message constantly conveyed by the Vichy hymn '*Maréchal, nous voila!*', with its mind-numbing assertion '*Pétain, c'est la France; la France, c'est Pétain!*' But if Pétain was France and France was Pétain, was this the real France? Or was it a nostalgic theme park – on a reservation?

When he arrived in London on 17 June 1940 and was cold-shouldered by his own embassy, de Gaulle felt 'alone and utterly bereft, like a man on the shore of an ocean that he was presuming to swim across'.[4] And while Churchill enabled him to make his far-sighted radio appeal the next day – in which he pointed out that France still had her empire and could combine with the British empire, which had the backing of the industrial might of the United States – he did not find the going easy. He appealed to two senior generals, Weygand and then Noguès, to take over the leadership of a Free French movement, but was rebuffed. Few of the French service personnel who had come to England after Dunkirk rallied to him, while the permanent French residents in London viewed him with suspicion. For who was this outlandishly tall maverick with his Cross of Lorraine symbol who seemingly came from nowhere yet presumed to speak in the name of France? Was he some sort of fantasist, a military adventurer or a would-be dictator, as Roosevelt – fed with damaging comments from his ambassador Leahy in Vichy – tended to think? And if Churchill admired his romantic gesture and set him up with temporary headquarters, was this not a blunder, as some in government and the Foreign Office thought? Would it not compromise their ability to put pressure on Vichy to cooperate by at least ensuring that its naval and colonial forces would not be used against Britain? And anyway wasn't this unclubbable character simply impossible?

Indeed, de Gaulle was not an easy man to deal with. He had never been to England and though he understood English he did not care to speak it; he was also awkward, arrogant and prickly. Moreover, he had the traditional

French view of Britain as a ruthlessly mercenary imperial power – and an unreliable ally with a large share of responsibility for the disaster in France. To the very extent that he was now dependent on Britain, he was suspicious of its intentions, so that his lordly manner, however irritating and bloody-minded his allies found him, was not simply a matter of temperament. It was also a tactical response to the very difficult hand he had to play and, if he often put off potential sympathizers, it was because he was over-anxious to protect his independence and his assumed status as leader of a resurgent France. This obviously placed him in a curious position in London and it is little wonder that Churchill, who often quarrelled with him in his colourful *franglais*, should have said that the heaviest cross he had to bear in wartime was the Cross of Lorraine. Nor is it surprising that the Foreign Office and the Americans should have looked around for some more congenial and more senior French figure with whom to replace him.

For, as de Gaulle was only too aware, there were real conflicts of interest between his allies and himself. While he aspired to be accepted as leader throughout the French empire, Churchill had his own empire to protect and would have little compunction in subordinating the French interest in North Africa or Syria to the primary aim of winning this world war. And, if de Gaulle was dependent on Churchill, Churchill was dependent on Roosevelt, who teased him for his patronage of this cardboard general with no troops to his name – and was in fact suspicious of the imperialist ambitions not only of de Gaulle but of Churchill himself. Roosevelt hoped to neutralize Vichy through his embassy there, but he had an unflattering view of the French in general and saw no role for either Vichy or de Gaulle in the post-war settlement, which he had decided would be determined by the four Great Powers: the US, Britain, the Soviet Union and the Nationalist China of Chiang Kai-shek. Overall, it was a situation in which de Gaulle – who was initially of little more than symbolic value even to Churchill – was the tail trying to wag a very large dog. He somehow had to get himself and his humiliated country taken seriously as an ally of these major powers.

De Gaulle's first concern was to ensure that any volunteers came under a separate French flag rather than be assigned to British regiments, so he persuaded Churchill to recognize him as leader of Free France within ten days of arriving in London. Set up in better conditions in Carlton Gardens, off the Mall, he then proceeded to organize the few forces available to him – volunteers from among French troops still in England or from the local French community, plus some units of the navy. The next step was to limit his dependency on London, get himself recognized as the leader of the French empire and establish a headquarters on overseas French soil. Though French North Africa remained pro-Vichy, partly due to the memory of Mers-el-Kébir, such central African colonies as Chad, Cameroon and French Equatorial Africa had rallied to him, and this led him to mount a joint expedition with Churchill in September 1940 to take over the important French West African port of Dakar.

While Churchill's interest was to prevent the Germans from using it as a base in the Battle of the Atlantic, de Gaulle thought a takeover could start a domino movement across all of the French territories in Africa and provide him with his new headquarters. But it turned out to be a fiasco and, though the final plan was Churchill's, de Gaulle was blamed because loose talk on the Free French side had enabled Vichy to send naval reinforcements in time. Churchill stood by him, but the disaster damned him in the eyes of Roosevelt and Vichy had a field day, presenting itself as the defender of the French empire against this traitor. The effect on de Gaulle of seeing Frenchmen fire upon Frenchmen was such, according to a colleague, that 'he was never the same man again, never happy again'.[5]

For all that, the course of the war and developments

within France itself gradually began to operate in his favour. Resistance began slowly, though there would eventually be over 200 networks of all kinds, whether independent, Gaullist, socialist or communist in inspiration – with the Communists entering the scene after Hitler's invasion of Russia in June 1941. La Résistance is in fact an umbrella term, covering all sorts of activities by all sorts of individuals – from writing graffiti or publishing underground news-papers to passing intelligence to London or committing sabotage. But sizeable organized networks were gradually emerging, such as the Comité d'Action Socialiste, Francs-Tireurs, Libération, Combat and the Communist Front National. While this development was encouraging, it also posed problems for de Gaulle. One was that these networks were receiving money and weapons from the British Special Operations Executive (SOE), so that he was cut out of the loop. This he countered by setting up his own parallel intelligence and supply service, but the problem of dealing with these independent and politically diverse groups was much trickier. His own focus had essentially been on building up a Free French force outside France to take its place alongside the Allies and he had no political programme for the post-war period.

He sent Jean Moulin, the former prefect of Chartres – and one of the great names of the Resistance – back to France in January 1942 to try to coordinate several non-Communist groups. But he was rather at a loss when the Socialist trade unionist Christian Pineau turned up in March to demand a proclamation of post-war aims. If de Gaulle despised Vichy, he was also no admirer of the unstable Third Republic, and it took weeks of haggling before he produced a declaration promising a restoration of democratic freedoms and the introduction of social security, central economic planning and votes for women. This was very well received when it was published in the underground press and, by demonstrating that he was no dictator, it strengthened the hand of Jean Moulin.

What with that and the Free French forces distinguishing themselves in June 1942 with the defence of Bir Hakeim in Libya, enabling the British Eighth Army to reorganize and defeat Rommel at El Alamein, things were looking up. So de Gaulle was all the more taken aback to find himself kept in the dark about the Allied invasion of French North Africa in November 1942. Roosevelt had decided to replace de Gaulle with his own man in the form of General Giraud, who was anti-German but who had Vichy sympathies. So Giraud had been smuggled out of France via Gibraltar, given the code name 'Kingpin' by General Eisenhower and lined up to be commander-in-chief of the French troops in North Africa – which numbered almost five times de Gaulle's force of 50,000.

This was a body blow to de Gaulle, to which he reacted with characteristic energy. He demonstrated the breadth of his own appeal to those other French territories which had rallied to him, he made overtures to the Russians, and he radicalized his own political line in opposition to that of Giraud. Since the Free Zone had been occupied by the Germans in November 1942 in response to the Allied landings, Vichy seemed less and less relevant and there was increasing internal resistance, so he could easily demonstrate that, unlike himself, Giraud had no appeal to the internal Resistance. He was helped by the fact that Jean Moulin – though he would later be captured and tortured to death – finally succeeded in creating a unifying National Council of the Resistance.[6] He was helped even more by the fact that Giraud was wooden, lacking in guile and so politically obtuse that he offended even the Americans. De Gaulle moved his headquarters to Algiers and more or less obliged Roosevelt and Churchill to make him joint president of the National Council of the Resistance – and plead with him to at least shake hands with Giraud for the sake of the cameras at the Casablanca Conference in June 1943. But he was already on the way to sidelining Giraud and it was clear by the end of that year that he was the unchallenged leader of the Free French. He had played his weak hand against the big players with great determination and increasing skill. But the game was not over.

Nor was it yet over for the leaders of Vichy, even though the Free Zone had disappeared from beneath their feet, for in the national vacuum thus created Vichy went on officially while the Germans tightened the screws. The systematic deportation of Jews and others was now well under way. The deportation of 4,000 Jewish men had been followed in July 1942 by the spectacular 'Spring Breeze Operation', in which the French police played its part in rounding up 12,884 Jews, of whom some 7,500 – including women and children – were held in stifling heat for five days in the covered cycling stadium, the Vélodrome d'Hiver, with no lavatories and with a single water tap. Some were driven to suicide, while others were shot trying to escape. And the deportations were continuing with the help of the new black-shirted Vichy Milice, a militia set up in January 1943, which worked alongside the Gestapo and was almost indistinguishable from it.

Meanwhile, whole industries were working for the German war effort, with the result that by 1944 more than 4 million Frenchmen including prisoners-of-war and requisitioned labourers – which amounted to 37 per cent of the male working population – were working directly for Germany.[7] But the introduction in February 1943 of the Service du Travail Obligatoire, or compulsory work service in Germany for twenty-year-olds, sharply increased the developing hostility to Vichy and sent a lot of young men into the *maquis*, or bush, to escape the draft. Yet even if people disliked Laval, who had publicly declared his hope that Germany would win the war, many still saw Pétain as the national hero nobly sacrificing himself for his people. And indeed this view was largely reflected in the post-war assessments of those who defended Pétain, in which he was viewed as the 'shield', as he described himself, protecting the French from far greater suffering at the hands of the enemy. If he made mistakes on occasion, these tended to be attributed to the influence upon him of the wily professional politician Laval.

Yet it is hard today to see the marshal as the transcendent figure above politics that he was made to seem. For his initial action of imposing his National Revolution upon a captive nation with no parliamentary means of expression and no free press was surely a piece of gross political opportunism. Since the terms of the armistice did not call for constitutional change, the French administration – as in other countries conquered by Hitler – could simply have maintained basic services, postponing any political change until the country was free again. Instead, as Robert Paxton argues, Vichy 'launched partisan initiatives of political revenge and exclusion'.[8] Again, it was a highly political decision to formalize his commitment to collaboration at his meeting with Hitler in the Führer's special train at Montoire on 24 October 1940 – after which he told the nation, 'it is with honour and to preserve the unity of France within the framework of the new European order that I am today entering on the path of collaboration'.

But it was a fool's bargain. Pétain thought that he could regain status for his defeated country and put it back on the side of history by becoming a partner in Hitler's new European order. By making this offer to the Führer, 'as between soldiers', he hoped to obtain the freeing of prisoners and the reunification of the two Zones to make France whole again. He was also, as an inducement, offering to commit the reduced French army to a combined Franco-German attack against the British in Africa. But Hitler, more concerned with invading Britain and then Russia, had no interest in a partnership with this defeated France that he despised. He simply wanted to hold it hostage through the prisoners while milking it economically – and, if he could rely on Vichy resisting any Free French move on North Africa, so much the better. So he happily accepted the old marshal's offer to collaborate, but made no real concessions. On the contrary, he piled on the pressure. While de Gaulle played his weak cards cleverly, Pétain naively threw away his ace at the beginning and lost his bargaining power. For no gain, the 'hero of Verdun' had turned his country into a satellite of Germany. After Montoire, he and Laval would at best be reduced to playing the losing game of trying to find some margin of independence within an undignified dependency.

There remained a tension between Pétain and Laval, who tended towards the harder, more ideological strand of collaboration represented by declared Fascists like the writers Robert Brasillach and Drieu La Rochelle, the newspaper *Je suis partout* or the influential Radio-Paris. These people thought Vichy's National Revolution too soft and backward-looking, as did Laval himself – which got him dismissed in December 1940, to be replaced after a brief interval by the anti-Semitic, Anglophobic Admiral Darlan, who was more supportive of the marshal's views and who introduced an innovative planning approach. It was during Darlan's tenure that Pétain sought to legitimize the regime by means of a show trial designed to prove that the leaders of the Third Republic had been responsible for the defeat. Hitler approved, wanting it to show rather that France had been responsible for the war itself. But it was a fiasco, for Léon Blum turned the trial upside down by demonstrating at length that it was the general staff and not the political leaders who were to blame. A furious Hitler had it stopped, Blum and Daladier were handed over to the Germans, to end up in Buchenwald concentration camp, and Laval was back at Hitler's demand for the endgame and the completion of the 'Final Solution of the Jewish problem'.

It has been claimed that Pétain's 'shield' at least protected many of the French Jews, but of course he had from the start taken oppressive measures against the Jews on his own account and, at German request, had set up a department for Jewish affairs, the Commissariat Général aux Questions Juives, which came to employ 2,500 people. This was ultimately the most damaging action of all, for by establishing a whole database, which the Germans could not have done without an enormous expenditure of manpower, Vichy was doing their work for them – and doing so voluntarily, following an agreement on police collaboration. By July 1944, almost 80,000 Jews had been deported and neither Laval nor Pétain had displayed much curiosity as to what happened to them, even if part of the public was disturbed. And Laurent Joly is surely right, at the end of his exhaustive study of the Commissariat Général, to conclude that 'after Romania, Vichy France is certainly the satellite country that played the most criminal role, quite voluntarily, in the Nazi policy of genocide'.[9]

With the Liberation looming in the spring of 1944, and with the Americans still largely keeping him out of the picture, de Gaulle could see even greater challenges ahead of him. Even though the Free French forces had risen to 120,000 in the Italian campaign of 1943 and to over 300,000 by the time of the invasion of France in 1944, they were still relatively marginal. So how could he gain some sort of equal status with those Allies, to ensure that France would immediately be restored to independent French control rather than come under Allied occupation? How, as D-Day approached, could he demonstrate to the Americans that the French population wanted him and not Vichy? And, as perhaps the greatest challenge – especially since the Communists were coming to the fore with Russian victories in the east – how could he bring the internal Resistance to lay down its weapons after the peace and respect the authority of the State?

The Vichy problem was solved by the Germans themselves. While Pétain had made a pathetic attempt to arbitrate and Laval was attempting to pre-empt a Gaullist takeover through a last-minute patched-up republican government, they were taken captive on 20 August 1944 and carted off to Germany, which discredited them further. Meanwhile, a Free French army under General de Lattre de Tassigny was prominent in the invasion in the south, an armoured division under General Leclerc was fighting alongside Allied armies in the thrust from Normandy and General Koenig was active in Brittany – and their warm reception by the population was obvious. In addition, the internal Resistance groups were sabotaging German transport, harrying German columns and fighting some real and costly battles. The combined contribution of these forces was recognized by the Allied commander Eisenhower when he said that the Resistance in Normandy was worth fifteen divisions. De Gaulle still had difficulty getting into France, but he managed to make a brief visit in mid-June and the enthusiastic reception he received in Bayeux demonstrated his popularity. He was now invited to Washington where Roosevelt, however reluctantly, recognized unofficially that his provisional government 'was qualified to administer France'.

But when he returned to France on 20 August, by which time the rising against the Germans in Paris had already begun, he found Eisenhower still intending to bypass Paris and drive on at top speed towards the Rhine, arguing – with some embarrassment, as de Gaulle thought– that a detour to the capital would mean losing valuable time. But with his mind set on the symbolic value of French forces recapturing the city, with the possibility that it could be destroyed by the retreating Germans – and with a premature rising there reviving the fear of a Communist takeover – de Gaulle persuaded Eisenhower to detach the armoured division of General Leclerc. So French troops retook the city, de Gaulle made his triumphal progress down the Champs-Élysées on 26 August 1944 and, while making it clear that the Resistance was now subservient to the reconstituted State, announced grandly at the Hôtel de Ville that the liberation of the capital had been carried out by the French, by the French alone and, should there be any misunderstanding, by nobody but the French.

It was a magnificent bluff which transformed the Resistance, real as it was, into a controlling national myth and which enabled de Gaulle boldly to assume control. It also enabled France – with a little help from Churchill – to be recognized at the Yalta conference in February 1945 as one of the victorious Allies and therefore entitled to share in the occupation of Germany. This proud, difficult man had taken a miserably defeated, shamed country and pulled it up by its bootstraps – or, as Malraux expressed it more starkly, had 'held up its corpse and persuaded the world that it was alive'.[10] It was a formidable achievement.

There followed a settling of accounts. Laval was condemned to death after a botched trial and was shot after a failed suicide attempt. Pétain's death sentence was commuted to life imprisonment by de Gaulle, who regarded the marshal as senile. Of collaborationist writers, Robert Brasillach was executed and Drieu la Rochelle committed suicide. Stars of the stage such as Sacha Guitry and Arletty or of the music hall, such as Maurice Chevalier, saw their careers suffer, while Louis Renault had his car firm nationalized. Some went into hiding in France or in Spain. Around 100,000 people were condemned to penalties ranging from loss of civil rights to death, although less than 800 were executed. But of course there had already been an uncontrolled unofficial purge of '*collabos*' – by Resistance fighters shooting members of the Milice, local groups lynching apparent traitors and shearing the heads of women who had slept with German soldiers, or simply individuals for personal reasons taking revenge on a neighbour. It was not pretty.

And then France forgot. This was for reasons of state in the case of de Gaulle, who wanted to speed up the recovery. He formally took the view – as later did President Mitterrand – that the Republic itself had no involvement in the deportations or other actions of an illegal Vichy regime. So there would be no official history of the Occupation, since that would have undercut the helpful myth that the French had all supported the Resistance, and that collaboration had involved only aberrant individuals who were in any event under pressure from the Germans.

It took over twenty-five years for this comfortable state of denial to begin to be questioned both by foreign historians such as Robert Paxton and by films such as *Le Chagrin et la pitié* (*The Sorrow and the Pity*), the TV documentary by Marcel Ophuls of 1971 and Louis Malle's *Lacombe Lucien* of 1974. *Le Chagrin et la pitié* was only permitted a limited showing in the cinema, while Louis Malle always felt that the French never forgave him for showing the comparative ordinariness of collaboration. And official tolerance of former Vichy figures meant that René Bousquet, the police chief responsible for the great round-up of 1942, Maurice Papon, also responsible for deportations, and Paul Touvier, the leader of the Milice responsible for civilian murders, did not have to face an adulterated and almost posthumous justice until the 1990s. Touvier had been hidden for years by a wing of the Church, while Bousquet was friendly with Mitterrand and Papon had since served as Prefect of Paris and a minister.

President Chirac did make an apology in 1995 for the State's responsibility in the deportation of Jews – and the Church apologized for its support of Vichy – but the controversy was stirred up again at the time of Papon's death in 2007 and it was only in February 2009 that the direct responsibility of the State was finally recognized by the highest court in the land, the Conseil d'État. That the state of denial should have lasted for over half a century is indicative of the depth of the wound to the national psyche.

11

THE FOURTH REPUBLIC IN COLD WAR AND COLONIAL CRISIS

The Fourth Republic, which began in January 1947 after a post-war provisional government under the presidency of de Gaulle, does not have a good name and indeed was the butt of many a weary joke in its own time. So why was this so?

One reason was the proportional voting system adopted after the war. This fragmented the electorate and imposed coalition government upon a collection of disparate political parties which found it difficult to work together. The result was no fewer than twenty-six governments between the Liberation and the collapse of the system in 1958 due to its inability to deal with the Algerian crisis, which led to its replacement by the Fifth Republic. The regular defeat in the National Assembly of these coalition governments, which could only be replaced by all-too-similar coalition govern-ments, led to intermittent crises and widespread public cynicism. The country could be left without a government for as much as a month while the cards were shuffled and reshuffled as all-too-familiar candidates tried and failed to obtain the approval of the Assembly for a proposed new government. There was a quite farcical vocabulary for this ritual game of musical chairs, whereby each would-be prime minister in turn did a consultative *tour de piste*, or run around the track, but failed in turn because the crisis was 'not yet sufficiently ripe' – *la crise n'est pas mûre* – until eventually some sort of compromise was cobbled together. This was not parliamentary democracy at its best.

Yet this alone gives a one-sided and false picture of post-war France. For a start, it makes no allowance for the difficulty of getting the country on its feet again after the destruction caused by the war. However great the damage caused by the First World War, it had affected only the northern and eastern parts of the country, but the destruction now extended over a far wider area, due to the fighting itself as well as to several years of Allied bombing, German reprisals, Resistance sabotage and, of course, the damage done at the start of the war in 1940. Also, while the overall figure of 580,000 deaths was lower this time, almost half were of civilians. Cities such as Caen and the Channel ports had been devastated, the railway system was in ruins, factories had been wiped out and millions left homeless. With industrial production in 1944 only half of the already low 1938 figure and agricultural production also down, the national finances were severely affected and rationing continued until 1949. Moreover, the weakness of France after this global conflict had not gone unnoticed in the empire; in French Indochina Ho Chi Minh was attempting to set up a Republic of Vietnam, while similar stirrings of independence were emerging in Algeria, Morocco and Tunisia. In fact, a weakened France was now discovering that the post-war world was not at all that of 1939.

A fundamental difference was the emergence of Soviet Russia as a dominant presence in Eastern Europe and the parallel rise of the Communists to become the largest party in France. With the old right-wing parties now discredited by their support for Vichy, and the Radical Party entering a decline because of its association in the public mind with the failures of the Third Republic, de Gaulle was left to form a government with the three groups arising out of the Resistance that were also the clear winners in the election of October 1945. The Communists won 159 seats, the Mouvement Républicain Populaire, or MRP, 150 seats and the Socialists 146 seats. While the Church hierarchy had supported Pétain, there were many liberal Catholics who had gradually become involved in the Resistance, and the MRP – despite its rather implausible motto '*La Révolution par la loi*', or the revolution by legal means – would become an influential party over the following years. But of course, as de Gaulle was sharply aware, the three parties were ill-assorted, not just because of the rivalry between the Communists and the Socialists, or because those two parties believed in secular education while the MRP brought back the vexed question of support for Catholic schools, but because the policy of the Communists – several of whom, including their leader Maurice Thorez, now held important ministerial posts – was felt to be dictated by Moscow.

The Communist Party had stood aside from the 'capitalist' war for two years following the Hitler–Stalin pact of 1939 and was only drawn into the Resistance by the German attack on the Soviet Union in 1941. It had even asked the Nazi Occupation authorities for permission to publish the previously banned *L'Humanité*, while Maurice Thorez had deserted on the advice of the Communist International, or Comintern, and spent the war in Russia. However, the Communists had become very prominent in the Resistance, even if the claim to be the 'party of 75,000 martyrs' was an exaggerated one. With their powerful support among the workers and in the unions, they now presented themselves as a great patriotic party. The embarrassment of portraying Maurice Thorez as the leader of the 'party of the Resistance' was lessened by pretending that he had not left for Moscow in 1939 but only four years later in 1943. And this was particularly important because the Stalinization of the party, in parallel with that of the Russian party, had developed the 'cult of the personality' to the point that the party was often presenting itself as *le parti de Maurice Thorez*.

Thorez, who never knew his real father, was born in the Pas-de-Calais area in 1900 and went to work in the manner of the time at the age of twelve, doing various jobs including a brief stint in a coal mine before becoming an official in the Communist Party. A bright and willing worker, he became a member of the political executive in 1925, the year in which he made his first visit to the Soviet Union, and by 1930 he had become general secretary of the party. In the following year, the Comintern dispatched to Paris a group of three specialists and five instructors to educate the French party in the ways of democratic centralism and, in particular, to groom its new general secretary into the kind of charismatic, authoritative leader required.

Over the following years the leader of the group, the Czech Eugen Fried – the other two specialists being a Soviet and a Pole – not only professionalized Thorez but became personally very close to him, to the point that when Thorez parted with his wife Aurore, Fried moved in with her. The great opportunity to promote the image of Thorez came with the party's involvement in the Popular Front and the occasion was grasped to produce his book *Fils du Peuple* in 1937. This, as the title suggests, was an official rather than a purely personal autobiography, designed to transform this 'son of the people' into the exemplar of the coming 'communist man'.

It was successful – so much so that studies of Thorez have tended not to get beyond the myth thus created in order to obtain a clear view of the man himself.[1] Ghosted by Jean Fréville, the literary critic of *L'Humanité*, it emphasized his part in the central industrial activity of mining – though he had worked in the mine for less than a year and did not care for physical work – and it screened out early activities that did not fit the picture. It turned him into an ideal type, the incarnation of the party, the perfect blend of worker and 'intellectual of a new type' – one grounded in social reality, unlike the 'bourgeois intellectuals'. Yet for all the image-making, it would be wrong to view Thorez as the hollow man or totally manipulated puppet that some have seen in him. He was intelligent, methodical, hardworking, widely read and highly rated by de Gaulle as a minister – partly, no doubt, because each in his own way looked beyond parliamentary politics. The trouble was rather that he became imprisoned not only within an authoritarian Stalinist machine that would eventually implode, but within his own image, to the point of enjoying the lavish lifestyle that went with it. In the immediate post-war period, however, the image and the disciplined party machine were not a weakness but a strength.

Although there were fears of a Communist takeover at the Liberation, that had been ruled out by Stalin, as one informed observer explains, on the grounds that 'only de Gaulle could achieve a national union able to reduce the grip of the Anglo-Saxons'.[2] And the new government implemented a whole raft of measures that would fundamentally shape post-war French society. The social security system and votes for women were brought in, as promised, while Électricité de France, Gaz de France and Air France were created. And the State took control of much of the economy with the nationalization of the Banque de France, Crédit Commercial, la Société Générale, over thirty insurance companies and the automotive business Berliet, to add to the already nationalized Renault. Since de Gaulle in January 1946 also appointed Jean Monnet to be head of a national economic planning commission, the basic mechanisms for future prosperity were in place. Except that three rapid changes in the situation began to make governing this new Republic very difficult.

The first was a clash over a new constitution between de Gaulle, who as president wanted a strong executive to avoid instability, and the MRP and the Socialists in particular, who wanted a strong parliament as a democratic safeguard. When de Gaulle saw that he was likely to lose a referendum on the issue, he resigned suddenly in January 1946 – gambling that the shock would force a rethink and that he would be called back. But while he was indeed called back, it would not be for another twelve years. A second and fundamental change was the start of the Cold War in April 1947, which envenomed the atmosphere and led to Communist ministers being dropped when they refused to support a government led by the Socialist Paul Ramadier, which collapsed in November of that year.

The third change was the setting up by de Gaulle in that same month of his Rassemblement du Peuple Français, or RPR – a 'rally of the French people' presented as a 'movement' rather than a mere political party. De Gaulle himself was therefore adding to the instability, for the country now had to be governed by a group of MRP, Socialists and Radicals squeezed in the centre and under attack from the Communists on the left and the increasingly right-wing Gaullists on the right. That there were ten changes of government between 1948 and 1952, even if they largely involved a turnover of the same cast of characters, hardly enhanced the image of authority of the State.

France was a major battlefield in the Cold War, which was basically a war between the US and the USSR fought by proxy in Europe in the late forties and fifties, before it switched to Asia with the Korean and Vietnam wars. Since direct military confrontation in Europe raised the spectre of mutual destruction through the use of the nuclear weapons now possessed by both sides, the war was fought essentially in ideological, political and economic terms. But there was always the fear that a shooting war could break out, if only because of some diplomatic blunder, so the atmosphere in Europe was tense. And it was particularly so in France with its large Communist Party, leading to fears of an internal *coup d'état* as well as of a Russian invasion of Western Europe – a concern which led some intellectuals in Paris to keep their bags packed. Certainly, there was in those years a disquieting line-up of forces with, on one side, the Marshall Plan of aid for Europe and the creation of NATO and, on the other, the setting up of the Cominform as a new version of the Comintern and the Russian blockade of Berlin in 1948–9. And at the centre of this struggle in Europe was the problem of a divided Germany and the question – an agonizing one for the French – as to whether it could ever be allowed to rearm.

All this brought the country to the edge of civil war. Thorez returned from a meeting of the Cominform in October 1947, having heard the Russian Jdanov lay down that there was now a worldwide ideological fight to the finish between Soviet communism and American imperialism. He had himself been heavily criticized there for not doing more to prevent the Marshall Plan, but had been given no authority to attempt a *coup d'état* – which presented him with a tricky path to tread. As it happened, his return coincided with a wave of strikes that developed spontaneously across the country, in protest against low living standards and rising prices. With the aid of the union, the Confédération Générale du Travail, or CGT, he managed to redirect this social protest towards an attack on America and on the French regime itself. The strikes became extremely violent, with rioting, sabotage, blockades and confrontations with armed police. But the derailing of a mail train, which caused several deaths and many injuries, proved to be a step too far. It frightened the public into believing that this was a communist takeover on a par with that taking place in Czechoslovakia, and led to a split in the CGT itself, with the more moderate element breaking off to form the Socialist

FO: Force Ouvrière, or workers' strength. And it enabled the government, by calling out the army, by introducing measures to improve living standards and by presenting the Communist Party as the creature of Moscow, to survive.

This rapid sequence of Occupation, Resistance, Cold War and ongoing political strife, to say nothing of the horrors of the concentration camps, inevitably coloured the work of writers, artists and even popular singers of the period. Indeed an iconic image of the immediate post-war years is of Le Tabou nightclub in St-Germain-des-Prés, Paris, with 'the Muse of Existentialism' Juliette Gréco, dressed with suitable severity in tight black sweater and slacks, singing Jean-Paul Sartre's chilling little number about an executioner, 'Dans la rue des Blancs-Manteaux', for the delectation of intellectuals such as the writers and song-writers Jacques Prévert and Raymond Queneau.

French *chanson* was of course vastly more grown-up and sophisticated than the Anglo-American pop song of the Bing Crosby era, and it reflected the deeper anxieties and political conflicts of the time – Gréco herself, having seen her mother and sister deported, had been worked over by the Milice and thrown on the street at the age of fifteen. It is true that, in the fevered atmosphere of the time, existentialism became something of a chic fashion – Boris Vian caricatured Sartre as the guru 'Jean-Sol Partre' in his novel *L'Écume des jours* (*Froth on the Daydream*) – but that was because the challenge of the time had brought philosophy into the big wide world and major figures such as Sartre and Albert Camus also wrote novels and plays. Certainly these two – like Simone de Beauvoir with her landmark study of the inferior status of women in *Le Deuxième Sexe* (*The Second Sex*) – made an impressive effort to come to grips with the apparent worldwide clash of ideologies as defined by Jdanov.

For even though France was beginning to absorb American Marshall Aid money, as well as American jazz, cinema and of course chewing-gum – popularly pronounced '*schwangum*' – Marxism was increasing among intellectuals and in the universities. This was partly because of the visible strength of the Communist Party – *L'Humanité*'s annual outdoor gala, '*la fête de l'Huma*' was an enormous affair. More profoundly, the war had thrown up further questions about European civilization and there was an often messianic hunger for some new and more inclusive kind of society, so that Marxism became a home for some and an object of fascination for others. Inevitably, this involved debate about the reality of the Soviet regime itself and, with details of Stalin's labour camps beginning to leak out – though they would not be widely believed until Khrushchev's stunning revelations of 1956 – Cold War debate could become very hot indeed. Sartre and Camus themselves had a famous row about these issues in 1952, following a critique in Sartre's magazine *Les Temps Modernes* of Camus's book *L'Homme révolté* (*The Rebel*). And their differing approaches illustrate the difficulty for serious writers of dealing with the central problem of the decade.

Sartre's approach is in some ways a curious one. In his lengthy wartime work *L'Être et le néant* (*Being and Nothingness*) – which is more entertaining than it sounds – he presents a bleak existentialist picture of the individual as living in a godless world where there is no purpose to his existence. He can either conceal this fact from himself through 'bad faith' or attempt – since he is in some sense forced to be free – to try to give his life a meaning. But his situation is the more tragic in that he can neither know himself fully nor know others, since Sartre – as also in his play *Huis clos* (*In Camera*) – tends to portray human relations as virtually impossible.

Clearly, it is a long way from this extremely subjectivist starting point to Marxism, with its emphasis on historical and social determinism. But Sartre, feeling a moral imperative to engage with the pressing issues of the time, attempts the transition by means of two curious shortcuts. First, by saying that, in willing my own freedom, I am by implication willing the freedom of everybody else. Secondly, by oddly conflating ideas with historical fact, as when he describes the working classes as 'the *reality* of Marxism' and of them as '*living* Marxism, *implementing* Marxism'.[3] Since he also argues, in determinist fashion, that Marxism is the necessary philosophy of the time, he becomes an uneasy, if somewhat romantic fellow traveller who, when disappointed by Soviet Russia, transfers his hopes to China and, when further disappointed, to Cuba – before deciding finally that it was all like a strange dream.

For various reasons Camus, though he too started with an absurdist portrait of alienation in *L'Étranger* (*The Outsider*), never dreamt that dream. He had been more active in the Resistance as editor of *Combat*, he had a French Algerian working-class background and had more experience of ordinary people. It could be said that his allegory of war in *La Peste* missed the point that war was not something impersonal like a plague, that he never quite clarified his position on the colonial problem, and that his argument for revolt rather than revolution in *L'Homme révolté* was lacking in specifics, but he could already feel vindicated by the time of his death in a car crash in 1960.

The great irony of the Fourth Republic is that the governmental instability barely mattered in regard to the reconstruction of the country, nor did it prevent the emergence of a quite visionary foreign policy. And the inspirational figure in both areas was an unelected individual from a family of brandy producers in Cognac, who left school early, was no great writer or speechmaker, but who 'succeeded more than anybody in the world ever had', according to one barely overstated claim, 'in becoming the intimate of a prodigious number of heads of state and of government'.[4] Though similar to de Gaulle in age and background, and though his achievement was at least as important, they were as different as chalk and cheese. Jean Monnet was not interested in History with a capital H or in the primacy of the national state, but in pragmatic ways of bringing together peoples to prevent destructive wars. He was the counterpart to de Gaulle also in that he was a widely travelled cosmopolitan who got along with the 'Anglo-Saxons'. Since that alone would have made him suspect to de Gaulle, it is to the general's credit that he put him in charge of the national reconstruction plan just before he resigned in January 1946.

But then Monnet's extraordinary career spoke for itself. After studying business practice in England for two years in his late teens, he sold his cognac across the world from Russia to the US. In the First World War, as French representative to the Inter-Allied Maritime Commission in London, he created a strategically important pooling system for imports. In 1919, at the age of thirty-one, he became assistant secretary-general of the League of Nations, before leaving in 1923 to reorganize the family business. In the years leading up to the Second World War, he was variously involved in setting up a bank in San Francisco, assisting the economic recovery of several Eastern European countries, and spending two years in China at the invitation of Chiang Kai-shek, helping to reorganize the railway network. When war broke out he became head of a Franco-British committee to coordinate war supplies, working closely with Churchill, to whom, in a last-minute attempt to avert a French surrender, he suggested the idea of a Franco-British union. But when the armistice was signed he did not join de Gaulle – telling him that they would not see eye to eye – and went to Washington. He now became a close adviser to Roosevelt, whom he persuaded to supply arms under the 'Victory Program', which was said by the economist Keynes to have shortened the war by a year. In 1943 Roosevelt sent him to Algiers, to work with the Free French administration, groom Giraud and keep the peace between him and de Gaulle.

The nationalizations of the autumn of 1945 provided a favourable backdrop to Monnet's economic plan, but he was keen to avoid bureaucracy and turf wars between ministries, so he presented the task of reconstruction as an essentially administrative one and got his commission accepted as an independent body of technical experts reporting directly to the prime minister. Working in an informal atmosphere with a small team of dedicated specialists in regular consultation with employers and unions, he produced a five-year plan to revive the economy. In practice, since the country was bankrupt, the plan needed the lifeline offered by the Marshall Plan in 1947, which came with economic conditions that were challenging, even if ultimately beneficial. Not only did the US require France to balance its budget and keep inflation under control, but it insisted on free trade, which in practice meant obliging a rather backward, protected economy to open up its markets to American goods. Since this entailed importing the American way of life in the form of Coca-Cola and Hollywood films, the culture shock was considerable. For all that, Monnet – who had been the link man with Marshall – incorporated the American funds intelligently and flexibly into his own plan, giving priority to basic industries and the infrastructure. If initial results were mixed, the first five-year plan of 1947–52 brought output up to pre-war levels, while the second of 1953–7 began the expansion that would lead to the thirty post-war years being dubbed the '*trente glorieuses*'.

But the problem of Germany was coming to the fore again, partly because a dispute with France over control of iron and steel production in the Saar and the Ruhr raised the spectre of war once more, and partly because Germany had been excluded from NATO, set up in 1949 to create a unified command for the forces of the Western Alliance. With speculation growing about a possible European solution, the 1948 conference at the Hague called for a United States of Europe, reviving a term used by Victor Hugo at a similar conference exactly 100 years earlier. The motivation was at once to achieve Franco-German reconciliation and to create a prosperous, independent Europe between the two super-powers, the US and the USSR.

It was characteristic of Monnet's approach that he decided to solve the two problems at one go and from the bottom up by creating concrete realities on the ground. He found an ideal partner in French Foreign Minister Robert Schuman, who had lived in Germany and had family connections there. In 1950 they put forward what became known as the Schuman Plan for a common European market for coal and steel, the two basic resources of the economy at that time, to be controlled by an independent authority. Six countries – France, Germany, Italy, the Netherlands, Belgium and Luxembourg – joined this European Coal and Steel Com-munity, which was presided over by Monnet.

And the remarkable Monnet – who for so many years, as his biographer reminds us, had the ear of government whatever its political complexion – was behind the next move towards European integration.[5] As the Cold War spread with the outbreak of the Korean War in 1950, the Americans put increasing pressure on Western Europe to do more for its own defence. This opened up the unwelcome issue of German rearmament, the more intractable in that it raised the question of war not only between two nations but between East and West. Schuman himself was opposed to allowing Germany to join NATO and rearm under its umbrella, but Monnet again sought to resolve the issue by placing it in a larger context. He proposed a European Defence Community, which would run a European army including German troops. This was an ingenious compro-mise which also emphasized Europe's independence of the Americans – whom Monnet had to mollify. The treaty was duly signed in Paris in 1952 by the government of 1952–3 of Antoine Pinay, who was something of a novelty because he was a traditional conservative who had voted for full powers to Pétain. But the country which had put forward the proposal did not find it so easy to get its own parliament to ratify the treaty.

This was partly due to political weakness. Although Pinay brought price inflation under control, this limited the profits of small shopkeepers, who were now organized into a strong political movement by the right-wing agitator Pierre Poujade, a populist who constantly threatened to 'get his jacket off'. There were also violent protests against American pressure to rearm Germany. The lack of authority, which was such that neither Pinay nor either of his two successors over the next two years would risk putting the ratification before the Assembly, was exposed to ridicule by the presidential election of 1954, when resplendent Republican guards were lined up in freezing weather by the Pont de Saint-Cloud to escort the new president into Paris, only to have to come back day after day until a thirteenth ballot produced the unexciting figure of René Coty. But then the issue of a European army was a highly symbolic one which unleashed passions of almost religious intensity. While it had the support of the Christian Democrats of the MRP, it was attacked by the Communists as a threat to the USSR, and by the Gaullists on the grounds that, without its own national army, France would no longer be a sovereign state. The other parties were divided, with many deputies concerned that a European army would inevitably lead to a united Europe.

To make matters worse, this dispute collided with the equally divisive colonial issue following the devastating defeat by the Viet Minh at Dien Bien Phu in May 1954. Questions about France's viability as an imperial power were now added to doubts about its status in Europe. France had a poor record in Indochina and, as the conflict merged into the Cold War with the Chinese support of the Viet Minh, its war effort was being financed by the US to the tune of 80 per cent.[6] And this humiliating military defeat at the hands of the Viet Minh was rendered the more embarrassing by the long list of French captives published in *Le Monde*, which included so many Foreign Legionaries with German names. In fact, the situation was so serious that President Coty had to ask Pierre Mendès-France to become prime minister. For the paralysis of the system was such, as Raymond Aron acidly remarked, that 'the very qualities that enabled Mendès to be a good prime minister left him little chance of becoming one'.[7] He was a quite charismatic, impressive figure with excellent Resistance credentials, who had been a minister under de Gaulle and had the support of the influential magazine *L'Express*. But he was from the small Radical party and was viewed as a Cassandra – too independent, too clever by half and Jewish into the bargain.

Certainly, Mendès dealt with the Indochinese problem in spectacular fashion by announcing that if he had not resolved it within a month he would resign. With great energy, patience and skill, he negotiated with the Viet Minh, the Soviets and the Chinese, while keeping the British and the Americans on board. The negotiations went down to the wire – though the clock had to be stopped for three hours at the end – but he managed to secure an acceptable partition of the country which avoided immediate military disaster. While some Christian Democrats criticized him for abandoning the Catholic part of the population to communism, and while the extreme right raged that the empire was being sold out by a Jew, the public approved. And when he proceeded in the same style to negotiate internal autonomy for Tunisia, his standing in the country was extremely high. But that left the problem of the European Defence Community and, for once, he hesitated. Arguing that it would be too divisive to put its ratification to the Assembly, he tried unsuccessfully to modify it and finally, without putting the weight of the government behind it, put it forward – to see it voted down amid exultant singing of the 'Marseillaise'.

Nevertheless, for opponents of the treaty, this decision was self-defeating, since West Germany joined NATO in

1955 and began to rearm in any case. Even so, in large measure due to the impulsion of the Germans themselves, the problem would once again be absorbed into a larger fusion with the expansion of the European Coal and Steel Community into the more elaborate European Economic Community by the Treaty of Rome of 1957 – ratified by the Socialist-led government of Guy Mollet, against the combined opposition of Communists, Gaullists and Poujadists. So that, by a circuitous route, Jean Monnet's dream was beginning to take shape.

The year 1956 was a turning point in several ways. It was a bad year for the Communist Party, which had already been ridiculed for Maurice Thorez's announcement, just when living standards were visibly rising, that the stage of the 'absolute impoverishment of the proletariat' had now been reached. His blustering reaction to Khrushchev's shattering recital of the crimes of Stalin at the Twentieth Congress, as well as to the crushing of the Hungarian revolt, was never likely to limit the outflow of intellectuals with which the gradual decline of the party now began. Nor was it a good year for the new Republican Front coalition government under the Socialist leader Guy Mollet – which began in January 1956 and lasted eighteen months – even if it raised the annual paid holiday to three weeks. For the joint Franco-British attempt to prevent Colonel Nasser of Egypt from nationalizing the Suez Canal proved to be a humiliating fiasco when both the US and the USSR threatened reprisals, forcing them to bring their troops home. The harsh lesson was that they were no longer imperial superpowers able to fall back on the old gunboat diplomacy.

It was a lesson that the new French government – which had come to power with the aid of large wall posters declaring 'Against the dirty colonial war, vote Socialist'– might more profitably have applied to Algeria. Admittedly, the demand for independence in Algeria posed formidable problems since, unlike Tunisia and Morocco, Algeria had been formally part of metropolitan France since 1881, with three *départements* under the jurisdiction of the minister of the interior. And of the population of some 10 million, 1 million were the 'French–Algerians' of mostly southern European extraction – or *pieds-noirs*, because of the black boots worn by early settlers – who regarded themselves as being as French as those on the mainland. The difficulty for the French policy of assimilation from the late nineteenth century onwards was twofold. On the one hand the Muslim majority feared that French citizenship would deprive them of their identity and customary rights under Islamic law and, on the other hand, the dominant French Algerians feared that any move towards independence or equal status would see them swamped by Muslims.

Ironically, it was in the freer atmosphere of the mainland that Algerian nationalism began to be seriously organized from the 1920s onwards. Algerian Muslims had fought for France in the First World War, while hundreds of thousands of them came over as workers and were to an extent politicized by the hard economic conditions of the 1930s. There was both a radical tendency under the workers' leader Messali Hadj and a moderate one under Ferhat Abbas, from a wealthy integrationist background. But, as the collapse of France and the arrival of US troops in Algeria in 1942 opened up new perspectives, Ferhat Abbas issued a manifesto in 1943 demanding full internal autonomy for Algeria, which soon saw him interned. While some concesssions were made, the French response was consistently too little too late. There was a largely spontaneous rising in 1945, which left over eighty European Algerians dead and was savagely repressed. This set the pattern and, after France reaffirmed the principle of assimilation in 1947, the discontent grew until it burst out in the wholesale guerilla war launched by the newly organized National Liberation Front, or FLN, in 1954.

It may seem odd today that there should have been such a large measure of agreement over Algeria across France's otherwise divided political parties – including the Communists initially. Yet for French politicians the loss of Algeria was as unthinkable as the loss of Alsace-Lorraine, and neither Mendès-France nor the future President François Mitterrand took the idea of independence seriously, believing rather that the problem was one of economic backwardness. And Prime Minister Mollet invoked France's 'civilizing mission' when he wrote:

> ... withdrawal is unacceptable for France, which would become a diminished second or third rate power deprived of its world role. And even more unacceptable for a socialist, for these countries rely on us to strengthen their democracy, guarantee their infrastructure and their economic expansion, develop their educational system and train civil servants.[8]

And he goes on to say that, if the French left, the US or the Soviets would only move in. This entrenched attitude meant that the war was seen as a quasi-civil war, for which the conscript army would be used to make a total of half a million men – thus in effect involving the whole nation and raising the stakes so high that the government could not afford to lose.

And that was the origin of the tragedy, since it meant that there could be no political accommodation with the FLN. Mendès-France's answer to attacks on Europeans had been to send Jacques Soustelle as governor-general in February 1955, but Soustelle exacerbated the situation by decreeing the summary execution of rebels caught with weapons. Mollet promised reasonably that there would be free elections, after which the future status of Algeria would be decided by the elected representatives of the Algerian people, but that would be within the framework of the French Union and only after order had been restored.

However, this took little account of the realities on the ground, as Mollet himself discovered when he went to Algiers in February 1956 and found himself pelted with tomatoes by a French-Algerian crowd which had no interest in elections that would inevitably favour the Arab majority. He now weakened his position by appearing to give in to the mob. For, although he had already appointed, as resident minister in Algeria, General Catroux, a moderate figure not congenial to the *pieds-noirs*, he now accepted his resignation, appointing in his place the Socialist deputy Robert Lacoste, to whom he gave full powers.

Lacoste, a rough diamond from the Dordogne, whose scurrilous exchanges in cabinet with Overseas Minister Gaston Defferre horrified the proper President Coty, announced on arrival that he was going to 'screw' the rebels.[9] While he did set up social and economic programmes and tried to Algerianize the administration, his immediate concern was to quell the rebellion. To this end he gave General Massu in January 1957 a free hand to deploy his 8,000 paratroopers in a ruthless campaign to root out dissidents which lasted eight months – and is the subject of Pontecorvo's well known film *The Battle of Algiers*.[10] But it is is here that the contradictions of the French attempt to present this war as just an internal action against wayward criminals reveal themselves. For it became painfully clear that the population was largely supportive of the FLN and that the necessary intelligence could therefore only be obtained through duress. Which made the systematic use of electrical torture – claimed to be a 'clean' form of torture and practised on women as well as men – central to the pursuit of the war.[11] By alienating the population, torture meant that morally, as well as militarily, the aims were nullified by the means.

And since by 1957 the Algerian crisis had become a crisis of the regime, the political price would be high. For the publication of accounts of torture, of local French opponents as well as of insurgents, led to increasing dismay on the left, to the rise of clandestine networks of support for the FLN and to a general sense that the war might be unwinnable. This in turn led to fears by the army and by the right of a sell-out by the government. To forestall this, rebel officers and right-wing elements brought Algiers to a standstill with a mass strike in May 1958, took over the Governor-General's palace and set up a Committee of Public Safety under General Massu – this being the initial stage of a plan, called Resurrection, for toppling the regime in Paris and bringing back de Gaulle.

The general was kept closely informed of the plot, but did not involve himself directly since he wanted to take over by legal means. His position was therefore formally correct, if somewhat ambiguous, and in any case he did not have to wait long. With the government having lost control of the army and under the threat of invasion, President Coty saw himself left with no option but to call on de Gaulle.

12

DE GAULLE'S GOLDEN DECADE ENDS IN TRAGI-COMEDY

It is not for nothing that de Gaulle has given his name to the Paris airport at Roissy or to the commanding roundabout in which stands the Arc de Triomphe at the head of the Champs-Élysées. With the passage of time since his death in 1970, the controversies surrounding him have faded and he has emerged as the dominant French statesman of the past century, one who ranks in the public mind alongside Louis XIV or Napoleon and who still influences the terms of political debate in France today. And, if this is obviously due to his achievements as a statesman, it is perhaps above all due to the idea of himself and of his country that he embodied. While he could seem stubborn, arrogant and dictatorial, he was also bold, farseeing and above the battle, an all-or-nothing man who was not drawn to power for its own sake and was prepared to relinquish it if he could not exercise it on acceptable terms. If he was a traditional social conservative, he was also a republican and one who had little interest in the rewards and fripperies that come with high office – he was far from wealthy when he died, having chosen to accept only the pension of a colonel rather than that of a former president. While he was no saint, he did leave the impression of a solitary, noble and incorruptible figure – perhaps even a tragic one – who consistently placed his country's interests above his own.

For all that, he worked his way back into power in the feverish atmosphere of May 1958 with cool calculation and studied ambiguity. While he responded to the insurrectionist cries of 'Vive de Gaulle' in Algiers by announcing that he was prepared to assume control, he answered fears that he was bent on dictatorship by declaring that he would only take power if invited to do so by the existing government. Initially he held the office of prime minister, but he insisted on having emergency powers for six months and a referendum for a new constitution. There was opposition from the Communists, from a section of the Socialists and from a new socialist-inclined group set up by Mendès-France and François Mitterrand, but since the failure of the regime to deal with Algeria now threatened France with an army-led civil war, it was widely accepted that only a powerful new government enjoying widespread national support could deal with the problem. De Gaulle declared that to be his priority, but his abiding concern was to achieve a strong central power untrammelled by what he saw as ineffectually squabbling parties and, mindful of his earlier failure to control them, he had no intention of missing this second, golden opportunity. His new constitution was designed to change the rules of the game.

De Gaulle's view was that:

the State needs a head, a leader, in whom the nation can see the man who is managing its essential affairs and directing its destiny. Nor should such an executive head, being in the service

of the community as a whole, come from parliament, which is
an assortment of special interests.[1]

And, if that sounds a little like Louis XIV, it is fair to say
that he was proposing to derive his legitimacy, not from God
through his family, but directly from the people. So, rather
than be merely the nominee of a leading party, he should be
designated by the nation as a whole, have the right to consult
it by referendum or through a broad electoral college, be free
to appoint ministers as he saw fit, and be entitled to take
emergency powers when France was in danger.

The constitution hastily drafted along these lines by
Michel Debré was less than clear, notably in relation to the
relative powers of the president and the prime minister, and
it has raised questions ever since, but it corresponded both
to the exceptional status of de Gaulle and to the dramatic
collapse of a parliamentary system paralysed by the endemic
polarization of opinion and by electoral fragmentation. So it
is somewhat beside the point for a hostile commentator to
argue that 'de Gaulle only achieved democratic legitimacy
on the day he resigned, following the lost referendum of
1969'.[2] Not just because there was no plausible alternative,
but because de Gaulle, though a traditionalist by background, was a republican by choice.

With a majority of almost 80 per cent for the constitution
and for himself as president, he now had significant powers
over the parliament. Its ability to amend legislation was
seriously reduced and the president could retain overall
control by having the right to appoint the prime minister and
dissolve parliament. While he did appoint many party
leaders as ministers, he began to depoliticize the government
to a degree by appointing technocrats and other unelected
figures to posts, including that of prime minister – a practice
which would become traditional in the Fifth Republic. He
was inevitably accused of Bonapartism, but he stayed within the democratic framework by having the support in

parliament of a new Gaullist party – l'Union des Démocrates pour la République (UDR) – which emerged as the largest group in the new elections, inflicting a heavy defeat on the left-wing parties. With this level of legitimacy, de Gaulle was less a dictator than a kind of republican monarch, although his ascendancy became such over the following years that it sometimes seemed eerily not only that de Gaulle had become France but that France had become de Gaulle.

Initially, de Gaulle did not know what to do about Algeria. He could see that this 'ball-and-chain' he had inherited was not only tearing the country apart, but burdening its economy and discrediting it diplomatically. Yet there was no consensus even among the Gaullists – if André Malraux or Edmond Michelet foresaw that independence might be the necessary outcome, his own prime minister, Michel Debré, and his information minister, Jacques Soustelle, were passionately against. So he played for time, first by going to Algeria and telling a vast cheering crowd from the governor-general's balcony that he understood their position – the famous Delphic ambiguity *'je vous ai compris'*, which would leave a bitter aftertaste in the mouths of the cheering *pieds-noirs* beneath him.

He then tried to enlarge the context of the problem by touring French Africa and by building into the referendum on the new constitution a provision for the colonies to vote either for separation or for independence within a new French Community, one not unlike the British Commonwealth. Since all the French African colonies, with the exception of Guinea, chose to remain within the Community, this provided the framework for an eventual solution. Meanwhile, he granted French citizenship to the Algerian Muslims and announced in Constantine a strengthening of the existing plan to provide them with improved services and jobs. But it was all too late and was hardly compatible with the harsh pacification measures taking place on the ground. The FLN was beginning to mount terrorist attacks within

France itself, and the war was not only divisive at home but damaging to France's standing abroad. So, in September 1959, he offered Algeria the same choice that he had offered to the other French territories.

Predictably, this brought forth cries of betrayal and unleashed a violent political struggle that would last for two years. It began with a 'week of the barricades' in Algiers in January 1960, a *pied-noir* protest against the recall to Paris of General Massu, who had been inciting insurrection. De Gaulle, increasingly powerful on television, having learnt his script by heart, appeared dramatically in military uniform and the protest fell apart after nine days. But with the fighting dragging on and opposition coming from former comrades like Georges Bidault and Jacques Soustelle, he was forced to cut the knot and recognize publicly in November that the outcome would be an Algerian republic.

In January 1961, he obtained a 76 per cent majority for this position in a national referendum, but this inflamed senior army officers to the point that there was an attempted *coup d'état* in Algiers in April, led by four generals, including the former inspector general of the army, General Salan. With Paris itself under threat of a parachute drop, de Gaulle once again read the riot act on television, concluding with an emotional appeal to the people to help him. The coup collapsed within days and peace negotiations were begun in May, but they would drag on intermittently for another year during which there would be no relief from violence in France itself. For a secret army organization, the OAS, was now in existence, led by the now outlawed General Salan along with de Gaulle's former close associates Jacques Soustelle and Georges Bidault, who, ironically enough, now led a 'National Resistance Council' mimicking the wartime Resistance organization. Over the next year the OAS was to kill some 2,000 people in bomb outrages. Meanwhile, the Paris police also dealt brutally with Algerian protests – there was a shocking massacre in October 1961 when at least seventy demonstrators were flung dead or alive from the bridges into the Seine.

Eventually, however, in March 1962, the peace treaty was signed at Évian and was overwhelmingly endorsed by the Algerian population. That did not stop OAS elements attempting to assassinate de Gaulle and his wife by machine-gunning his car at the Petit-Clamart roundabout near Paris – one of almost thirty such attempts during his career – nor did it stop the brutal revenge visited by FLN fighters on those Algerians who had been incorporated into the French army. Add the bitterness of the many *pieds-noirs* forced to withdraw to France and the coming of independence to Algeria was less an easy birth than, by one colourful description, 'a bloody forceps delivery based on a tentative realpolitik approach'.[3] But it was all that this long-divided country could manage. Only de Gaulle could have managed it. And at least it left him free to pursue his larger designs.

Or almost free. For he had always said that the parties would try to get rid of him once the Algerian crisis was settled and he now had to face another test of strength – one which he largely provoked himself. His loyal prime minister, Michel Debré, known to favour keeping Algeria French, had provided him with convenient political cover for the first stage of his plan, but de Gaulle now replaced him with the banker Georges Pompidou. However, he had failed to consult the Assembly as required by the constitution and Pompidou, who was in any case not an elected politician, only just managed to survive an acceptance vote. And de Gaulle, with the memory of the machine-guns at Petit-Clamart fresh in his mind, created a further row when he decided to secure the presidency by having his eventual successors elected, not by the broad electoral college as had been decided, but by the whole nation. This again was not done in conformity with the constitution and Pompidou was forced to resign after losing a vote of censure.

De Gaulle, untroubled, dissolved the Assembly, trounced the opposition in the referendum and ended up with a handsome Gaullist majority in the chamber. Once again he had demonstrated his prestige and his popularity.

'It's no longer Monsieur Monnet who is giving the orders' said de Gaulle pointedly one day to Monnet's old colleague Étienne Hirsch.[4] It is ironic that the ardent nationalist de Gaulle, who dismissed supranational organizations as 'talking shops', should have come to power just as Monnet's old dream, the European Economic Community (or EEC), came into force as of 1958. But he realized that a policy of national *grandeur* called for solid economic foundations and he recognized the value of the economic inheritance that Monnet and his Planning Commission had given France. No economist himself, the general tended grandly to see Prime Minister Pompidou and Finance Minister Antoine Pinay as running the 'quartermaster general's department', but he appointed competent people and – apart from some odd Colbertian statements about bullion reserves and the 'universality of gold' – let them get on with it. Which, against the favourable background of an international economic boom, they did.

While the Gaullist regime did provide valuable political stability for the implementation of economic policy, it essentially followed the same path to prosperity as the Fourth Republic. Even the French nuclear deterrent, which de Gaulle embraced so enthusiastically, followed on a previous five-year plan of nuclear research and on the project for the creation of an atomic bomb set up by Mendès-France. There was no change in the dirigiste insistence on the central planning role of the State in the capitalist economy – an approach which led to a number of characteristically ambitious, occasionally over-ambitious *grands projets* such as the Caravelle passenger airliner and the Franco-British Concorde. But there was a new insistence on strict financial controls, signalled by the devaluation and replacement of the franc by a new 'strong franc' worth 100 old francs, designed to tell the world that in a rejuvenated France a disciplined financial team was now in place.

And a rejuvenated France was indeed what was emerging in this golden period of the *trente glorieuses*, as Jean Fourastié baptised the years 1946 to 1975, claiming that 'no country had succeeded in moving beyond traditional poverty and hardship more rapidly or more clearly than France'.[5] It was rejuvenated in a quite basic sense. The population increased by almost 30 per cent from 40.5 million to 52.6 million; infant mortality was reduced dramatically from 84.4 to 13.8 per thousand, and the length of life increased – from 61.9 to 69.1 years for men, and from 67.4 to 77 years for women. The main effect of these demographic changes was the explosion of the new baby boom generation, boosted by improved medical facilities and generous family allowances. Even if the third age generation was now living longer, France seemed suddenly to have become a young country.

All this, of course, depended on the prosperity created by what was virtually a new economy, based on high productivity. The government set out to modernize industry by shifting production away from the old semi-artisanal firms employing fewer than twenty workers towards larger, more efficient companies benefiting from increased mechanization, standardization and economies of scale. It encouraged the merger of companies in such fields as chemicals and textiles into large groups able to compete internationally and enhance exports, while it also initiated blue-sky research and production in key areas like defence, aeronautics and nuclear energy. De Gaulle's suspicion of 'talking shops' notwithstanding, the economy responded well to the competitive challenges presented by the European Economic Community, so that France increased exports fivefold to the rest of Europe while still retaining advantageous trade relations with its recently liberated colonies. Investment increased apace and the economy grew by some 5 per cent per year, not as much as Japan or West Germany during their own 'miracle years', but more than the US and almost twice as much as Britain, which now found its gross domestic product triumphantly surpassed by its old cross-Channel rival.

This rapid economic change naturally affected lifestyles. Since the successful mechanization of agriculture meant that it required fewer workers, a gradual exodus from the countryside began as France became a more industrial, urban society. There was a marked shift of employment towards the expanding service sector, in such areas as banking, insurance, public administration, transport and tourism. This sector, which also offered better job opportunities for women, promoted the development of a new managerial class and a more sophisticated workforce. Implicit in this and in the record number of young people was an increase in educational provision, both at the secondary level, with the number of *baccalauréat* certificates increasing from 32,000 in 1950 to 139,500 in 1970, and at university level, where the number of students rose from 200,000 in 1960 to 500,000 in 1968.[6] However, with the rising generation either too young to work or in education, the growing demand for labour of this new industrial society was met by immigrants, some 4 million of whom arrived between the end of the war and the late 1960s – mostly from Italy, Spain and north and central Africa. This influx dramatized the need for more housing and it was now that Paris and other towns began to be ringed by dormitory suburbs – the *banlieues* – consisting of impersonal high-rise housing blocks, creating a distinctive new commuter population. Within a decade, especially with the spread of television and the increasing Americanization of popular culture, French society was largely transformed.

This economic transformation provided de Gaulle in the 1960s with the springboard he needed in order to pursue his ambitious foreign policy aims. As he had previously raised up a France humiliated by the defeat of 1940, so he now aimed to expunge the successive humiliations of Indochina, the Suez adventure and Algeria, in order to restore France to its rightful place among the Great Powers. 'The French need to be proud of France', he told his confidant Alain Peyrefitte in 1963, 'otherwise they wallow in mediocrity and bickering. If France ceases to be a great power, and to behave like a great power, it is nothing.' And for de Gaulle that meant challenging the existing Cold War order. As a nationalist, he had no great opinion of the United Nations – '*le machin*', or 'thingumajig', as he called it. He saw himself as a realist who recognized where power in the Cold War world actually resided, and he intended to change the equation.

Insisting that policy had to be based on realities and not on appearances, he went on to tell Peyrefitte that there were three international realities. The first was an expansionist United States, seeking to maintain its world leadership and to reinforce its hegemony in Europe. The second was Russia, as he preferred to call the Soviet Union, which had doubtless given up trying to rule the world, following Khrushchev's failure to threaten the US by installing missiles in Cuba, but which did not want 'to be gobbled up, and rightly so'. What then was the third reality that de Gaulle perceived? It was not Great Britain, which was merely the Trojan horse by means of which the 'Anglo-Saxons' – by which he essentially meant the Americans – were seeking to get into the European Community and start running it in their own interests. It was France, for,

> . . . at this time we are the only ones, apart from the Americans and the Russians, to have a national ambition, to follow it through and to have the courage to declare it. Outside these three realities, there are only countries that are amorphous, divided against themselves, hesitant – perpetual wannabees.[7]

De Gaulle's foreign policy decisions in the 1960s were therefore not just the petulant gestures that the 'Anglo-

Saxons' often took them to be – even if he visibly enjoyed provoking them – but successive steps in a very deliberate plan. Not prepared to depend on the US for the defence of France, and believing that real power now came from the independent possession of nuclear weapons, he speeded up the existing nuclear project and was soon the proud possessor of his own strike force. This led to considerable acrimony with the Americans and to France leaving NATO while remaining a political member of the broader Atlantic alliance. So all US and Canadian bases in France were closed in April 1967, leaving France with its new missiles pointedly directed *tous azimuths*, to all points of the compass and thus towards *both* sides in the Cold War. He reinforced this intermediate position by recognizing Communist China and by making a State visit to Moscow in 1966, where he argued for a Europe without opposing blocs. Since the Americans saw his invocation of a 'Europe from the Atlantic to the Urals' as leaving Europe open to potential Russian attack without adequate Western defences, they were not amused – and they were even less amused, since it was France that had left them this poisoned inheritance, by de Gaulle's criticism of their war in Vietnam.

Naturally, since he could only accept a 'Europe of nation states', de Gaulle had to find a way of dealing with the European Economic Community. He could see that it provided a useful export market for French goods – and indeed that it could serve as a substitute for the lost empire if France could dominate it in alliance with the then diplomatically much weaker Germany. He first tried through the Fouchet Plan to replace the EEC's supranational structure with a simple inter-governmental organization. When that failed, he blamed the 'Anglo-Saxons' and blocked Britain's entry into the organization both in 1963 and again in 1967 – although this was also a convenient way of protecting France's backward agriculture, which he further tried to protect by threatening to leave the EEC over agricultural tariffs. Again, in 1965–6 he practised a boycott in protest against an extension of the role of the European Assembly which threatened individual national vetoes. He fought so stubbornly because he felt that France could only be the 'third reality' and potential arbiter in world affairs if it was the leading force in Europe.

It can certainly be said that de Gaulle tried hard to make the rhetoric of *grandeur* come true. And it could be noted that, however provocative his manner, he did usefully point the way beyond the confrontation of East and West in the Cold War. But as he entered his late seventies he perhaps became rather self-indulgently mischievous, as when on a visit to Canada in 1967 he expressed support for the French separatists with his famous '*Vive le Québec Libre*' – a diplomatic blunder, as his own ministers recognized, which saw him promptly hustled out of the country.

He still seemed very much in command in his New Year greetings for 1968, when he assured the country that France would continue to set the standard by the calm, efficient operation of its government. Little did he suspect that his very success in energizing the country had helped to bring about social and cultural changes which would coalesce into a challenge that would leave him and his government in shock only a few months later.

The Gaullist regime had a deliberate cultural policy, with the distinguished writer André Malraux as its first minister of culture. He was active in many directions, in giving State commissions to artists such as Chagall, in the cleaning of public buildings – to restore a cold grey Place de la Concorde, for example, to its original pleasant ochre – and, above all, in reviving a left-wing idea of the 1930s to create throughout the country a number of Maisons de la Culture. These enriched the provinces by stimulating theatrical and other cultural activities, while he also took measures to guarantee affordability of access and to increase the national stock of art treasures through inheritance tax reliefs. His impact was considerable.

Yet this well-intentioned policy was still a top-down approach which did not quite engage with the changes in this society and, in particular, with the startlingly different new sixties generation, one that was heavily influenced by the dreaded 'Anglo-Saxons'. They were taller, they were healthier, they had money to spend on colourful clothes and they had their own sub-culture, their own magazines, their own radio programme and their own language. And of course their own rock-and-roll and *yéyé* music – the star of 1962 was not an Édith Piaf or a Gilbert Bécaud but the teenage Françoise Hardy, singing 'Tous les garçons et les filles' for all the other teenagers out there. In this new urban society they were no longer constrained by the old family ties and lack of opportunity, they wanted to have moral freedom, they wanted the mini-skirt and the contraceptive pill – 'we can't pay for *that* out of social security' said de Gaulle, 'what will they want us to give them next, a free car?!'[8] They had only heard of the war, they were not afraid of Germans or Russians, and they simply took for granted the hard-earned improvements in housing and hygiene that had transformed life for their parents. They aspired to individuality, but they were living in a new society in which market manipulation standardized individuality. And if some commentators saw them almost as an alien species, others discerned in them a malaise due to prosperity, an uncertainty born of freedom.

And there was much to be uncertain about, for France was undergoing its own cultural revolution. There was a new wave in cinema and in the novel, broadly reflecting the idea that there was no ready-made objective reality waiting to be transcribed, but rather that a film or a novel was a search for reality. The young directors of the Nouvelle Vague in cinema such as François Truffaut, Claude Chabrol or Jean-Luc Godard were also theorists who believed in the *auteur* conception of film as a personal statement. They rejected

studio filming, with its montage, seamless editing and
continuity, in favour of outdoor location shooting and the
hand-held camera, while they varied jump-cut editing with the
use of the long take to draw attention to what was seen rather
than to the 'story'. For they were also concerned to turn the
traditional film inside out, to show how it worked, to
demonstrate that this was not life but a film, a search for a
structure of meaning. They burst on the scene at Cannes in 1959
with Truffaut's *Les Quatre Cents Coups* (*The 400 Blows*), about
a young lad kicking over the traces, Godard's *A Bout de souffle*
(*Breathless*), with its gleefully insolent opening, and Alain
Resnais's haunting *Hiroshima, mon amour*. Though Godard
later went in for some pedantic Maoist editorializing, the work
of this group, along with that of Chabrol, Agnès Varda and
others, marked a turning point in international cinema.

And similar preoccupations were even more strongly
represented in the Nouveau Roman, two of whose practi-
tioners, Alain Robbe-Grillet and Marguerite Duras, were
also active in cinema. These 'new novelists', while there were
differences of emphasis in their approach, aimed at a sort of
anti-novel shorn of the traditional features of fiction such as
social and political scene-setting, character-drawing and
linear narrative. So, instead of the usual narrator integrated
into the social world, understanding and reflecting on what
is happening, there is an implied narrator or point of view –
the protagonist of Michel Butor's *La Modification*, for
example, is called *vous* and therefore might or might not be
addressing himself. This implied narrator or entity, as
though uncomprehendingly encountering civilization for the
first time, is confronted either with the otherness of the
world through lengthy neutral, often geometrical descrip-
tions of things, or else with his or her own intense, often
obsessively repetitive engagement with it.

The reader is required to share in this often disquieting
phenomenological exercise, which can become a tragic
ontological drama of the failure to come to terms with

anything outside the self. It is significant that Robbe-Grillet, who was fascinated by Flaubert's impossible old dream of writing 'the novel about Nothing', runs into the same clash between objectivity and subjectivity as had Sartre before him. The more elaborately objective his description of a sliced tomato, or whatever, the more manically subjective it seems, while the more he seeks to exclude the psychology of character from the novel, the more he is simply displacing it back towards the implied narrator – and the narrator's narrator, Robbe-Grillet.

Needless to say, the cinema and the novel were reflecting ideas that were being treated elsewhere in more systematic form. Some of the more pessimistic themes of the Nouveau Roman were being reinforced by the new Structuralists of the 1960s, who had begun to apply linguistic theory to different disciplines. The psychoanalyst Jacques Lacan produced a reading of Freud which suggested that reason and self-knowledge were virtually inaccessible. The structural anthropologist Claude Lévi-Strauss looked for a universal logic underlying all myths, but, if he demonstrated brilliantly, for example, how abstract body painting in an Indian tribe corresponds to a social hierarchy, this underlying structure was not understood by either the painters or the painted. The epistemologist Michel Foucault argued that there was no continuity to history, since people were so locked inside their own period that there was no real communication across time, and that in consequence Man with a capital M was dead.

For some of the structuralists at least, there was still the belief that the determining underlying structures could be uncovered, but the so-called post-structuralists who took over in the 1970s went further. Already, with Roland Barthes, there was a shift towards the idea of the 'death of the author', the view that he or she had no control over the book's meaning – in effect that it was the book that wrote the author rather than the author the book. And, for others such as Gilles Deleuze, Jacques Derrida or Jean-François Lyotard, there was nothing beyond the text, no underlying reality or firm truth to be uncovered. This leap into a postmodern relativism, by denying the belief in reason and in a knowable external reality on which leftist politics traditionally depended, inevitably incurred criticism – and not just because their writing often seemed gratuitously difficult. In attempting to invest social science with the hardness of mathematics or the natural sciences, Lacan, Deleuze and others made heavy use of concepts that they were sometimes shown not to understand. While some of the criticism may have been unfair, it is clear that their influence has faded and that there has been a movement away from the universalist pursuit of grand theory towards a more empirical approach. Nevertheless, these were intellectually exciting and disturbing times.

However, leftists in the 1960s were more drawn to the various mutations and repackagings of Marxism that were occurring at this time. Even if many intellectuals were abandoning the Communist Party out of disillusionment with the Soviet Union, or because history had not borne out the proletarian model of revolution in industrial societies, Marxism was still present in one form or another. There was a Trotskyite strand which tended to lump together the Soviet Union and Western capitalist society as oppressive authoritarian bureaucracies, and there was even a 'Communist Anarchist' group. But the theoretical battle within the Communist Party was between those such as Henri Lefebvre who, on the basis of Marx's early writings, sought to recast him as a broad humanist, and purists such as Louis Althusser, who in his 'scientific' interpretation of Marx, tried to defend the orthodoxy. For the idealistic young, however, increasingly aware of themselves as an international protest group, the future lay rather with the peasant revolutions of Mao in China and Castro in Cuba, the romantic image of Che Guevara and the war of liberation in Vietnam.

*   *   *

The spectacular 'Events' of May 1968, so called because nobody was quite sure what else to call them, seemed to come entirely out of the blue. For there was no obvious political trouble in sight. It was true that there had been strikes from time to time, since progress did not favour all sectors equally, but these had been settled. And the Socialist François Mitterand had done better than expected in the presidential election three years earlier, but that was largely because de Gaulle had not deigned to campaign. And it was rather the absence of serious opposition that was reflected in an editorial in *Le Monde* in mid-March, which declared that the French were bored, especially the young, who felt excluded from the student protests they could see in America and all over the world – even if, as it added tartly, their own demand for male students at the new suburban campus of Nanterre to have free access to the female students' rooms suggested a rather limited conception of the rights of man.

Yet that was precisely the trigger for the explosion that occurred when the male students did occupy the women's quarters five days later. The university authorities reacted strongly, the students defiantly extended their occupation and the 'Events' began to acquire their own inevitability. The Nanterre campus was closed down, but that only led to the occupation of the Sorbonne, then to other occupations of universities and *lycées* across the country. The academic authorities were at a loss as the student saturnalia in the Sorbonne left it partly trashed and only really reacted when more organized Trotskyite and anarchist elements entered the scene. The police were called in to make arrests, but their rough tactics only increased sympathy for the students and turned the Latin Quarter into a battleground with barricades and flying paving-stones – providing a televisual feast for the whole of France and beyond. The Communists and Socialists were reluctantly dragged in, to try to canalize often utopian aspirations into trade union demands, and a general strike began which involved 10 million employees, occupied factories and brought the country to a standstill, leaving the government in a state of shock.

So 'how could it be', asked the influential sociologist and political commentator Raymond Aron, 'that a localized student protest turned into a national crisis which caused the regime to tremble, when no political party and no leader of a mass movement had any real intention of taking power?'[9] For, as he pointed out, revolutions now tended to take place only in less developed societies, the trade unions had become a conservative force in advanced industrial countries and, in any event, the Communist leaders were not only shocked by the cavalier attitude of these liberated young 'bourgeois' – there were bitter inter-generational disputes within left-wing families – but were quite happy with de Gaulle's anti-American posture. Moreover, many of the student protesters dismissed everyday politics as unreal. So was this 'revolution', with its revival of the old Surrealist slogans – 'it is forbidden to forbid' or 'the dream is the reality' – just a psychodrama, an innocent carnival, a theatrical gesture to the real national upheavals of 1789, 1830, 1848, 1871, 1936 and 1944? Or was it more grandly, as André Malraux and Prime Minister Pompidou called it, a 'crisis of civilization'?

Whatever it was, the government did not seem able to deal with it. Pompidou was trying to play off the unions against the students with large wage increases, but some of the president's officials were packing their bags, the Socialist leader Mitterrand was offering himself jerkily on television as a replacement for de Gaulle – and the general seemed mysteriously to have disappeared. Had he fled the country? In fact, for the first time in his life, as he later told Pompidou, he completely lost his nerve.[10] But he recovered it and added a little theatre of his own with a secret trip to Germany to consult General Massu and test the loyalty of the army. Reassured, he returned after three days and announced with the old authority that he would not resign and that there would be fresh elections. And, as though it had all been no more than a summer storm, the country sighed with relief. There was a mass demonstration in support of him on the Champs-Élysées, the general won a triumphant victory in the elections and everything was magically the same as before, only more so – not so much a case of *'après moi le déluge'*, the ominous prophesy attributed to Louis XV, as *'après le déluge . . . moi!'*

But not quite. It is true that the students had no coherent political project, that they were themselves the expression of the very social trends they were criticizing, and that their 'revolution' was something of a luxury in the light of the fact that, with sociology students now failing to find jobs, the first faint signs of the fading of the *'trente glorieuses'* – which would be brought to an end by the oil crisis – were already visible. But *Le Monde* failed to see that the original issue at this dreary overflow Nanterre campus was not so trivial as it appeared. On the contrary, it was a symbolic issue for students tired of a creaking university system which was heavily authoritarian, which had a very unfavourable staff–student ratio so that there was little or no interaction and which, with its segregated hostels, treated them like children. And their inhospitable new campus, thrown up in the middle of a grim shanty town on the edge of the city, was itself suggestive of the strains of rapid transition and of the gulf between rich and poor in the world at large.

And they had achieved quite a lot. For, by paralysing the country so easily, they had highlighted the hollowness of a paternalist presidential regime that was over-dependent on de Gaulle himself. They had demonstrated that it was failing to incorporate this new generation into the life of the nation. They had revealed the Achilles heel of authoritarian structures not only in education but in the workplace. They had shown that the virtual State monopoly of television alienated much of public opinion, despite the old monolith's mastery of the medium. They had brought to the fore new themes such as the environment and personal life balance and tried, however amateurishly, to get a little closer to the republican ideals of Liberty, Equality and Fraternity.

Whereas a large part of the victorious new Gaullist majority wanted him to clamp down on opposition, de Gaulle did see that this had been a crisis of transition, from one stage of society to another. He now spoke of the need to reform 'narrow and outdated structures' and he sought to implement a policy of 'participation'. The very competent Edgar Faure quickly began to decentralize and democratize education by granting some autonomy to universities and by introducing a representative committee structure. De Gaulle pushed that reform past a reluctant parliament, but his attempt to replicate it in the area of granting greater autonomy to the regions went wrong. This was partly because the proposal was tacked on to a reform of the Senate that offended certain groups there, and partly because de Gaulle seemed to be insisting on an unnecessary trial of strength by putting this less urgent proposal to a national referendum. He did realize of course that it was not a make-or-break issue and that he was taking a gamble. So why did he do it?

He did it because he felt outshone in the handling of events by Pompidou and he thought it necessary to test his own authority. He also did it because he felt old and tired – the cruellest suggestion on the banners had been that he be stuffed and stuck in a museum. As one observer shrewdly observes, there was a permanent conflict in de Gaulle between the pessimistic, puritan traditionalist and the decisive man of action, which explains both the tension in his personality and his recurrent bouts of discouragement and despair.[11] This realist had no illusions about people or about the difficulty of governing his fractious 'country of 246 different cheeses', but he felt less and less at home in this new society of the pill and the mini-skirt. And, even if he was a victim of his own success, was there any longer a place for de Gaulle in this evolving Gaullist regime?

He lost the referendum, as he half expected, resigned immediately and died the following year.

13

MUTATIONS OF THE 'REPUBLICAN MONARCHY': POMPIDOU TO CHIRAC

De Gaulle was a hard act to follow. Clearly, in the absence of another world war or national crisis on a par with the Algerian drama, no successor could pretend to his historical legitimacy and prestige. And this very fact revealed all the more sharply the apparent contradictions of the hastily drafted constitution of 1958 – tailored not only to a particular emergency but to a particular individual – which has raised questions of interpretation ever since.

De Gaulle, of course, had himself gone beyond the terms of his constitution in more ways than one. Although the prime minister was supposed to 'decide and conduct the policy of the nation', with the president acting as arbiter, de Gaulle had declared in 1964 that 'the indivisible authority of the state is entirely the responsibility of the president' – leading the Socialist leader François Mitterrand to attack what he called a 'permanent *coup d'état*'. And, whereas the prime minister was also stated to be 'responsible for national defence', de Gaulle simply decreed that foreign policy and defence were a 'reserved area' for the president. The end result was to emasculate parliament, which had no say either in the choice of a president elected by the whole nation or in the choice of the prime minister of a government including non-parliamentary ministers, and which faced the threat of dissolution if it held out against the president's proposals. In short, there was a real question with this hybrid republican constitution as to the democratic balance of powers.

In fact, no other leader of a Western democracy has been granted such political power as was conferred upon the presidents of the Fifth Republic, accountable neither to parliament nor to the law of the land, and with extensive powers of appointment to some 500 posts. So long as de Gaulle was in power, especially at a time of national emergency, these questions seemed secondary, but his disappearance brought them to the fore for his less illustrious successors. Could a prime minister with a strong party base be kept in such a subordinate position? Could this unchallenged power of the presidency be maintained? Was not a seven-year presidential term too long? What would happen if an unpopular president saw his parliamentary supporters defeated after five years in legislative elections? De Gaulle would certainly have resigned in such a situation, but what if a president insisted on completing his mandate? Was there even the bizarre possibility of a supposedly powerful executive president having to appoint a hostile prime minister? The present political system of France can fairly be said to have been born of necessity, given the failure of the Fourth Republic to muster the national energies to deal with a major crisis. It would demonstrate clear strengths, but it would also have its drawbacks.

De Gaulle's successors would have to operate within this system as best they might. And they would have to do so through the different phases of a world economy not only undergoing the transition to globalization, but disrupted by such events as Middle Eastern wars, oil crises and the collapse of the Soviet Union. The France of *grandeur*, which had largely succeeded in the sixties in maintaining an independent stance in world affairs and even in offering itself as a non-aligned arbiter, would now have to pursue those ends within the constraints imposed by the need to operate within supranational bodies such as the enlarged European Community and by the increasing interconnectedness of national economies.

Georges Pompidou, president from 1969 until his death in 1974, was a primary schoolteacher's son who graduated from the prestigious École Normale Supérieure. A cultivated individual with developed literary interests, he worked on de Gaulle's personal staff at the end of the Second World War and although not a professional politician – he worked for the Rothschild bank for several years in the 1950s – he remained close to de Gaulle to the point of acting as his secret peace envoy to the FLN during the Algerian war. Since he had also been his prime minister for over six years – quite a record – he certainly knew the ropes as regards the governance of this new republic. Indeed he knew them almost too well, for he had handled the 'Events' of 1968 with rather more aplomb than de Gaulle and been sacked for such lèse-majesté. His aim was to continue along Gaullist lines while satisfying the desire for inclusiveness that had been revealed by the 'Events' of 1968.

And with his prime minister Jacques Chaban-Delmas, the handsome former Resistance general and mayor of Bordeaux, who developed a project for a 'new society', he did take steps to modernize and liberalize the regime. With the relaxation of State control over television and radio, there were now phone-in programmes and more balanced political debates. Labour reforms included on-the-job training, the indexing of the minimum wage to economic growth and profit sharing at Renault while, in answer to the demands of the new feminist movement, there was a law granting equal parental authority to women. Also, the first ever Environment Ministry was created, while regional assemblies were set up. Again, there was an explosion of artistic activity at this time, notably of left-wing theatre – which, ironically, would not survive the arrival of a Socialist president in 1981. And Pompidou, like his successors, would leave monuments to his memory in the form of the colourful new inside-out Pompidou Centre and – much less popular with Parisians since it breaks the traditional skyline – the Tour Montparnasse.

The most striking change Pompidou made in foreign policy was to accept the entry of Great Britain into an enlarged European Community. Like de Gaulle, he had no great belief in supranational organizations, but he was concerned by the West German Chancellor Willy Brandt's 'opening to the East' and he calculated that Britain's entry would turn it towards Europe rather than the US, rebalance the continent politically and prevent France from becoming isolated. But he also took more obvious steps to meet the Gaullist aspiration to act as an independent world power. He maintained good relations with the Soviet Union, had a meeting with Brezhnev and was received officially in Beijing by Mao Zedong. He further followed de Gaulle's pro-Arab line rather than the American pro-Israeli policy at the time of the Yom Kippur war of 1973, feeding arms indirectly to the Egyptians via Libya, and attempting to do a separate deal with the OPEC cartel to obtain oil supplies.

However, the oil crisis of 1973 signalled not only the end of the '*trente glorieuses*', but the start of a new and troubled phase of the world economy, marked by the failure to coordinate exchange rates and by rampant inflation. France was particularly badly hit by rising oil prices, since it depended on imported oil for over 70 per cent of its energy requirements and, unlike Britain or Germany, had no share in the new North Sea oil discoveries. When it proved impossible to maintain a separate policy over oil supplies, it became clear that the Gaullist ambition to act as an independent force in the world had little chance of being realized without an alternative energy source.

Nor was it so easy to maintain the clarity of de Gaulle's hybrid part-presidential, part-parliamentary constitution. Pompidou's own attempt to 'cut the Gordian knot' in *Le Noeud gordien* – almost by definition, Fifth Republic presidents have a book or two to their name – is somewhat embarrassed. 'It is precisely because ours is a bastard system', he argues, 'that it may be more flexible than a logical system.' That may well be, but why is it necessary? It is because 'you only have to look at how the French behave to recognize their profound natural inability to let themselves be governed.' Yet people's behaviour is also determined by the structures within which they operate and he himself, a little later, suggests that the reason why France cannot have the usual two-party system is the existence of the Communist Party – which has little to do with the supposed French egocentricity.[1] In practice, he did try to redress the balance by improving the liaison with the parliament and by giving his prime minister Chaban-Delmas room to breathe, but this led to a difficulty which he would have found ironically familiar.

For Chaban-Delmas was becoming a problem, quite apart from the embarrassing revelation that he had managed, however legally, to pay no tax. He had a clear majority in the Assembly and his liberalizing 'new society' project was popular in the country, but the more right-wing Gaullists were suspicious of such ideas and felt that his standing was beginning to equal that of the president himself. Since Pompidou also believed firmly that there must be no diarchy at the head of the State, he did to Chaban-Delmas what de Gaulle had done to him and sacked him. He also yielded to the mystique of the presidency – that the president is transformed by the burden of this almost sacred trust, which he must bear alone – to the extent of concealing from the country for a whole year that he was being worn down by a rare form of lymphatic cancer, from which he died in office in April 1974. While this was hailed in *Le Monde* as the supreme sacrifice to the State, it may be questioned whether it was responsible – or whether Giscard d'Estaing's was not the more sensible view when he said that, in such a situation, he would have 'resigned on the spot'.[2]

Valéry Giscard d'Estaing, president from 1974 to 1981, was an independent republican with only a modest parliamentary group behind him who owed his presidency largely to a split among the Gaullists, which led to their official candidate Chaban-Delmas being undermined by a group favouring the more fundamentalist Jacques Chirac. Still only forty-two years old and known in the trade as 'le Bulldozer', Chirac was to build a formidable reputation for killing off political opponents – though only those in his own camp. In the event, his manoeuvring almost handed the election to his real opponents, since François Mitterrand had brought the Socialist party back from the dead, formed a common front with the Communists and the left-wing Radicals, and was only behind Giscard d'Estaing in the second round by 1.6 per cent. So Giscard d'Estaing was something of an accident and, insofar as he broke the Gaullist line of descent, a surprise.

Giscard d'Estaing, an indirect descendant of Charlemagne and a top tax expert, appeared a youthful forty-eight, dynamic, intelligent and – being a keen *'tennisman'* – very fit. Although one of nature's aristocrats, he wanted to introduce a less stilted style of politics and 'English' civility rather than harsh partisanship. And, even if his own informality could seem a little artificial, he did try to set the tone by having open days at the Élysée Palace, by dining occasionally with selected families and by having breakfast with road-sweepers. While he wanted to govern from the centre in order to create a new 'advanced liberal society', his problem, apart from a certain resistance to his ideas, was that he did not have the automatic backing of a majority party in parliament. However, he appointed Jacques Chirac as prime minister in order to keep the Gaullists sweet and set about his task with brio.

A number of domestic reforms were introduced at this time, in recognition of changing attitudes in the country. The monolithic control of the airwaves was broken up to provide competing radio stations and television channels. The age of majority was reduced from twenty-one to eighteen, which brought almost 2.5 million young people on to the electoral register. Divorce by mutual consent was introduced, along with legalization of abortion under certain conditions, and schools were standardized in order to give all children an equal chance. In foreign affairs, while Giscard d'Estaing continued France's neocolonial policy in Africa – and would be accused, possibly wrongly, of accepting valuable diamonds from the implausible Emperor Bokassa of the Central African Republic – he was a strong supporter of steps to strengthen the European Community.

But none of this was designed to please the Gaullists, who had initially been taken aback when Giscard d'Estaing only took four of them into his cabinet, preferring instead to appoint non-political specialists. Giscard d'Estaing may have wanted more political consensus, but he rivalled de Gaulle himself in the exercise of presidential power, even if he saw this as institutional rather than personal. He ran a private inner cabinet, appointed ministers without telling Chirac and did not even consult him about a government reshuffle in 1976 – so that one study could conclude that he 'wields more power today than any French head of state since Napoleon III'.[3] Chirac put up with being sidelined for two years and then resigned very publicly, declaring that he had simply 'not been given the means to carry out his job as prime minister'. He then proceeded to recast the Gaullist party with himself as leader, to gain a new power base by getting himself elected Mayor of Paris and, having set himself up as a rival to Giscard, watch him run into trouble over the economy.

The economy was indeed the decisive challenge, in France as elsewhere. Whereas in the early 1970s output was rising by around 7 per cent a year and almost 100,000 extra jobs were being created annually, ten years later production was down and over 200,000 jobs were being lost each year. Initially, Finance Minister Fourcade tried to cool off the economy by raising taxes and interest rates, while softening the effect on the poor by raising benefits. But, as of 1976, his successor Raymond Barre, while retaining the dirigiste approach in furthering the build-up of the nuclear industry, applied stronger neo-liberal measures designed to reduce the deficit, conquer inflation, remove the cushioning of subsidies to lame ducks and create a competitive modern economy. However, the resulting failures among small and medium enterprises created further unemployment and the situation was seriously worsened by the second oil crisis, arising out of the Iranian revolution of 1979.

With inflation approaching 14 per cent and unemployment at 1.5 million as Giscard d'Estaing approached the end of his mandate in 1981, national spirits were low. And, for all Giscard d'Estaing's modernizing efforts, the political commentator and broadcaster Alain Duhamel could still complain that France, though now an advanced industrial society, had an archaic, artificial, semi-developed political system suffering from excessive centralization of power and a lack of checks and balances.[4] Nevertheless, with the left divided, it was assumed that Giscard d'Estaing would win the forthcoming presidential election.

But that was to fail to take account of Chirac, who came a poor third in the first round behind Giscard, first, and the Socialist François Mitterrand, second. Even though he had

publicly criticized Giscard d'Estaing, he was still expected
loyally to urge his own Gaullist voters to support him in the
run-off to prevent a left-wing victory. This Chirac failed to
do, with the result that – to right-wing consternation,
left-wing rejoicing and a collapse on the stock exchange – he
handed the presidency to Mitterrand.

President Mitterrand, who served from 1981to 1995, tends
to be seen as a mysterious figure. An apparently shy young
man from a provincial middle-class Catholic background, he
had just completed his law studies when the Second World
War began. He was taken prisoner, escaped, started to work
for Vichy, but drifted towards the Resistance. He reached
London and met de Gaulle, but returned to France to play
a part in the internal Resistance – if he later seemed cagey
and even something of a fantasist, it may in part be due to
his experiences at that time. After the war he served in eleven
governments under the Fourth Republic, but lost his seat in
1958 and hit the headlines the following year when he
claimed to have escaped an assassination attempt by Gaullist
supporters of French Algeria because of his anti-colonialist
views. This curious imbroglio was widely seen as a publicity
stunt at the time and the recent memoirs of a senior police
insider tend to confirm that view.[5] In his subsequent period
in the political wilderness, he made scathing attacks on the
presidential regime and plotted his way back into power.

Was he a 'real' Socialist? When he took over the leadership
in 1971, there were those like Guy Mollet who thought he
had merely learned to talk the talk. Certainly he had little
time for socialist theory and had no real knowledge of
economics, but he did sympathize with the demand for a
fairer society and he was prepared to risk electoral failure by
insisting on the abolition of the death penalty. Above all, he
knew about power and thought he knew how to get it, the
main way being to embrace the Communist Party in order
gradually to swallow it. If he 'was a tough and single-minded

professional at home with power and driven by a libido dominandi' as David Bell puts it, that is not unknown among successful politicians.[6]

The 'mystery' of Mitterrand is not that he moved from right to left, that he kept secret the existence of an illegitimate grown-up daughter, or that he ended up delighting in presidential power to the point of following the kingly practice of not carrying money. It lies rather in the personality of a man not given to intimacy or teamwork, who not only kept his cards close to his chest but played simultaneously with different packs against people largely unknown to one another. A man who, like some inscrutable Renaissance prince, exercised power through a complex network of dependents, keeping them guessing and playing them off one against the other. A man who refused to resign when visibly ailing from cancer because he believed the exercise of power kept him alive.

But for the left, in 1981, it seemed that Mitterrand had created nothing less than a 'Copernican revolution', as one of his ministers Pierre Joxe called it, since 'before him the left in France had only known rare, brief "experiments", as they were called, that ended badly'.[7] Now, with seven clear years ahead of him, he seemed to have broken the spell of near-permanent conservative rule, especially since he immediately dissolved the Assembly and obtained a large majority. And the atmosphere was transformed by a whole series of measures that were set in train – to reform the prison system, decentralize to the regions, align higher education with the social and economic needs of the nation and, most immediately obvious, spread culture and jollity around the country. The new minister of culture, the racy Jack Lang, whose budget would increase five-fold over the next twelve years, allowed independent radio stations to set up, took steps to support the book trade and created the annual national music festival which enlivens Paris with outdoor music every 21 June. And of course the Mitterrand

presidency would inevitably set its name on even more
grands projets – including the Louvre pyramid, the attractive
Institut du Monde Arabe, the ill-conceived Bibliothèque
Mitterrand and the monumental, if windy, Arche de la
Défense.

Yet the real challenge was the economy and here the
change in approach under Prime Minister Pierre Mauroy
was dramatic. Everything was done to put the State in
control rather than the market, with a new national plan
emphasizing the modernization of industry and the public
services. To deal with unemployment, the government
increased demand by raising family allowances and State
pensions, and attempted to share out the available work by
increasing the annual holiday to five weeks and by reducing
the working week from forty to thirty-nine hours, this being
seen as a first step towards an eventual reduction to
thirty-five hours and a pensionable age of sixty. It was in fact
a bold attempt to change society: *changer la vie*.

It was recognized that France was alone in following this
policy, but it was assumed that any temporary difficulties
would be resolved when the full effect of the changes was
felt and when the world economy picked up again. Yet the
rise in purchasing power increased inflation and went largely
towards imports, so that the deficit increased, the franc had
to be devalued and unemployment went on rising. Business
complained about the taxes imposed to pay for the increase
in social benefits, unemployment caused anti-immigrant
feeling and an increased following for the far-right Front
National, and the government was forced to withdraw a
proposal on education perceived as an attack on Catholic
schools. Long before Mitterrand changed tack with a new
prime minister, Laurent Fabius, in 1984, it was all too clear
that this French attempt at 'socialism in one country' had
failed.

This was a significant moment, for it emphasized that
what the French now call *mondialisation*, or globalization,

was already a fact of life and that a Western country could not uncouple itself with impunity from the ebbs and flows of the world economy. This was the more the case in that France, whether through its defence, energy, banking or luxury industries, was now firmly embedded not only in the European but in the global economy. It was therefore a key moment for the Socialists, since it called in question the formal philosophy of the party and strengthened the hand of the social democratic tendency. And, to the dismay of the Socialist left and the Communists, the emphasis under the thirty-eight-year-old Laurent Fabius was now placed firmly on balancing the budget and modernizing the economy. This involved the socially painful exercise of cutting subsidies and switching government support away from declining industries such as coal and steel towards newer areas such as chemicals and information technology.

Fabius did bring down inflation, but unemployment began to seem immune to any treatment and it was clear that the left was going to lose the 1986 parliamentary elections. Mitterrand limited the damage in advance through the ruse of switching to proportional representation – which had the unintended effect of giving the Front National thirty-five seats, the same number as the declining Communist Party – but the left still lost the election. Which raised a large question, once again, about the Constitution.

Rather than resign as expected, Mitterrand appointed Chirac as prime minister, thereby bringing the Fifth Republic into the era of 'cohabitation'. And over the next two years he and Chirac used the Constitution against each other, with Chirac invoking his rights as prime minister to get his measures voted through, and Mitterrand using his presidential prerogative to thwart him as far as possible – all the while appearing to be grandly above the battle. Enthused by the policies of Ronald Reagan and Mrs Thatcher, Chirac now promised a no-nonsense neo-liberalism – involving the privatization of over sixty companies and banks, deregulation and the scrapping of price controls, exchange controls and the Socialist wealth tax. He also brought in controls on immigration to neutralize the Front National and reversed Mitterrand's electoral reform. However, the moderate right regarded his approach as extreme, he ran into a wave of protest strikes in 1986 and then the stock exchange collapse of October 1987, while Mitterrand shrewdly outmanoeuvred him, presenting himself as the protector of the nation in dangerous times. So Mitterrand was returned as president in 1988 and the rollercoaster could begin again.

However, it began on different terms. To get a working majority Mitterrand dissolved the Assembly, but the election only provided for a minority Socialist government supported by elements from the centre parties. He therefore appointed the very able planner Michel Rocard as prime minister, since as the Socialist Party's leading social democrat he could look for consensus, but Mitterrand also found it convenient to place a prime rival in a challenging position – and indeed he would undermine him during his tenure. Rocard restored the wealth tax, created benefits for those looking to get back into the workforce, and made a serious attempt to deal with the social security deficit. He also benefited from the change in mood due to the fall of the Berlin Wall and to the sense of national unity engendered by the first Gulf War. But, with the economy turning down again and clashes over policy within the party, Mitterrand dismissed him curtly in 1991 and appointed Édith Cresson.

As the first woman prime minister, Cresson had novelty value, as well as being intelligent and forceful, while as a critic of Rocard she also held out the promise of a more left-wing alternative. She was highly qualified, with a doctorate in demography, and had held several ministerial portfolios. But she encountered a certain misogyny, the more so in that she governed with close advisers, ran roughshod over the administration and – as when she declared on the basis of a visit to London that a quarter of 'Anglo-Saxon' men were homosexual – was quick to judge. It hardly took the defeat in the local elections of 1992 to force Mitterrand to dismiss her – though by this time the turnover of prime ministers was beginning to be reminiscent of the Fourth Republic.

The merry-go-round continued with the contrasting figure of Pierre Bérégovoy, an old working-class Socialist who had had left school at fifteen. Formerly Mitterrand's chief of staff at the Élysée, he took over as prime minister in the brief interval up to the parliamentary elections of 1993. These were clearly doomed in advance, even without a further crisis in the world economy and a spate of corruption scandals – one of which led Bérégovoy himself to commit suicide. Mitterrand, who had long since switched his attention to building up a strong alliance with Germany within the European Union, was now frail and visibly losing interest. And there was open warfare among the Socialist leaders between modernizers and traditionalists. So it was no surprise when the Socialists were routed with less than 20 per cent of the votes, leaving Mitterrand with no option but to swing once again to the right.

Since Chirac wanted to stay out of the firing line in order to build up a campaign for the presidency, it was Édouard Balladur, a centre-right figure with a background in industry and no attachment to the mystique of Gaullism, who became prime minister. He was a reassuringly calm and courteous figure, but also a shrewd tactician – Mitterrand described him admiringly as 'worse than me' in that regard.[8] Balladur brought in strong neo-liberal remedies with budget cuts and the privatization of public companies, including the Banque Nationale de Paris and the oil company Elf-Aquitaine, but he mollified the unions with a national loan to relieve unemployment. He eventually ran into widespread strikes with restructuring plans involving job cuts, and unemployment was still at 12.6 per cent at the end of 1994.

Nevertheless he had established himself as the obvious candidate for the right in the presidential election. But that, once again, was to forget Jacques Chirac.

Chirac, who was to become president from 1995 to 2007, dramatically attacked Balladur's support for the franc and balanced budgets and issued a kind of leftist Gaullist call for bold action to lower taxes, solve unemployment and heal a broken society. This was dismissed as demagoguery in political circles, but it was what the electorate wanted to hear and Chirac defeated the Socialist Lionel Jospin in the presidential election. Whereupon he appointed as prime minister the neo-liberal technocrat Alain Juppé and – not untypically – proceeded to do the exact opposite of what he had promised. Was this cynicism on the part of Chirac – the 'Weathercock', as 'le Bulldozer' was also called? Yes, but not of the grand Machiavellian kind, for it also reflects the fact that, as a biographer argues, 'he had no preconceived ideology, no coherent political programme'.[9] While Giscard d'Estaing saw him as 'a naturally jolly and warm man' who was ill at ease in his political role and was only himself when backslapping voters on campaign, Sarkozy saw him in not dissimilar fashion as being 'scared of demonstrations' and therefore tempted to leave things alone.[10] A populist opportunist with a hearty appetite and a preference for beer, he was always a reactive tactician rather than a strategist.

Even so, Chirac had his moments, notably in July 1995, when he made an admirable speech commemorating the notorious round-up of Jews in Paris in 1942, becoming the first president to recognize the responsibility of the French State in the deportations. Yet within months his presidency was in trouble. Juppé embarked on an extensive reorganization of State finances in order to meet the convergence criteria for the introduction of the euro across the European Union in 1999, but, since this threatened wages, benefits and pensions, it brought the country to a standstill with the biggest general strike since 1968. This did little for the popularity of Juppé, who was seen as arrogant and shown to be benefiting unduly from housing perks. So in order to provide him with a more solid majority with which to carry out his reforms, Chirac was persuaded to dissolve the Assembly – a major blunder which landed him for the next five years with a left-wing Assembly and a Socialist prime minister in the form of the austere Lionel Jospin.

Jospin had the good fortune to arrive in 1997 just as the world economy was moving into a period of growth, which would last until 2001. This not only enabled him to put Chirac in the shade by meeting the convergence criteria for the euro without the use of the harsh medicine prescribed by Juppé, but allowed him to bring in a raft of distinctively socialist measures. These included the thirty-five-hour working week and a job creation scheme for the young unemployed, which helped to bring unemployment below the 10 per cent mark. There were also significant modernizing measures such as civil unions for gay and lesbian couples and a law promoting gender equality, designed to increase the tiny percentage of women elected to political bodies. Meanwhile, Chirac was heavily discredited by the revelation of financial scandals reaching back to his time as Mayor of Paris, mostly relating to the illicit funding of the Gaullist party through fictitious jobs and kickbacks from companies tendering for public works, but also involving vote-rigging and having private work done at public expense. Controversially, he managed to obtain immunity from prosecution while president, but he kept a low profile – until the wind changed in 2001.

For the broader economy turned down again, with bankruptcies, the flight of jobs to low wage countries and another rise in unemployment, leaving Chirac with an opportunity to attack Jospin in good time for the 2002 presidential election. However, the combination of public disenchantment and a self-defeating electoral system turned the election into a disquieting farce. The figure of 28.4 per cent for abstention was the highest ever seen in the first round, while there were candidates from no fewer than sixteen parties, most of them tiny. They included three separate Trotskyite parties on the left and, on the right, a right-wing Christian homophobic Forum and a hunting-shooting-and-fishing party called Chasse, Pêche, Nature, Traditions. Even on the far right there was no unity, since there was now a breakaway branch from Jean-Marie Le Pen's Front National. With all this fragmentation, Chirac only obtained 19.88 per cent of the vote and Jospin even less with 16.18 per cent, while the candidate who slid into second place for the run-off was Le Pen with 16.7 per cent – which shocked the country and drove hundreds of thousands of protesters on to the streets. The abstainers returned in force for the second round and with gritted teeth, chanting 'rather the crook than the Fascist', helped Chirac to win with a record 82 per cent of the vote – a triumph that was also a humiliation.

Chirac had meanwhile brought about yet another mutation to the Constitution. Largely in order to improve his chances in the election, since he thought that the electorate might hesitate to grant another seven-year term to a man who would be aged seventy-seven at the end of it, he had aligned it by referendum with the five-year term for the Assembly. He had also, by obtaining his immunity, increased the power of the sitting president by making him unaccountable in law. Would these modifications allay the ongoing concerns as to the effectiveness of the political institutions of the Fifth Republic?

It is of course possible to exaggerate the importance of this issue. In a changing world, constitutions and institutional arrangements are never going to be perfect – Britain has taken a century over reforming its medieval House of Lords, while the US can suffer a stalemate between the president and Congress, and is tied to maintaining the right to bear arms in what is now an urban rather than a frontier society. Also, these two countries have been confronting similar international and domestic problems, have been facing the same tension between the free market and social protection in an increasingly globalized economy, and have shown similar swings between right and left in response – if not with the same zigzag rapidity as in France. In practice, the approach of Western democracies to what are basically the same challenges is likely to be similar. And, if the political system of the Fifth Republic arose out of an emergency situation, it has nevertheless endured for half a century. The supposedly logical French may well have an illogical Constitution, but the strong executive does have its advantages. In particular, it conforms to the country's longstanding economic dirigisme and makes for rapidity of decision-making – whether in relation to the build-up of the nuclear industry or to a project such as Eurostar.

Even so, the Constitution might seem to have created as many problems as it solved. There is the obvious 'conflict of legitimacy', as Chirac's biographer calls it, between that of a president elected by universal suffrage and that of a prime minister whose appointment has to be sanctioned by an Assembly also arising out of universal suffrage.[11] It was this contradiction, rather than a simple clash of personalities, that led directly to the damaging conflict between Pompidou and Chaban-Delmas, as between Giscard d'Estaing and Chirac. This became absurd as well as damaging under the system of 'cohabitation', with Mitterrand undermining his prime minister, Chirac, and Chirac undermining his prime minister, Jospin.

Again, if the system was designed to focus national opinion and reduce the large number of disparate parties, it has hardly done so. That problem would in fact have tended to correct itself, given the end of the Cold War, the collapse of the Communist Party and the fact that right and left have increasingly found themselves, if with different emphases, running the same market economy under the same global constraints. However, as was demonstrated by the farcical presidential election of 2002, the two-round voting system encourages a plethora of implausible candidates, who stand in order to get free media time, to build their party image for lesser proportional elections, and to acquire bargaining power. Even when they fall in behind one of the two leading candidates in the second round – and some will see no party interest in doing so – there is not a properly coherent majority of right or left. The system promotes fragmentation and public cynicism.

Yet the exceptional power embodied in the presidency creates another concern. While political corruption is not confined to France, there was an unprecedented spate of scandals over these years which brought the system into disrepute. Although many of these involved the Gaullist party, others involved Socialists. Some of these concerned the wholesale illicit funding of political parties – also a problem not unknown in other democratic countries – and this was tackled by imposing a ceiling on election expenditure. Others concerned covert action by the State, as in the sinking of the Greenpeace ship *Rainbow Warrior* by the French intelligence services to prevent it from interfering with a nuclear test in Mururoa or the secret sale of arms to Angola in return for oil rights, in which Mitterrand's son Jean-Christophe was involved. Many, especially since ministers in the dirigiste economy were so close to major companies, were due to personal greed – as in the colourful case of Bernard Tapie, also charged with fixing football matches for his team Olympique de Marseille, and that of Roland Dumas, whose mistress, a lobbyist and conduit for kickbacks for the oil company Elf-Aquitaine, famously dressed him in wildly expensive Berluti handmade shoes. Courageous investigating magistrates encountered obfuscation and intimidation, Giscard d'Estaing, Mitterrand and

Chirac were all stained by scandal, there were two ministerial suicides and the satirical weekly *Le Canard Enchaîné* –
the 'Chained Duck', or 'Chained Rag' – had a rich diet of
scandal. One can only conclude with the view of Colombani
and Portelli that such a succession of scandals was due to
'this way of exercising power and to the absence of adequate
institutional, political, social – and above all moral – checks
and balances'.[12]

The reduction of the presidential term to five years as of
2002, combined with the fact that the presidential election
would from now on be closely followed by the legislative
elections, effectively got rid of the confusions of 'cohabitation'. But of course this simplification, by making the
president even more powerful, merely sharpened the old
questions about the role of a prime minister and about
accountability to an elected parliament.

14

THE 'FRENCH EXCEPTION': REALITY OR ILLUSION?

So what's French about the French? And what about the so-called 'French exception'? Generalizations about national identity are subject to caution. France covers a large area, with a great deal of climatic and cultural variety. Brittany is different from Alsace, Picardy from Provence and Paris from all of the provinces. Indeed, at the end of his vast study *L'Identité de la France*, the recent great historian Fernand Braudel was left to conclude not only that France is diverse, but that 'its diversity is manifest, enduring and structural'.[1] Some of the earlier French historians, on the other hand, have not helped by encouraging an essentialist view of the national history with such expressions as 'the soul of France', 'eternal France' and 'the French genius', as though there pre-existed a quintessential Frenchness determining historical developments rather than the reverse – whereas, if it was a quintessential national spirit that expressed itself by, in turn, resisting the Romans, cleaving to the Church like St

Louis, undermining the Christian world through the Enlightenment and then trying to impose a new world through Napoleonic conquest, it must have been a little confused.

Nor has it been helpful to speak, for example, of the 'genius of the language', as though that dictated the quality of the thought expressed. French is in fact a charmingly quirky, idiosyncratic language, with a more restricted register than English enjoys with its dual Anglo-Saxon and Norman vocabulary, so that a word like *chalumeau* means both a drinking-straw and a blow-lamp – although the context should normally help to avoid using one for the other. The 'logic' and the 'clarity' of French are the logic and the clarity of a mode of thought derived from a particular education system, just as French fashion derived historically from royal patronage rather than spontaneously from the innate flair of stylish women or designers. National identity, in short, is not something given but a historical construct. Neither has it helped that 'the French exception' has become such a popular term that it has been used to designate French differences or superiority as regards 'road safety, gynaecology, the banking system, the constitution, culture, the treatment of AIDs, the Grandes Écoles, the shooting of migrating birds and cryptography' – to mention only some of the usages listed by one contributor to a useful study.[2]

And then there is the final irony that the 'French exception' only became a regular subject of discussion following the announcement of its demise – by François Furet in particular, in the collective work *La République du centre: la fin de l'exception française*. Published in 1988, a year before the fall of the Berlin Wall and just before the first version of Francis Fukuyama's *The End of History*, it argued that with the fading of the bitter internal political conflict following the collapse of the Communist Party, the acceptance of the Republic by the traditionalist right and the new involvement in a united Europe, France could now drop its 'theatrical' geo-political posturing, stop seeing itself as special, and behave like the medium-sized country it was.[3]

This of course was in line with the attempts to move towards the centralist politics of Chaban-Delmas, Giscard d'Estaing and others, as with the new model of 'cohabitation', but it was not designed to appeal to everyone. And almost twenty years later, in his swansong presidential address of March 2007, we find Chirac reasserting his belief in the French exception when he declares, 'France is not like other countries. It has special responsibilities, inherited from its history and from the universal values which it has contributed to forging.' And he ends with a salute to 'this France which, take my word for it, has not finished astonishing the world.'

So has there ever been a 'French exception'? And if so, does it still exist?

France is not 'exceptional' merely because it has had a violent internal history – Germany, Russia and Spain have hardly been free from political violence. More pertinent is the fact that it is the only major country in the European Union which retains costly overseas departments and territories in line with its self-image as a world player.[4] For the policy of *grandeur* in one form or another has been a constant aspiration since the seventeenth century, when France was after all the richest, most heavily populated and most powerful country in Europe. The 'French exception' is a paradox in that France has seen itself as exceptional not simply in the ordinary sense of being different from other countries but rather, through its adherence to universal values, as being exemplary – the model for other countries. At the heart of this notion is the ambition, accepted as a national destiny, to be the highest expression of civilization.

The template for this exemplary society was laid down during the *grand siècle*, when France began to see itself as the modern equivalent of ancient Rome. Louis XIV's declaration *'L'État c'est moi'* worked both ways, in that the notion of divine right established the status not only of the king but of the State, the area in which he must work out his contract with God. And, since absolute rule implied absolute responsibility, it fell to the central State to control and coordinate commerce, culture, architecture and every aspect of society down to the language itself. Colbert's economic dirigisme and the attempt to codify artistic creation or the pursuit of linguistic rigour by the Académie Française were in their different ways implicit in the will to raise civilization to a condition of order and harmony. In short, the 'French exception' meant a universalism implemented by a centralist state.

But of course in the following century the Enlightenment, by undermining religion and the authority of the Church, threw up a competing universalism. In an age of discovery, when Europeans were learning about other cultures scattered across the planet, this was a universalism which went beyond the nation itself and which obviously threatened an absolutist Catholic monarchy claiming to rule by divine right. At a time when the American Revolution was also encouraging radical political ideas, the Encyclopédistes were establishing the theoretical basis for the great Revolution of 1789 and for its universalist Declaration of the Rights of Man and the Citizen, which proclaimed the right to freedom and equality of all people everywhere. All of this, obviously, seemed to be the very opposite of the universalism claimed by Louis XIV's monarchical state. Ironically, however, the pressure of circumstances and its own internal dynamic led the Revolution to transform itself under Robespierre into an absolutism that was the mirror image of the monarchical state it had set out to replace. So once again there was a fusion of the authoritarian state with universalism, in an expansionist France which saw its mission as being to spread Liberty, Equality and Fraternity throughout Europe and beyond.

In broad terms, the history of France over the past two centuries has been the history of the conflict between these two universalisms. In a country such as Britain, which became Protestant and which was industrialized earlier, the dividing factor in politics has essentially been social class. If the French situation is confusing, it is because class difference was overlaid by two irreconcilable forces – Catholic conservatives and monarchists on the right, and republicans and revolutionists on the left. The violence that burst out in the revolution of 1848 or the Commune of 1871, like the extraordinary hatreds unleashed by the Dreyfus Case or the Popular Front, was the by-product of this clash of universalisms – a clash rhetorically mythologized by extremists on both sides. A further by-product was the Bonapartist strand in French politics, emerging in recurring attempts to bridge this historic gulf in opinion by means of an authoritarian populism: Napoleon as emperor bedding down the essential achievements of the Revolution, Napoleon III, the follower of the Utopian Socialist Saint-Simon playing at autocracy, and de Gaulle, the traditionalist military man going against his former mentor Pétain and restoring the Republic. All these at moments of crisis rode over the 'normal' party politics of conservatives, socialists or whatever.

In fact, the conflict between these two polarized views of the nation was in large measure settled by the Second World War. France is of course the country where since 1789, as one commentator reminds us, 'every political regime has ended in a *coup d'état*, revolution or war and there have been fifteen different constitutions'.[5] But the Catholic conservative tradition was heavily discredited by Pétain's collaboration with Hitler, by his setting up of a regime akin to the Fascist model of Franco's Spain, and by the sending of French citizens to their death at the hands of a foreign power. From the Liberation onwards, despite strains during the Cold War and ongoing questions about the working of the Constitution, there has been general acceptance that France is a republic. And it is a republic which, in the eyes of Chirac as of de Gaulle, remains the 'French exception' by virtue of its universalist mission and its belief in the directing role of the strong state.

Those aspects of French life which tend to puzzle outsiders become clearer when seen in the context of the role played by the state. For the French State is a construct with its own theoretical logic and internal coherence. As defined in the preamble to the constitution of the Fifth Republic, 'France is a republic which is indivisible, secular, democratic and social'. The terms of this declaration, and indeed the order in which they are placed, are significant in that they define the specific character of modern France. For a start, the very idea of a *republic* means obviously that there is no recognition of the hereditary privilege and class system inherent in monarchy and aristocracy. It should be remembered that the declaration of rights was 'of the Rights of Man and the Citizen'. French people – unlike the British before 1948, for example – are not subjects but citizens having equal rights and responsibilities. And this means, not merely that they are entitled to be addressed as 'Monsieur' or 'Madame' whatever their social position – though that in its time was a significant advance – but that they are defined as members of a collectivist society.

That is immediately reinforced in the Declaration by the first term: *indivisible* implies a centralist, non-federal state in which an individual is not defined by region or by adherence to any minority cultural or ethnic group, but purely as a citizen of the Republic. That is why the State was reluctant for so long to loosen the control it exercised through the prefects by granting any separate powers to the regions; it was only in the interests of more even economic development that elected regional councils were eventually set up by a law of March 1982, supplemented by a law of July 2006 granting them financial autonomy.

Similarly, regional and minority languages such as Breton or Occitan were denied any official status and only finally recognized as 'part of the national inheritance' in July 2008. Although France has recently begun to speak approvingly of linguistic pluralism, that is essentially a tactic in its long struggle against the world domination of English. Again, if a commission was set up in March 2009 to consider ways of establishing France's ethnic make-up, that is because official census forms did not require indication of ethnic or religious affiliation, so that the government did not really know, for example, how many Muslims or Hindus there were in the country. Quite apart from bad memories of the Vichy census, which sent so many Jews to the gas chamber, this reflected the rejection of multiculturalism in favour of a policy of integration, the idea being that citizens should relate directly to the State and not have their interests represented for them by some self-elected ethnic or religious organization or lobby.

This obviously leads directly to the second term of the declaration: *secular*. This marks an important point of difference with Britain and the United States, where religion may well be in decline but secularity has never been enshrined as a constitutional principle. The reason for this 'exception', clearly, is the unusually prolonged struggle that took place before the State freed itself from the political and social control of the Catholic Church, but that does not mean that secularity is merely a formal notion – on the contrary, it has important consequences.

While the State recognizes the right of citizens to have religious views and therefore does not oppose religion, it treats this as essentially a private matter. The public domain is seen as a neutral republican space in which people interact as equal citizens, so it is inappropriate to provide religious education or, since a law of 2004, to allow the display of divisive religious symbols such as the wearing of Islamic headscarves in state schools. This decision, together with the campaign of 2010 against the wearing of the burka in public service areas, seemed strange to many outside France, but similar issues have since arisen elsewhere and it is noticeable that Britain, for example, has drawn back somewhat from its earlier multiculturalist stance. So it is not by chance that in the Declaration the term *secular* comes before the term *democratic*. The underlying belief is that democratic liberty, equality and fraternity can only be guaranteed by shared citizenship within the neutral public space provided by the secular republic.

Finally, it was inevitable that a republic seeking to unite freedom, equality and fraternity should describe itself, to quote the last term of the definition in the preamble to the Constitution, as *social*. The linking notion here for those early republicans looking for a middle way between nineteenth-century German authoritarianism and British small-state liberalism, as has been well documented, was that of solidarity.[6] It is in the name of this republican value, reconciling freedom and justice, that France has tended to assume more responsibility than other countries for the welfare of its citizens. Chirac, when in America, always had an eye for a good hamburger, but he was shocked that in such a wealthy society there should be some 47 million people without access to proper health care. Solidarity is the cement which holds society together – and why the French tend to be more tolerant than others of inconvenient transport strikes. And it does not simply underlie the 'French social model', or État Providence as it is tellingly known. It is part of the blueprint for the good society which also involves State economic planning or State promotion of culture as related aspects of the 'French exception': the idea that the Republic has a special responsibility before the world for carrying forward the cause of universal human rights as defined by the French Enlightenment and the French Revolution.

That of course is the theory and, in its way, it is an admirable one. But, in an ever-changing world, the theory tends to be overtaken by reality and it is not too difficult for the Marxist sociologist Saïd Bouamama, in his 'autopsy of a national myth', to point to the paradoxes inherent in France's position.[7] An obvious example is the '*mission civilisatrice*' in the colonies, based on the period Eurocentric assumption that it was a duty to impose advanced Western standards on the 'backward' countries of Africa or Asia. As ideological justifications go, this was not entirely ignoble, but it did not sit well with the economic motivation involved or with the practice of the French in the territories. The maintenance of an overseas empire was also seen as an imperative in upholding France's status as a world power, and even today a strong reason for retaining at considerable cost the four overseas departments – Martinique, Guadeloupe, French Guyana and La Réunion – is their potential strategic value. Above all, France's bloody withdrawal from Indochina and from Algeria did nothing to validate the idea of a 'civilizing mission'. However, happier times have come with the development of the French Community, and it is of value to its members as well as to France that there should be as many French speakers outside the 'hexagon' as within it. Of course colonialism is a two-way process and an immigration crisis was to arise damagingly in 2005 – there being little advantage in being granted formal equality if you cannot find a job.

Another area where republican universalism has tended paradoxically to be exclusionist is that of gender difference. As feminist critics can fairly argue, 'France collapsed differences of gender, ethnic group and sexual orientation into white, male heterosexual self sameness.'[8] Since the Revolution failed to pass a declaration of gender equality and Napoleon consigned women to the home, it was only in 1881 and against Church opposition that the first *lycée* for girls was opened, while it is only within the last fifty years that women's rights in relation to the family have gradually been recognized. And it was only in 1967, with the State concerned to build up the population, that the law forbidding contraception was repealed, while abortion became legal in 1975.

There has been a strong feminist movement in France, with writers such as Julia Kristeva, Hélène Cixous and Monique Wittig following the lead given by Simone de Beauvoir's ground-breaking work of 1949, *Le Deuxième Sexe* (*The Second Sex*). The approach, given the French intellectual climate, is not so much pragmatic as philosophical and literary – or psychoanalytical as with Luce Irigaray's study of the mother–daughter relationship. However, there has been considerable opposition from the far right to the changes in the law, with the Front National campaigning for salaries for mothers in order to get women back into the home, not to mention raids on abortion clinics and boycotts of pharmaceutical companies manufacturing the morning-after pill. It has been a long-drawn-out struggle.

As is the case in comparable countries, women are now generally better qualified than men in educational terms and they are also better adapted to the changing skills required in the workplace. But as elsewhere they tend to opt for courses in the arts rather than in the sciences and they are more prominent in such areas as teaching, the social services or secretarial work. While the situation is improving, women are still faced with the 'glass ceiling' as regards promotion, they are virtually absent from the boardroom and they earn on average 12 per cent less than men for similar work – although the pay gap is even bigger in Germany with 22 per cent and in Britain with 20 per cent. However, France has fewer women in parliament, with 18.5 per cent of seats in the Assembly and 22 per cent in the Senate. In part, this reflects the fact that French women only obtained the vote in 1945, but over the fifty years to 1995 the figure for women in the Assembly only rose to 6 per cent. After Jospin decided that two-thirds of Socialist candidates should be women, the figure rose to 10.9 per cent. In 1999, the principle of parity of representation was passed by the Assembly after bitter

controversy, but the Senate was still holding up implementation ten years later. At least it has been officially correct
since 1998 to speak of *la ministre* or *la gendarme*, instead of
the masculine *le ministre*, or whatever. So *Madame la Juge*
or *la Capitaine* no longer has to feel that the language itself
renders her invisible. And of course President Sarkozy broke
the mould when he appointed seven women as ministers
along with eight men in 2007.

Is there anything in France's imperial history or in its
attitude to gender differences to suggest a 'French exception'? Only in the negative sense, perhaps. The 'civilizing
mission' gave it a sense of ownership which led it to hang on
to its colonies for too long with disastrous results, while the
masculinized discourse of rights prevented it from recognizing obvious inequities. But then, since France was operating
in the same competitive world as imperial Britain and since
its story on women's rights is broadly the same as that of
comparable countries, it would be naive to expect anything
else. The 'French exception' is an idea and, in the real world,
is best seen as an aspiration. But it is an aspiration that has
left a distinctive mark on French politics and society.

Essentially, the aspiration to create the exemplary society is
embodied in the planned coordination of economic
dirigisme, State education and social welfare. It is on the
interaction of these three areas and on the extent of its
success in implementing republican values that the claim to
exceptionality ultimately depends.

There is of course nothing new or specifically socialist
about dirigisme in France. State economic planning took
place under Colbert and under Napoleon, while in the
nineteenth century public capital assisted in the development
of mining and heavy industry. In the 1930s the Popular
Front government nationalized the railways and the arma-
ments industry, creating a precedent for the wholesale
reconstruction required after the Second World War. The

Monnet plan, while it never involved nationalizing more than a minority of industry, brought about a rational reordering of the economy by such means as incentives, conditional loans, and price and exchange controls. Particularly important, since the pre-war economy was relatively backward and fragmented, was the restructuring and merging of companies in order to obtain economies of scale and create groups able to withstand international competition. It was in strategic areas that the government intervened more directly, in infrastructure, transport and defence. It nationalized the railways as well as Electricité de France (EDF) and Gaz de France (GDF), and made the country a leading force in the defence field.

While this policy of unalloyed dirigisme was markedly successful in the expansionist period of the 'trente glorieuses', it had to adapt to the changed international situation following the oil crisis of the mid-1970s. This was made brutally clear by the failure of Mitterrand's attempt at 'socialism in one country' in the early 1980s, when the French discovered that their economy was now so integrated into the new global economy that an entirely independent policy was impracticable. It was evident that the strong dirigiste approach depended on growth, that without growth the government was left propping up losers and that, with the increasing globalization of companies and the freeing up of international credit, the national State no longer possessed the same control.

Nor was this due simply to the new neo-liberal orthodoxy – which dictated the privatizations carried out by Chirac and Balladur in the 1980s and 1990s – for there were also the constraints imposed by membership of the European Union. Not only did France fail to get its European partners interested in French-style job creation measures, but the Commission's competition authority clamped down on State subsidies to industry – Renault being a case in point – as well as on the preferential treatment of national firms for State contracts. Still, the wily French read the game well, with the result that, as one observer points out, 'the privatization process has been pursued in a dirigiste manner, with state actors exploiting elitist networks to ensure that controlling holdings end up in safe hands'.[9] And, in fact, in the name of 'economic patriotism', the State continued to have core holdings in key sectors such as banking, energy, transport, telecommunications and vehicle production – a kind of dirigisme-lite.

While the French economy is strong in many areas, the planned integration of strategic sectors in the service of national independence shows up particularly well in the way in which its aircraft industry, one of the foremost in the world, not only blends the civil with the military, but merges into the nuclear field and thence into space research. The resulting technological complexity calls for a high level of synergy between some of France's world leaders in this area – so much so that it is almost surprising to find an independent private group such as Dassault, a major player with a presence in more than seventy countries and best known for its fighter planes such as the Mirage and the Rafale. Related groups with a strong world footprint are SNECMA, specializing in aircraft engines, rocket propulsion and satellites; Safran, prominent in rocketry and telecommunications; and Thales, a frontrunner in information systems for aerospace, defence and the security market.

With MBDA, the second largest missile producer in the world, and Alcatel Alenia Space and Arianespace selling satellites abroad, the French aviation industry covers the whole spectrum, from transport planes and helicopters to drones and military satellites. As for the government-promoted nuclear industry, the now part-privatized EDF is the largest operator of nuclear establishments in the world and – apart from building reactors in Britain – works in conjunction with Areva, which builds reactors as well as mining uranium, and has manufacturing centres in forty countries as well as partnerships in China and the US. While the French developed nuclear energy to make up for their lack of fossil fuels, they now happily market it as clean energy responding to the global warming crisis and as guaranteeing safety of supply in an uncertain world.

All this is to say nothing of Airbus or of the other successful areas of activity which combine to give France its high rank – fifth, just ahead of Britain – among the world's advanced economies. The French economy has its specific problems – notably a persistent level of unemployment bearing heavily on ethnic minorities – but it has strengths far beyond its outstanding infrastructure and its world leadership in tourism. It is telling that over recent years there should have been a Frenchman at the head of the European Central Bank, the World Trade Organization and the International Monetary Fund.

So how does State education serve the exemplary society? The answer is not straightforward, for France's revolutionary history has left it with a uniquely divided higher education system, in which the small and prestigious sector of the Grandes Écoles produces the meritocratic elite which runs the country, while the main university sector caters rather indifferently for the rest. Historically, the system has been quite monolithic, as illustrated by the legendary story of the minister of education in the Third Republic who could look at his watch and say just which passage of Cicero pupils of the same age were construing at that precise moment in every school across France. The curriculum was laid down centrally and even universities had no autonomy. The hierarchical rigidity was relaxed to a degree following the student uprising in 1968, but President Sarkozy's proposal to grant independence to universities was still encountering widespread opposition in 2010.

Republican values are positively expressed in the excellent Maternelle, or nursery school system. This is heavily frequented since about a third of children start there from the age of two and, by the age of three, around four-fifths are already in attendance. Thereafter, school is less fun, the emphasis being strictly on learning rather than on sport, character-building or seeing the school as a community. Secondary schools are State-run, apart from some 13 per cent of Catholic or 'free schools', which the State subsidizes on condition that they adhere to the national curriculum, while equality dictates that there should be mixed-ability teaching. After the nursery stage, the École Élémentaire goes up to entry to the secondary level at the age of eleven, after which the Collège, or junior high school, has a four-year course leading to the Brevet, or junior diploma. This guarantees admission to the *lycée*, with its three-year course leading to the *baccalauréat* – '*le bac*' or '*le bachot*' – normally taken at eighteen. While there is a strong emphasis on mathematics and while philosophy is famously studied in the final year, there are three types of *lycée*. The Lycée Général, for those bound for university, has three streams: the literary, the economic and social, and the scientific. The Lycée Technologique leads towards a two-year course in an Institut Universitaire Technologique, while the Lycée Professionnel leads towards apprenticeships.

On the face of it, this system is successful in that most of a year group end up with a secondary diploma of some sort. But it is at this point that the lack of balance and inadequate career guidance begin to cause major problems. With over a quarter regularly failing the *baccalauréat*, the system is cluttered up with students trying to repeat their exams. This weakness is then compounded by the lack of career guidance at university level. Since State education is virtually free, since admission to university is automatic for anyone having passed the *baccalauréat*, and since the standard university course carries more prestige than the shorter technical or trade courses, students deprived of careers advice often choose a quite unsuitable course. The result is that some 50 per cent fail the examination at the end of their first year and some 40 per cent of those still studying, including repeaters, fail to obtain the intermediate diploma at the end of their second year, so that the overall higher education drop-out rate is unusually high. Ironically, by using student failure as a filtering mechanism, a system which ostensibly rejects selection in the name of republican equality of access has been practising selection by the back door. And that is only one aspect of the gulf between the universities and the Grandes Écoles.

This unique two-tier structure is a direct result of France's history. Since the pre-Revolutionary university was essentially clerical and not given to exploring modern disciplines, the Grandes Écoles were set up alongside them to provide a brand new administrative class – the École Polytechnique and the École Normale Supérieure both date from 1794. The latter, which essentially produces academics these days, counts among its alumni many of the great names of the Republic – from scientists such as Louis Pasteur to philosophers such as Henri Bergson or Jean-Paul Sartre. The students in science and engineering at the Polytechnique are also the crème de la crème, since here too admission is by national competition for a strictly limited number of places after special post-*baccalauréat* training lasting at least two years. These courses are extremely demanding on the students, who are formidably hardworking and who are in practice operating at postgraduate level by the time they arrive and become paid as trainee civil servants.

Over 200 specialist Grandes Écoles have since arisen, together commanding 30 per cent of the higher education budget for less than 5 per cent of the students. While the system certainly produces highly trained people, it has its disadvantages. Not only does it bleed the universities of money and of the best students, but it bleeds them of research, which is essentially carried out in the Écoles or in separate national research institutions. This means that the system, at a time of academic interchange, does not conform to the normal university pattern and consequently shows up badly, if rather unfairly, in international comparisons.

Crowning the whole structure of the Grandes Écoles is the extremely selective École Nationale d'Administration (ENA) with just over 500 students, which was set up by de Gaulle in 1945. This was designed to produce the top decision-makers of the Republic in what was seen, in the dirigiste spirit of the time, as the interchangeable fields of politics, diplomacy, nationalized industry and banking – *énarques*, as the alumni are known, have included not only Giscard d'Estaing, Chirac, Balladur, Jospin and more recent politicians such as Villepin and Ségolène Royal, but Jean-Claude Trichet of the European Central Bank and Pascal Lamy of the World Trade Organization. However, l'ENA too has encountered the criticism that it is unrealistic in the modern globalized economy to attempt to produce all-purpose mandarins who can move easily without the relevant experience from one sector to another. The government has taken some note of the criticisms and, while it would be most reluctant to weaken the great strengths of the Grandes Écoles, it is moving gradually towards bringing its universities into line with the general world pattern – if only to try to correct the anomaly that its statist elitism has in some measure conflicted with the larger value of republican equality.

What then of the most discussed element of the 'French exception', the 'social model'? This, according to Chirac in his Bastille Day interview of 2005, 'has a great ambition which is permanently to level up' and is 'in a way our national genius and a necessity which we must keep'. It may well seem an odd claim since other West European countries also have reasonable welfare systems, and it may seem the odder in that the social model, as it crystallized after the Second World War, is not specifically French at all but an obvious hybrid. While it adopted basic elements of the German Bismarckian social insurance model, such as income-related benefits and contributions collected through the employer, it added some features borrowed from the British Beveridge Plan, such as standard allowances in some instances and an admixture of financing through national taxation. In short, the social model is a complex hybrid which in itself is not at all specific. What is specific, as we have seen, is rather the social and moral vision which it embodies and the republican context in which it operates.

Yet if the French welfare system is a complex one, it is not simply because it was a hybrid in the first place, but because there have also been accretions as time went on. Over the past thirty years in particular, in an attempt to respond like other European welfare systems to new challenges – higher unemployment, increasing longevity, a more demanding public and the cost of more sophisticated treatments – there have been various measures of reform. The result is that the social model is not at all the monolithic State organization that it is often assumed to be, but rather an aggregation of systems and sub-systems held together as much by agreement between groups of stakeholders as by coordination through the State. In short, it is a patchwork of services rather than the completely unified system that those over-impressed by the French reputation for clarity and logic might expect.

The main branch of the system, the Régime Général, caters for salaried workers who constitute about 80 per cent of the population, but there are minor branches for other workers. In addition, there has always been a surprisingly large number of Régimes Spéciaux, special group schemes which until recently covered 5 million people ranging from civil servants to employees of the port of Bordeaux. Over recent years, the government has struggled to bring these groups, with their generally privileged pension arrangements, into the mainstream. Postal and France Télécom workers were incorporated in 2004, civil servants in 2005 and finally, in late 2007, President Sarkozy confronted rolling strikes to bring into line the remaining 500,000 in areas such as public transport and the energy sector.

The Régime Général is administered by funds, or caisses, dealing separately with health, family and retirement. Since the money is raised from both the employer and the employee, the funds are run by a joint committee of representatives from the employers' organizations and the trade unions. The employer's contribution covers a whole list of extra items such as accident insurance, public housing, education, supplementary pension plan and private social security top-up plan. This obviously dwarfs the contribution of the employees, who therefore find themselves in a disproportionately strong position on the joint committee. In fact, the trade unions only represent around 8 per cent of the workforce, but they are largely concentrated in the public sector and firmly embedded in the social security system, where they have enjoyed something approaching a power of veto. Since any company employing more than fifty people must also have a *comité d'entreprise*, or union-controlled company committee, to organize such services as sports events or summer camps for children, it is clear that the social model places the employee at the heart of the system.

That is the basis of the exceptional quality of the French social model. Its health system is regularly rated the best in the world by the World Health Organization. Its family allowances, such as its six-week maternity allowance and two-week paternity allowance, are generous, as are its pension arrangements. There is a basic State pension with a 'complementary pension' to which can be added a company or private pension, while the official retirement age has been sixty and the official length of service forty years, although both are due to rise in response to increasing longevity. With the best available healthcare, a very high birth rate and a longer retirement – to say nothing of the five-week paid holiday and the still official thirty-five-hour working week – the French have produced a republican social model that, as indicated by the remarks of Chirac, has support across the political spectrum. Yet it is also clear that this system, admirable as it is, is costly.

The 'French exception' then is not an illusion, but neither is it an achieved reality. And behind the perceptible unease in French opinion over recent years there lurk the obvious questions as to whether it can be maintained, if not consolidated. Will France's dirigiste control of its economy be lost in the new globalized economy? Will it be able to reform its university system without losing the high standards inherent in its Grandes Écoles? And will its economy be strong enough to support the social support which it sees as essential to its republican model of civilization? These are the questions confronting its leaders in the twenty-first century.

15

FRANCE IN THE NEW GLOBAL ORDER

The French tend to say that the French – themselves excepted, needless to say – are *rouspéteurs*, or incorrigible complainers. And President Chirac's second term, following as it did the farcical election of 2002, was never likely to deprive them of opportunities to complain. The population was said to be suffering from '*morosité*', a term so widely used as to acquire an almost clinical quality. There was much talk of national decline by 'declinists' – or 'declinologists', as they were contemptuously dubbed by the flamboyant foreign minister Dominique de Villepin. Of course some of the concerns were also those facing similar countries in a changing world, but others were more specific. There was an immediate concern about rising crime, there was the ongoing worry about the apparently insoluble problem of unemployment and, in view of Chirac's weakened authority, there was tension within the government. Not only would Chirac find himself in competition with his own minister of the interior, the bouncy action man Nicolas Sarkozy, but there would be harsh infighting between Sarkozy and Villepin. With a failed attempt by a disturbed right-winger to assassinate Chirac on Bastille Day 2002 and the problem of Iraq boiling up at the United Nations, it promised to be an interesting time.

In June 2002 Chirac appointed as prime minister Jean-Pierre Raffarin, a modest figure more versed in provincial politics. Sarkozy proceeded vigorously to tackle crime, through increased funds for the police and harsher penalties for juvenile delinquency. Raffarin and his minister of labour, the Anglophile François Fillon, then made yet another attempt to deal with unemployment and reduce the deficit to meet Eurozone requirements. This meant undoing, as far as was politically practicable, the Jospin measures of worker protection, not replacing posts in the public services and bringing in further privatizations, notably of Gaz de France and Air France. While they did not risk reversing the thirty-five-hour working week, they nibbled at it by allowing increased overtime and exemptions for small businesses.

They then tried to contain two major areas of runaway expenditure: public sector pensions, where they raised the qualification to the forty years of service standard in the private sector, and then the health service, where they increased contributions, imposed a small payment for visits to the doctor and – with the French being among the heaviest users of medication in the world – sought to limit excessive prescriptions. Predictably, all this was resisted by the unions and much of public opinion, while an attempt to decentralize more powers was suspected to be a ploy to offload on to the regions the levying of some taxes hitherto raised by the State. And, with the measures themselves being slow to take effect, the regional elections and then the elections for the European Parliament, both in 2004, were disasters for the government.

Meanwhile, Chirac had been busy ensuring that France's presence was still felt in the international arena. After the attack on the Twin Towers of 2001, he had immediately proclaimed his solidarity with the US, but as Washington moved closer to the invasion of Iraq he declared himself unconvinced. France was not alone in its opposition, of course – it was joined by Germany, Russia and China. But its threat to veto the operation in the United Nations Security Council was particularly resented by the Americans and a part of the British press. While in America french fries were renamed 'Liberty fries' and late-night comics like Jay Leno joked about 'cheese-eating surrender monkeys', in Britain the populist tabloid *The Sun* ran a cartoon representing Chirac as a prostitute in blonde wig and high heels being solicited by a kerb-crawling Saddam Hussein – and even the self-consciously serious *Spectator* ran a cartoon on similar lines. Why so much bitterness – and why the disrespect, which drew complaints from the French? Of course, both France and the US have long seen themselves as competing models of civilization and the Americans have tended to see the French – not always incorrectly – as thinking themselves more refined. But the basic reason was that the US felt that it had been badly let down by an ungrateful traditional ally. So for much of American opinion this was the same old posturing Gaullist France, trying to punch above its weight in world affairs and delighting in creating trouble for the 'Anglo-Saxons'.

For not only had Chirac declared in advance that he would use his veto on the Security Council – where Villepin's stylish and strongly applauded speech rammed the message home – but he had actually coordinated the opposition. And it was suggested that this was not mere diplomatic opportunism, but that it was dictated by the desire to protect French interests in Iraq. Of course it is true that France, as a legacy of empire, maintained an exceptionally large diplomatic presence around the world and had longstanding strategic interests in the Middle East. It is also true that Gaullist France had a pro-Arab rather than a pro-Israeli stance and had given refuge to the future leader of the Iranian revolution, the Ayatollah Khomeini. In particular, it is true that, following an official visit by Chirac in 1975, France had supplied Iraq with fighter aircraft and Exocet missiles – and indeed with the Osiraq nuclear reactor which the Israelis bombed before it could be commissioned in 1981. But then France was competing with other Western countries for defence markets and oil supplies in the Middle East, while the US had itself supported Saddam Hussein during the Iran–Iraq war. Whereas Chirac was prepared to cooperate on intelligence, he was alarmed at what he saw as the messianic tone of the neo-conservatives and President Bush, he felt that they had no realistic sense of the upheaval such an invasion would create and, declaring that he had seen no convincing evidence that Iraq possessed weapons of mass destruction, he argued that in these circumstances it would damage the United Nations to proceed.

Even if he felt vindicated by subsequent events, Chirac had not succeeded in imposing his idea of a 'multi-polar world' as opposed to one dominated by a single Great Power. And he was to be shocked, like much of Europe, by France's rejection in a referendum of the new Constitution for the European Union in May 2005. France was after all one of the six founding countries and one of the largest. Even if it had not been able to impose a European version of its own social model, it had largely succeeded in dominating the Union diplomatically and the constitutional commission had duly been chaired by the former French president Giscard d'Estaing. Moreover, an indicative vote within the Socialist party had shown a majority in favour, while it was assumed that the Gaullist and centrist parties were also in support. So why was the referendum rejected by 55 per cent to 45 per cent?

On the left, there was a developing power struggle in the Socialist Party between potential candidates for the 2007 presidential election such as Laurent Fabius, Dominique

Strauss-Kahn and Ségolène Royal. Arguing for a notional Plan B, the former right-winger Fabius now unexpectedly split off to lead a leftist faction to vote against, alongside Communists and Trotskyites who saw the European Union as a neo-liberal capitalist enterprise. On the right, the opposition came not only from the Front National and nationalist groups but from a part of the Gaullist party itself. So the left's fear of outsourcing and the right's fear of immigrants merged in the symbolic figure of the 'Polish plumber', the foreigner perceived to be a threat to French jobs. Of course most voters did not read the unwieldy constitutional proposal and simply followed their usual practice of voting against the government. But there was an underlying unease about the continuing unemployment, the effect of globalization, the possible loss of identity as well as jobs due to a proposed enlargement of Europe to include Turkey, and about the visible loss of influence in the existing Europe with its reunited and increasingly independent Germany. In fact there was a touch of despair about this converging nationalism of far left and far right, a feeling of being diminished and rather lost in a rapidly changing world.

A weakened Chirac appointed Villepin prime minister and gave Sarkozy a special status as number two and minister of the interior. This was a balancing act intended to strengthen Villepin's position against that of his increasingly formidable rival Sarkozy, who had already made clear his intention to stand for the presidency in 2007. They made an interesting study, these two equally ambitious figures. The glamorous, cultivated Villepin, a former diplomat and long-time close adviser to Chirac, was not an elected politician and was rather disdainful of those who were, so that he could be seen, in one view, as a 'peacock, a musketeer always ready to unsheathe his blade for his master' and as the 'Don Quixote of Gaullism'.[1] Sarkozy, on the other hand, described by the traditional Gaullist Philippe Séguin as 'a spontaneous neo-liberal, a pragmatist without theory, preconceptions or taboos', was no gifted amateur but a hard-driving professional who had come up the hard way and who had already defied Chirac's wishes by getting himself elected leader of the Gaullist party, now renamed the Union pour un Mouvement Populaire (UMP).[2] But for the moment the spotlight was on Villepin who, in an echo of his hero Napoleon, publicly gave himself 100 days to restore trust in the government. Which to a degree he did, with proposals for tax changes and measures to reduce youth unemployment, so that he was ahead of Sarkozy in opinion polls by the autumn – when it all went wrong.

For the general sense of insecurity was brought back with a vengeance by the explosion of immigrant violence in the *banlieues*, or outer city estates, in October 2005. The *banlieues* that ring Paris with their functional Soviet-style blocks have become so separate from the central part of the city that inhabitants there became aware of the riots only through television. The trigger for the riots was the death in Clichy-sous-Bois of two teenagers who, attempting to evade a police identity check, climbed into an electricity substation and were electrocuted. A violent protest began which, with the police over-reacting, soon spread around the outskirts – notably to Épinay-sur-Seine where a visiting engineer was beaten to death in front of his wife and daughter – and then to Marseille, Lille, Toulouse and other cities. In the course of three weeks tens of thousands of cars were burnt, many public and commercial buildings were set on fire and hundreds of rioters were arrested. They tended to be young people, often minors of second or third generation North African extraction – known as *beurs* – and most of them, significantly, had French citizenship.

The initial response was to treat the original incident as a minor burglary gone wrong, but as the violence developed Minister of the Interior Sarkozy fanned the flames by saying that the rioters were *racaille*, or scum, who should be cleared out with high-pressure hoses, and by presenting the riots as having been planned and coordinated. In fact, as an official report from the security services would conclude, the local Islamic groups were not involved and the riots had developed spontaneously. This was more alarming in its way, although it should hardly have come as such a surprise since there had been occasional incidents of car-burning for years. But it was still a shock to the country, which Chirac recognized when he spoke of an 'identity crisis' and of the need to abolish discrimination and create equal access to employment. The extent of the alienation could be measured by the spectacle on television of the rioters setting fire to the very schools, youth centres, gymnasia and even small businesses set up to provide for them – wrecking their own environment because it signified this France in which they did not feel themselves to be full citizens. They were in effect asking whether the republican claim to equality and solidarity could be real if it did not apply to them.

If Sarkozy had become a hate figure for the immigrant population, he was increasingly seen as a strong man by the right, and he could now watch while Villepin attempted desperately to find some answer to the questions posed by the riots. Villepin proposed further privatizations and introduced taxes on services to try to reduce the national debt, while practising 'economic patriotism' by forcing a merger of the conglomerate Suez with Gaz de France to forestall a takeover by the Italian company Enel. Above all, he tried to deal with youth unemployment by introducing a two-year 'first job contract' designed to encourage firms to employ people under twenty-six. Yet if firms might have been tempted to take on beginners by the possibility of being able to dismiss them, if unsuitable, without written justification or compensation, the unions and the students reacted with a huge protest strike in the spring of 2006. Villepin made the mistake of pushing through the measure by an emergency procedure and of failing to engage with the unions, with the result that Chirac was eventually forced to ask him to withdraw it. This discredited both of them and left Villepin, who felt that he had been sabotaged by Sarkozy, deeply humiliated. It also left the outside world with an impression of paralysis, since the French seemed to have treated themselves to a mini-revolution not in order to effect change but to preserve a much criticized status quo.

And it was at this point that the power struggle between the top Gaullists hit the headlines with the breaking in May 2006 of the particularly murky Clearstream scandal, soon dubbed a 'French Watergate'. The affair went back to a judicial investigation begun in 2001 into bribes linked to the sale of six French frigates to Taiwan, but it was in 2004 that the two judges charged with the investigation received anonymously a list of suspect accounts held by the Clear-stream clearing bank in Luxembourg. The list of politicians and industrialists presumed to have received kickbacks contained the name of Sarkozy – and indeed that of Dominique Strauss-Kahn. On discovering this Villepin, though this was strictly outside his brief as foreign minister as he then was, ordered the top intelligence figure General Rondot to inquire secretly into the matter and was alleged to have asked him to pay specific attention to Sarkozy.

The list was proved to be fraudulent – and may in part have been an attempt to invent a political scandal to blur the issue of the bribes – but it was alleged that even after he knew it was false Villepin had sat on the information for fifteen months. It also transpired that the anonymous source was Jean-Louis Gergorin, vice president of the aerospace company EADS and a long-time associate of Villepin. Rondot denied that Villepin had asked him to investigate Sarkozy, but his own notes of the meeting, leaked to the press, suggested not only that his denial was false but that Chirac himself was involved. All of this was denied by both Chirac and Villepin, but the damage to them and to public confidence had been done. A furious Sarkozy filed a suit against the 'person or persons' responsible for the fraud and emerged unopposed as the right-wing candidate for the 2007 presidential election.

The election of 2007 marked something of a sea-change in French politics as a seemingly exhausted system sought to renew itself. And the change was perhaps most apparent in the Socialist party which, with the Chirac presidency so unpopular, might have been expected to have its house in order and its candidate lined up for an easy win. In 2004, after all, the left had romped home in twenty of the twenty-six regions in the regional elections, while the Socialists had won thirty-one seats in the European elections, to become the largest national contingent in the European Socialist group.

For all that, the internal split over the European constitutional referendum – which resulted in Laurent Fabius being excluded from the executive – had been a traumatic experience. Not only had it revived the fundamental question of the party's attitude to globalization, but it had raised concerns about the failure to persuade its European partners to espouse its dirigiste views on macro-economic planning and employment creation. Also, this was a largely middle-class party, with no fewer than seven or eight identifiable left, moderate, right or green ideological strands, so that it was not easy for its first secretary, François Hollande, to hold it together. But he reformed the party machinery and started a recruitment campaign which brought in almost 100,000 new members who, since they were predominantly young and well educated, in effect increased the middle-class bias of the party. This, together with a certain disaffection with the established leadership contenders – or 'elephants', as they are engagingly called – led to a surprise result by which Hollande's partner Ségolène Royal comfortably won 60 per cent of the internal party vote, with only 21 per cent for the social democrat Dominique Strauss-Kahn and 19 per cent for the leftist democratic socialist Laurent Fabius.

Yet the novelty of a female presidential candidate was only one of the changes from 2002. The 85 per cent turnout in the first round was the highest for thirty years. With the emphasis this time on 'voting usefully', the minor parties were heavily squeezed. On the left, the three Trotskyite parties, the once-powerful Communist Party, the Greens and the colourful anti-GM crops candidate José Bové got less than 10 per cent between them. Surprisingly, since his group held only 27 of the 577 seats in the Assembly, the rather unexciting centrist Jean-François Bayrou obtained 18.57 per cent, suggesting that some voters were looking for a way between left and right. Less surprising was the fact that the Front National was down to 10.44 per cent, since Sarkozy siphoned off many of Le Pen's votes by promising to set up a Ministry of Immigration and National Identity, as well as by taking a hard line on crime prevention and on work-shy 'scroungers'.

However, it was rather implausible that Royal, Sarkozy and Bayrou, in their fifties, should present themselves not only as the new generation but as clean-break candidates and even outsiders. For Sarkozy had only recently been a minister at both Finance and the Interior and had not been a conspicuous success at either. Royal, a contemporary of Villepin at the prestigious ENA, had been minister for the environment, then education and finally family and children's affairs. Bayrou was a former minister of education and had been president of his centrist party for nine years. These people were hardly political newcomers, so why the insistence on the clean break: *la rupture*? Why did Sarkozy and Royal both imply that they were also standing against their own parties?

They were responding to a widespread awareness that the context of politics had changed, a sense that no government, whether of the right or of the left, had full control of the national economy in this new age of globalization, with its mergers and outsourcings. There was a related recognition that, if France enjoyed the benefits of membership of the European Union, it was also bound by its constraints. And the novelty that Ségolène Royal's power base was the presidency of the Poitou-Charente region was symptomatic of the fact that decentralization had begun to drain away power from the central State. In this situation, the historic differences between right and left seemed less important, especially since the two sides had been drawn closer in their rather desperate attempts to solve the same basic problems – Sarkozy's non-ideological stance and Royal's new emphasis on participative rather than on parliamentary democracy were evidence of that. Furthermore, the new five-year constitutional arrangement for both president and parliament ensured the personalization of power in the hands of the president. All of this led to a situation in which the voter was inclined to vote not so much for the party as for the person. And both Sarkozy and Royal, each of whom had a professional publicity team, were very much aware of it.

For, while the French had scoffed at the personalization of politics and the charismatic image-making of figures such as Clinton, Blair or Berlusconi, they now found themselves hit by a wave of glossy so-called 'people' magazines – *people* or *pipol* being the new word for celebrity – with come-on titles such as *Closer*, *Gala*, *Public* and *Voici*. The resulting *pipolisation* of politics turned the election into something approaching a showbiz soap opera in which there was little about the personal lives of 'Ségo' and 'Sarko' that we did not know. We knew that Royal's feminism was aroused by an estranged autocratic father, whom she had actually sued at one point. We knew about the tensions between her and François Hollande and how his affair was leading to a separation. We knew about the sexist opposition she sensed among her Socialist colleagues, but also about how attractive and telegenic she looked, either in the trademark white suit which led some to think of her as a virginal Madonna, or in the turquoise bikini in which she was snapped surreptitiously, but decided to allow to be published. Of course all this chimed with the twenty-four-hour multi-channel world, but she seemed as much victim as beneficiary of this exposure.

And that was even truer in the case of Sarkozy, who was seen radiant with his wife Cécilia, desolate when she left him, radiant when she returned, desolate when she left again, radiant with Carla Bruni. There was nothing we did not know about Sarkozy. We knew from the playwright Yasmina Reza, who went with him on campaign, that he had a hang-up about being short, that as a jogger and cyclist he never touched alcohol but did smoke cigars, that he adored sweets and chocolates, that he saw himself as a right-winger but no conservative, that he had lowbrow tastes and that he believed that love was all that mattered.[3] We knew from a second account that he saw himself as 'shaped by the humiliations of his childhood', since his philandering Hungarian aristocrat of a father abandoned the family when Sarkozy was four, diminishing the social status of his much-loved mother.[4] And we knew from a third account of his driving resentment against Chirac and the grandees of Gaullism:

... they have never accepted me as the candidate. I haven't the right face, the right education or the right style. I'm an outsider and they will never accept me. But I should thank them for the favour they have done me, for it is precisely because I'm an outsider that I will pulverize them.[5]

But this outsider was president of the Gaullist party and his witnesses for his first marriage were members of two of the richest industrial families in France. The emphasis on the private was everywhere obscuring the political.

Neither Sarkozy nor Royal was entirely convincing as a candidate. Royal appealed directly through her website to the mass membership and to the public at large. Her call for direct democracy, combined with broad concepts

such as motherhood, the family and the nation, made her seem
an attractively different kind of politician. But the traditional
left tended to see her campaign as populist and even as a
marketing operation based on opinion polls – her real 'clean
break', it was said coldly by Emmanuel Todd, was 'with the
socialist tradition of ideological discussion'.[6] It is fair to say,
however, that the divided party's own line was not so clear as
to be helpful to her. Never strong on economic issues in any
event, she found herself arguing for a better society while
offering no plausible means of achieving it. She also misjudged
a key television debate when, in trying to unsettle Sarkozy,
she succeeded only in appearing both garrulous and peremp-
tory.

Sarkozy, of course, had the problem of making a 'clean
break' with himself as a government member and, in trying to
appear to be above politics, with the UMP of which he was
president. And there were other contradictions, as when he
declared himself an economic liberal and an admirer of the US
and Blair's Britain, but also expressed protectionist views on
industry and agriculture. Yet for all the showiness, the bling
and the tendency to act as a one-man-show, Sarkozy showed
himself to be a highly intelligent, experienced and well-
intentioned politician. And he won comfortably by 53 per
cent to 47 per cent for straightforward reasons. He was the
better prepared, he was the shrewder tactician and he seemed
more urgently aware of the national crisis. Above all, he
looked like a man who knew about power – and had no
inhibitions about exercising it.

While he duly appointed the faithful François Fillon to the
much reduced post of prime minister, Sarkozy immediately
set the stamp on his presidency by surrounding him with a
rainbow cabinet including non-Gaulllist centrists, a female
minister of justice in the person of Rachida Dati, of North
African extraction, and several Socialists, including Bernard
Kouchner, the founder of Médecins sans Frontières, who

became foreign minister. The Socialists were not amused, and even less so when Sarkozy continued the practice by appointing the writer Frédéric Mitterrand, nephew of the former president, as minister of culture in 2009. But this was more than an attempt to emasculate the main opposition party – tactically useful though it obviously was – for this new Bonapartist president did not really believe in parties.

'If I didn't exist, they would have to invent me', Sarkozy told Yasmina Reza.[7] And indeed, by presenting himself as the no-nonsense pragmatist unburdened by ideology and ready to stop the rot, he fitted neatly enough into a national situation where there was confusion and discouragement to left and right. But those with no formal ideology have an implicit ideology and it is interesting that Chirac should have criticized him not only for being 'too neo-liberal and pro-American' but for being 'too multiculturalist'.[8]

For Sarkozy's earlier harsh comments about immigrants, or even his much noted attack on the wearing of the burka in 2009, do not make him an earnest republican secularist. On the contrary, in *La République, les religions, l'espérance* (*The Republic, Religions and Hope*), he speaks of the inadequacy of post-Enlightenment thought and, as though unaware of the republican social model, asks 'if the French Church does not care for the poor, who will?'[9] In a speech in Rome in December 2007, he invoked France's 'Christian roots' and called for a 'positive secularism' rather than a 'tired, fanatical one', while in Saudi Arabia a few weeks later he praised Islam and spoke of the 'transcendent God present in the mind and heart of all people, who is a rampart against the folly of men'. It was as though, while not himself pious, he regarded religion as a cultural fact, thought one religion as good as another, and was prepared to accommodate Islam in France so long as it respected local practice.

All this, as the prominent academic Sami Naïr argues, represented 'a break with the whole of French republican culture and the idea of the nation'.[10] It was indeed a break with

Gaullism which, in its aspiration to *grandeur*, saw itself optimistically, like the left, as a developing historical project. But Sarkozy's hectic activism sprang, ironically, not simply from a private need to prove himself to those who had disparaged him, but from the sort of philosophical pessimism often associated with the radical right. Neo-liberal and pro-American, as Chirac had perceived, he moved towards the 'Anglo-Saxon' model in search of economic solutions and, like a new-broom company executive, took ideas from left or right with no regard for political labelling. He virtually dismantled the thirty-five-hour week, gave tax reliefs to the workers but also gave the wealthy a large reduction in inheritance tax, and then offset this slightly with a tax on dividends to help those on low income. He attempted to cut the deficit by starting a programme of staff reductions in education, the courts and the army. He continued the programme of aligning the privileged special pension schemes for transport workers with those in the private sector, and introduced the requirement for a minimum service on transport and in schools during strikes. The unions protested, but he bought them off with pay rises and they received little public support – especially since Sarkozy, while bold in his proclamation of a reform, was actually quite flexible in its implementation.

Yet that was only part of a whole battery of innovations, introduced at startling, sometimes excessive speed. He tidied up the Constitution, to give some more formal rights to the Assembly, to confine presidents to two five-year terms, to limit their traditional right to nominate to official positions and grant amnesty – and, in effect, to rationalize and stabilize his own approach as president. He introduced selection criteria into immigration, restricting admission to those with economically useful occupations and expelling 25,000 illegal immigrants each year. He organized an elaborate conference which led to an ambitious action plan on the environment. His justice minister, Rachida Dati, drove through his promised reforms of closing a number of courts deemed to be surplus to requirements and bringing in minimum sentences for repeat offenders, but unfortunately – given her symbolic importance as an ethnic minority minister – she offended advisers and magistrates by her authoritarian manner and had to be eased off to the European Parliament in 2009.

Nor, predictably, was the passage of reforms in education an easy affair. The minister of education, Xavier Darcos, had to deal with opposition to his plan to prioritize literacy and numeracy in primary schools and, similarly, to reorganize the curriculum around basic subjects in the *lycées*. And the minister for higher education, Valérie Pécresse, whose brief was to grant independence to universities, create special centres of excellence and revise conditions for lecturing research fellows, had a prolonged struggle with students and some lecturers who regarded this as introducing capitalist competition. It should be said that her task was not eased by some scornful comments from Sarkozy, whose tastes did not run to classical literature, about *La Princesse de Clèves*, France's first psychological novel. Inevitably, this increased sales of the novel, led to public readings from it outside the Panthéon, and had students walking around with badges proclaiming their dedication to the chaste Princesse de Clèves when they were on strike for five months in the early part of 2009. Sarkozy's undiplomatic directness, shocking to some but refreshing to others, did embarrass his ministers from time to time.

On the international front, he was equally capable of ruffling feathers – German, Chinese, British, you-name-it – but there was no doubting his drive and effectiveness. No sooner was he in office than he was negotiating with rebels in Columbia for the release of the politician Ingrid Betancourt, or striking a deal with Libya for the extradition of Bulgarian nurses – and the purchase of French nuclear power stations. He also visited London and Washington, to emphasize that the old Gaullist quarrel with the 'Anglo-Saxons' was over.

And he put France and Europe firmly at the centre of
events with a tremendous display of energy as rotating
president of the European Union (EU) in the second half of
2008, when the EU had to respond to a whole series of crises
including the Irish rejection of the Lisbon Treaty, Russia's
invasion of Georgia and, above all, the global banking and
economic crisis. He intervened personally to secure a ceasefire
in the conflict between Russia and Georgia, he helped to
finesse a second Irish vote with a view to saving the Treaty
and, along with the British prime minister Gordon Brown, he
persuaded the EU's member countries to act together to
refloat their banks – even if there remained basic differences
between them on the running of the economy.

Sarkozy, as he said, loved that job, and found it a revelation.
While he viewed Europe as an alliance of nation states rather
than in federal terms, he had seen the possibility of making it
a much stronger political force in the world. However, he had
had another, chastening revelation. For he found his original
neo-liberal assumptions dented by the shattering implosion of
the global financial system and its damaging social and
political effects in Europe and across the world. France was
fortunate to some extent in that its economy was not so
export-oriented as that of Germany or so dependent on
complex financial engineering as that of the US or the UK.
But it soon had its own illustration of the workings of what
now seemed to be a global casino with the case of Jérôme
Kerviel, a young trader who – to practise his skills rather than
to achieve any personal gain – lost the Société Générale 5
billion euros by reportedly gambling more than the entire
market value of the bank. Before the combined Assembly and
Senate at Versailles in June 2009, Sarkozy declared grimly that
the Anglo-American financial system he had admired was a
'dead end' and that 'the crisis had put the French model back
into fashion'. 'Nothing' he told them starkly, 'will ever be the
same again'.

*   *   *

This was a turning point which changed the whole political landscape for Sarkozy, now that his radical reformist project seemed to have been invalidated by events. As the banking crisis developed into a worldwide recession he found himself driven back to the basic problem with which his predecessors, Gaullist or Socialist, had struggled for decades – that of maintaining the French republican model while yet adapting the economy to meet the challenges of a globalized world. And he had to do so not only in less favourable circumstances but in the face of increasing national disillusionment and scepticism from both left and right. So he perhaps sounded more like Chirac than Sarkozy when he reverted to the standard republican rhetoric in his New Year address to the nation for 2010. For he not only praised the social model, but he also invoked the 'French exception' when he declared: 'the ideas put forward by France will mark the search for a new world order: more balance, more regulation, more justice and peace. These ideas impose upon us a responsibility to set the example.'

And in his usual spectacular fashion he did try, notably at the EU summit on the Eurozone's sovereign debt crisis in the following March, to place France's stamp on attempts to reform the system. Loudly attacking the role of credit rating agencies, bonuses and hedge funds, he argued strongly for a new pan-European system of regulation. He also, of course, with his finance minister Christine Lagarde, had to tackle France's own problems. So it was announced that the budget deficit of 8 per cent of gross domestic product would be reduced to 3 per cent by 2013, although this was simply to meet the standard Eurozone rule to which France had previously paid little attention and it was not clear how it would be achieved. In June, since longer life spans were pressing on pensions costs, a plan was put forward to eliminate the shortfall, partly by gradually raising the legal retirement age from sixty to sixty-two and partly through extra taxes. While this was strongly opposed by the Socialists and the unions, the French budget cuts were markedly less severe than those of Germany, Britain and some other EU countries. One reason was that the French were concerned that the sudden application of unduly harsh austerity measures might actually prolong the recession. The other reason, obviously, given the inevitable opposition to these plans, was political expediency.

Having abandoned his neo-liberal stance Sarkozy, with an eye to the next presidential election coming up in 2012, had to tack to right and left more carefully than before. This was especially so since his hyperactive approach, now that like other political leaders he had been diminished by the sheer scale of this global crisis, had become less credible. Nor did he possess the gravitas of the reassuring father figure who could authoritatively persuade the nation of the necessity of taking painful measures. And he had made political mistakes. He was accused of nepotism when he tried to push the candidature of his son Jean, a local councillor but a second-year law student aged twenty-three, for the chairman-ship of the public body running La Défense, France's prime business centre and one of the largest in Europe. He also caused a furore by appearing to intervene for his own political advantage in the sale of the famously independent newspaper *Le Monde*. Again, he raised a hornet's nest when he launched a 'great debate' on France's national identity. Since this coincided with the campaign against the wearing of the burka, it predictably revived anti-Islamic feelings, turned the exercise into an often sour debate on immigration – and inevitably created suspicion as to Sarkozy's motives.

Although he had previously successfully united the right at national level under a single umbrella, there were some mutterings in the UMP following its heavy defeat in the regional council elections in March 2010. Not only had the centre-left coalition won in all twenty-two mainland regions with the exception of Conservative Alsace, but the Front National was back with 7 per cent of the vote. Naturally enough, the Socialist leader Martine Aubry – the daughter of the former president of the European Commission, Jacques Delors – saw this victory as a repudiation of the government and as a launch pad for the left's return to presidential power in 2012. And then there was Villepin. Sarkozy's personal involvement as plaintiff in the Clearstream affair had kept his high office embroiled in legal controversy even beyond the four months of the trial – at which, if lesser figures were found guilty, Villepin was cleared for want of evidence. Since the public prosecutor had launched a more or less automatic appeal, the gossip about the feud would linger for the rest of Sarkozy's term as president, especially since Villepin – who would set up a rival grouping, République Solidaire, in the summer of 2010 – was bent on revenge.

While the victory of the left alliance, the Gauche Solidaire, was striking, there does tend to be a disjunction between national and regional politics in France, since the issues involved are different and it is easier to form electoral alliances at the local level. Also, while the turnout was low, this did not mean that disenchanted conservative voters would desert Sarkozy in the presidential election in 2012. Nor did it imply that they would turn to Villepin, though he might siphon off some of the more purist Gaullist support. Again, it was difficult to achieve unity and coherence in a new left alliance which brought together the Socialists, a grouping of Green and other ecological groups under the heading of Europe Écologie, and a smaller Front de Gauche consisting of various far left groups. There was as yet no very clear programme for achieving, in the face of such economic difficulties, the 'radical transformation of society' promised.

While a poll suggested that Martine Aubry might defeat him in a presidential election, Sarkozy still had the benefit of office and could project himself advantageously when he hosted the G20 summit in November 2010. However, it might be a different matter if the former Socialist minister Dominique Strauss-Kahn, now head of the International

Monetary Fund, were to stand. Also, damaging stories of government extravagance were emerging, with one minister costing the taxpayer a sizeable fortune for cigars. More serious, there was the colourful affair of the L'Oréal cosmetics empire, a family drama involving accusations of tax evasion and illicit political funding which cast doubt on the Labour minister Éric Woerth, just when he was trying to push through the unpopular pensions reform, and even on Sarkozy himself.

So as France advanced into the second decade of the twenty-first century, the immediate economic outlook was daunting – so much so that external pressures might dictate the policy of a government of any complexion – and the political prospects uncertain.

What then are the longer-term prospects for France? In a world where the globalization of information and entertainment makes it difficult for any country to retain its cultural identity? Where the globalization of the economy suggests that the major agents are often giant international companies rather than nations? Where countries under these pressures are necessarily tied into international arrangements or organizations? Where only collective action can solve the looming problems arising from global warming? Where the principle of economic growth is itself being called into question?

In these circumstances the fortunes of France, as of other countries, will be heavily dependent on whatever international agreements and controls may be forged to meet the larger challenges of the years ahead. It may be increasingly unrealistic for individual countries such as France or Britain to attempt to project power on a global basis. It seems over-ambitious, for example, for each of these countries to operate at great expense a nuclear submarine fleet, as indeed the recent preliminary talks on defence cooperation recognized. However, the Eurozone crisis has thrown doubt on the

European project, brought out latent conflicts of interest and slackened the important bond between France and an increasingly self-assertive Germany. And it was striking, once the European Treaty had finally been ratified, to observe Sarkozy and German Chancellor Angela Merkel manoeuvring to ensure that they each got one of the 'real' jobs for their country, leaving the two nominally top European posts to go to relatively minor figures. This persistent competitive nationalism within a jigsaw European Union may no longer be in tune with the larger political realities, for it was painfully obvious that, in the world climate talks in Copenhagen in December 2009, Europe itself – even though it was hosting the talks – was brushed aside while the deal was made between the US, China, India and Brazil.

Meanwhile, it is clear that the famous *morosité* from which the French were suffering stemmed from doubt about the viability of their economic and social model, a measure of the uncertainty being the disconnection between the activity of French companies, which happily embraced globalization, and the protectionist tone of the political rhetoric on both right and left. It seemed to many since the end of the Cold War that the deregulated free market system of the most obviously comparable country, Britain, was more successful. But the credit crunch encouraged French commentators, in their turn, to criticize Britain's over-dependence on financial engineering, its high levels of debt, its poor pensions and what Jacques Monin saw as its tendency to reduce everything to monetary value.[11] The fact, of course, is that each country had been facing the same basic problem of trying to balance the economy, and that each approach had advantages and disadvantages, with the British system offering more jobs and commercial opportunities in the expansionist phase and the French offering greater protection in the downturn. The problem for each is doubtless now to find a realistic middle way.

The merits of the French model hardly need restating. Its State-directed long-term strategic planning approach has endowed it with an enviable infrastructure, as well as with a leading role in nuclear energy and related industrial fields. With an excellent health and benefits system, and with less inequality than in Britain, it is a more cohesive society. But there has been a price to pay for this large public sector. In 2007, the last year before the recession changed the game, public spending represented 52 per cent of gross domestic product, as opposed to 45 per cent in Britain. As a result, the tax burden was one of the highest in Europe and the annual rate of growth – at 2.2 per cent as opposed to Britain's 3.1 per cent – was below the OECD average. Since the burden on business of high social security contributions deterred companies from taking on permanent staff – and since the top-down dirigiste approach tended to leave less room for start-ups – there was a clear connection between the size of the public sector and unemployment. Politically this was particularly damaging, not only because it caused 20 per cent unemployment in the under-twenty-six age group, but because so many of those involved were from the ethnic minorities – and were in effect outside the social model. While the problem of the outsourcing of jobs might call for agreements at European level, there appears to be no reason in principle why France could not preserve its social model within an open trading world through a trade-off between taxation and unemployment. It is not politically sustainable in the medium term to have a social model that protects the majority against the minority.

A greater challenge for the French may be to retain their cultural identity. They themselves have not been slow over the past twenty years to speak of the decline of their culture. Why, they ask, does France no longer have writers of the stature of Sartre or Camus, or thinkers to compare with Foucault or Lévi-Strauss? It is true that the reputation of post-modernists such as Jacques Lacan, Julia Kristeva or Jean Baudrillard has been dented, notably because of the tendency to frame their work rather portentously in ill-understood concepts from the natural sciences.[12] Nevertheless, France did produce an extraordinary collection of influential philosophers, sociologists and literary theorists in the decades up to the 1980s, and it is understandable that the French should look back to that time as the heyday.

However, it is rather beside the point to blame television for transforming intellectuals such as Bernard-Henri Lévy into all-purpose public commentators 'elevated into the conscience of our time' as one attempt to 'psychoanalyse' France puts it.[13] For the fact is that the national and global contexts have changed. The work of those writers and thinkers corresponded to a particular historical moment. Sartre and Camus lived through the Second World War, the Occupation and the great ideological cleavage of the Cold War – if Sartre attempted to synthesize existentialism and Marxism, it is because it seemed urgent at the time. Also, the centralization of intellectual life in Paris created a critical mass of work which in rapid succession produced a dialectical sequence of intellectual orthodoxies from Marxism, through structuralism and post-structuralism, to postmodernism. But with the change in the historical situation, and the opening up of French intellectual life to outside influences, the debates have moved on.

The real challenge to France's cultural identity is rather the threat of domination by English as the world language. For, as the French have been aware since the Marshall Plan, this comes with the whole economic and cultural baggage that they tend to call 'Americanization'. Their language may be so corrupted as to turn into the linguistic porridge of *franglais*. Their firms may have board meetings in English. Their films may be sidelined even in their own country if the distribution networks are owned by international chains. Their television screens may be filled with dubbed American programmes and with McDonald's invading their boulevards and Disney setting up its elaborate Disneyland – described by the theatre director Ariane Mnouchkine as a 'cultural Chernobyl' – they may feel that their national identity is under threat. For a country which also sees itself as being a 'cultural exception', in the sense that its culture aspires to have a universal rather than a merely local resonance, that presents a formidable challenge, especially since films, TV programmes, music and the internet represent an increasingly important dimension of the international economy.

Fortunately, France has fought successfully to ensure that cultural products are not seen as mere commodities. While there is now general acceptance of the need to protect cultural diversity since the UNESCO agreement of 2005, it was France which from 1993 onwards led the battle against strong American opposition to achieve this, at the negotiations of the General Agreement on Tariffs and Trade and the World Trade Organization. It can therefore protect the space for home production in various ways. It imposes quotas of French music on radio channels to prevent its singers – some of whom have had to build their careers by singing in English – from being drowned out by English-language performers. It supports French cinema by requiring major TV companies to show at least 50 per cent French films, and it also requires them to contribute a percentage of their turnover to the financing of such films. As part of its support for literature, it helps small publishers and booksellers by imposing uniform pricing to prevent discounting. What with this, its France 24 world television service and its own programme for digitizing books – though it has now yielded control to Google – France has largely held its own. And it has done so without becoming parochial or chauvinist in its cultural attitudes. On the contrary, it is far more open to the whole range of international writing and cinema than either Britain or America.

It may no longer be quite the case that, as Thomas Jefferson said, 'each man has two countries, his own and France', but one might almost think that it is, to judge by the visitors who flock to France each year – almost 80 million, making it the first tourist destination on the planet. They go for the food and the wine and the glimpse of a different lifestyle, but the millions who throng Versailles or Chartres or the Conciergerie also recognize that this is a country which has had a central role in the defining conflicts of European civilization. And, as a nuclear power with a seat on the United Nations Security Council, a highly advanced economy ranked fifth in the world and a commercial and cultural presence worldwide, this resilient country still has a role to play. However, France will doubtless have to change as the world changes. As the Copenhagen climate change negotiations rather brutally underlined, there are now major political forces rising in the world which will begin to dwarf the power and influence of the single European state. Surprisingly perhaps, Sarkozy's insight into the potential power of a more closely organized Europe, when he was briefly rotating president of the European Union, might even hint at a new direction. If so, it would be the final victory of Jean Monnet over Gaullism.

NOTES AND REFERENCES

Chapter 1. Cro-Magnon Man, Roman Gaul and the Feudal Kingdom

1. André Leroi-Gourhan, *The Dawn of European Art* (Cambridge: Cambridge University Press, 1982), p. 75.
2. R. Dale Guthrie, *The Nature of Paleolithic Art* (Chicago, IL, and London: Chicago University Press, 2005), p. 270.
3. For the conflicting presentations of Vercingétorix, see Paul M. Martin, *Vercingétorix* (Paris: Perrin, 2000) and Christian Goudineau, *Le Dossier Vercingétorix* (Arles: Actes Sud/Errance, 2001).
4. Manuel Armand, 'Des archéologues révèlent une veritable métropole arverne', *Le Monde*, 29 August 2007.
5. Julius Caesar, *The Gallic War and the Civil War* (trans. John Warrington) (London: Heron Books, 1969), p. 201.
6. Edward James, *The Origins of France: From Clovis to the Capetians, 500–1000* (London: Macmillan, 1982), p. 139.
7. Voltaire, *Essai sur l'histoire générale et sur les moeurs et l'esprit des nations* (ed. R. Pomeau) (Paris: Garnier, 1963), Vol. 1, p. 685.

Chapter 2. A Nation Born in Blood

1. Aliénor features notably in Shakespeare's *King John*, in Jean Anouilh's play *Becket* and in the film *The Lion in Winter*, with Katharine Hepburn and Peter O'Toole, from the play by James Goldman.
2. Father of Simon de Montfort, Earl of Leicester, who led the baronial revolt against Henry III of England.

3. Peter de Rosa, *Vicars of Christ* (London: Transworld, 1988), p. 165.
4. Notably Ronald Millar's play *Héloïse and Abelard* (1970), based on Helen Waddell's novel *Peter Abelard* (1933).
5. Richard A. Newhall (ed.), *The Chronicle of Jean de Venette* (trans. Jean Birdsall) (New York: Columbia University Press, 1953), pp. 48–9.
6. Colette Beaune, *Jeanne d'Arc* (Paris: Perrin, 2004), p.10.
7. Norbert Elias, *The Civilising Process: State Formation and Civilisation* (trans. Edmund Jephcott) (Oxford: Blackwell, 1982), p. 44. See also pp. 8–12 and 117–61.

Chapter 3. Renaissance, Reformation and the Wars of Religion

1. Among others Victor Hugo in *Le Roi s'amuse*, which inspired Verdi's opera *Rigoletto*, and a succession of French films featuring such well-known actors as Sacha Guitry and Jean Marais.
2. Joachim du Bellay, first line of 'Invocation à la France', in *Les Regrets*.
3. For an account of this long-running controversy see R. J. Knecht, *Catherine de' Medici* (London and New York: Longman, 1998), especially pp. xi–xiv and 163–5.
4. Lucien Febvre, *Le Problème de l'incroyance au 16e siècle: la religion de Rabelais* (Paris: Albin Michel, 1942), p. 212 and the section on 'Les limites de l'incroyance au XVIe siècle', pp. 361 ff.
5. François Rabelais, *Gargantua* (Pantagruel, Paris: Arléa, 1999), p. 57.
6. Michel de Montaigne, *Les Essais* (Paris: Arléa, 1992), pp. 67, 157.

Chapter 4. The Grand Century of the Sun King

1. Cardinal de Retz (Paul de Gondi), *Mémoires* (ed. G. Montgrédien) (Paris, Garnier, 1935), Vol. I, p. 49.
2. Ibid., p. 87.
3. Jean-Christian Petitfils, *Louis XIV* (Paris: Perrin, 1995), pp. 434–7.
4. Comtesse de Boigne, *Mémoires* (Paris: Mercure de France, 1971), Vol. I, p. 37.
5. *Ridicule* (1996), directed by Patrice Leconte, with Charles Berling, Jean Rochefort and Fanny Ardant.
6. Jean-Marie Apostolidès, in *Le Roi-machine: spectacle et politique au temps de Louis XIV* (Paris: Editions de Minuit, 1981).
7. Peter Burke, *The Fabrication of Louis XIV* (New Haven, CT: Yale University Press, 1992), p. 13.
8. Louis XIV, *Mémoires* (Paris: Tallandier, 1978), p. 42.
9. Ibid., pp. 111, 203.

Chapter 5. The Enlightenment and the Fall of the Monarchy

1. Madame de Maintenon, *L'Allée du Roi: souvenirs de Françoise d'Aubigné, Marquise de Maintenon* (arranged by Françoise Chandemagor) (Paris: Juilliard, 1981).

2. Madame de Pompadour has been played on film by a range of stars from Lillian Gish in 1927 onwards, as well as inspiring a German operetta, the shape of the standard champagne glass and a Californian wine. Biographies include those of Evelyne Lever (Paris: Perrin, 2000) and Nancy Mitford (New York: Random House, 1953).

3. Michel Foucault, *Surveiller et punir: naissance de la prison* (Paris: Gallimard, 1975), pp. 9–11.

4. Voltaire, *Candide* (Paris: Bordas, 1969), p. 147.

5. Of the various English-language studies of French and British views of each other, the fullest is that of Robert and Isabelle Tombs: *That Sweet Enemy* (London: Heinemann, 2006).

6. Madame Campan, *Mémoires sur la vie de Marie-Antoinette* (Paris: Nelson, nd; reprint of original 1823 edn), pp.57–8.

7. Louis de Saint-Just, speech to the National Convention of 3 March, 1794, in *Oeuvres complètes* (Paris: Lebovici, 1984), p. 715.

8. Bertrand Russell, *History of Western Philosophy* (London: Allen & Unwin, 1946), p. 723.

9. In Jean-Pierre Poirier, *Turgot: Laissez-faire et progrès social* (Paris: Perrin, 1999), p. 343.

10. Louis XVI, *Journal* (ed. Louis Nicolardot) (Paris: Dentu, 1873), p. 136.

Chapter 6. From the Revolution to Napoleon

1. Georges Lefebvre, *La Révolution française* (Paris: Presses Universitaires de France, 1951); Albert Soboul, *La Civilisation de la Révolution française*, 3 vols (Paris: Arthaud, 1970–1983).

2. François Furet, *Penser la Révolution française* (Paris: Gallimard, 1978).

3. Jacques Godechot, *Les Révolutions (1770–1799)* (Paris: Presses Universitaires de France, 1963).

4. Ibid., see especially pp. 371–3.

5. Dominique Godineau, *Citoyennes tricoteuses: les femmes du peuple à Paris pendant la Révolution française* (Aix-en-Provence: Alinéa, 1988).

6. See Bailey Stone, *Reinterpreting the French Revolution* (Cambridge: Cambridge University Press, 2002).

7. In J. M. Thompson, *English Witnesses of the French Revolution* (Oxford: Blackwell, 1938), p. 231.

8. This was the first occasion on which an observation balloon – on the French side – was used in a battle.

9. Theda Stocpol, *States and Social Revolutions: a Comparative Analysis of France, Russia and China* (Cambridge: Cambridge University Press, 1979).

10. Georges Lefebvre, *Napoléon* (Paris: Presses Universitaires de France, 6th edn, 1969), p. 583.

11. Martyn Lyons, *Napoleon Bonaparte and the Legacy of the French Revolution* (London: Macmillan, 1994), p. 298.

Chapter 7. Revolutionary Aftershocks and Another Napoleon

1. Arnold Hauser, *The Social History of Art, III: Rococo, Classicism and Romanticism* (London and New York: Routledge, 1999), p. 155; Jacques Barzun, *Classic, Romantic and Modern* (Chicago, IL: University of Chicago Press, Phoenix edn, 1975), p. 14.
2. Frank E. Manuel and Fritzie P. Manuel, *Utopian Thought in the Western World* (Oxford: Blackwell, 1979), p. 588.
3. Karl Marx, 'The Revolution in Germany', from *Neue Rheinische Zeitung* in David McLellan (ed.), *Karl Marx: Selected Writings* (Oxford: Oxford University Press, 1977), p. 273.
4. Jean Sagnes, *Napoléon III: le parcours d'un saint-simonien* (Sète: Éditions Singulières, 2008), p. 541.
5. Éric Anceau, *Napoléon III* (Paris: Tallandier, 2008).
6. See Roger Price, *The French Second Empire: an Anatomy of Political Power* (Cambridge: Cambridge University Press, 2001), pp. 250 ff.

Chapter 8. The Third Republic: *Semaine Sanglante* to the First World War

1. In Eugene Schulkind, *The Paris Commune of 1871: the View from the Left* (London: Jonathan Cape, 1972), p. 27.
2. Jacques Rougerie, *La Commune* (Paris: Presses Universitaires de France, 1988), pp. 118–20.
3. See Colette E. Wilson, *Paris and the Commune 1871–78: the Problem of Forgetting* (Manchester: Manchester University Press, 2007), pp. 208–10.
4. Karl Marx, 'The Civil War in France', p. 307; Friedrich Engels, 'Introduction' to same, p. 259, both in Marx and Engels, *Selected Works* (London: Lawrence and Wishart, 1968).
5. Robert Tombs, *The Paris Commune, 1871* (London: Longman, 1999), p. 215.
6. Bernard Dorival, *Les Étapes de la peinture française contemporaine*, Vol. 1 (Paris: Gallimard, 1948), pp. 22 ff.
7. T. J. Clark, *The Painting of Modern Life: Paris in the Art of Manet and his Followers* (London: Thames and Hudson, 1984), p. 267.
8. In the review '*Évolution* of 1931', reproduced by Jean-Baptiste Duroselle, in *La France et les Français 1900–1914* (Paris: Éditions Richelieu, 1972), pp. 34–40.
9. Jean-Jacques Becker, *Les Français dans la Grande Guerre* (Paris: Éditions Laffont, 1980), p. 305.

Chapter 9. 1919–1940: Defeat Out of Victory

1. John Maynard Keynes, *The Economic Consequences of the Peace* (Introduction David Felix) (New Brunswick, NJ, and London: Translation Publishers, 2003), p. 37.

2. Jacques Bainville, *Les Conséquences politiques de la paix* (Paris: Éditions de l'Arsenal, 1995), pp. 21–2

3. Pierre Renouvin, *Le Traité de Versailles* (Paris: Flammarion, 1969), p. 117.

4. Paul Valéry, 'La Crise de l'esprit', in *Variété*, I (Paris: Éditions de la Nouvelle Revue Française, 1924), pp.11–12.

5. André Malraux, *La Tentation de l'Occident* (Paris: Grasset, 1927), p. 29.

6. André Breton, *Les Manifestes du Surréalisme* (Paris: Sagittaire, 1946), p. 72.

7. Gilles Morin and Gilles Richard (eds), *Les Deux France du Front Populaire* (Paris: L'Harmattan, 2008), p. 4.

8. Stéphane Sirot, 'La vague de grèves du front populaire: des interprétations, divergentes et uncertaines', in Morin and Richard, *Les Deux France du Front Populaire*, p. 57.

9. Jean Brunet, *Histoire du Front Populaire* (Paris: Presses Universitaires de France, 1991), p. 122.

Chapter 10. The Second World War: Collaboration and Resistance

1. Jean-Paul Sartre, 'La République du silence', in *Situations III* (Paris: Gallimard, 1949), p. 11.

2. André Figueras, *Philippe Pétain, devant l'histoire et la patrie* (Paris: Éditions de l'Orme Rond, 1985), p. 86.

3. Rod Kedward, *La Vie en bleu: France and the French since 1900* (London: Penguin, 2005), p. 252.

4. Charles de Gaulle, *Mémoires* (Paris: Gallimard, La Pléiade, 2000), p. 71.

5. Jean Lacouture, *De Gaulle* (Paris: Éditions du Seuil, 1969), p. 89.

6. Another member of the network, René Hardy, captured at the same time but released, was twice tried and cleared on the charge of having betrayed Moulin. The controversy about the circumstances of his death has continued to the present time.

7. See Philippe Burrin, *La France à l'heure allemande: 1940–1944* (Paris: Éditions du Seuil, 1995), p. 470.

8. Robert O. Paxton, *Vichy France, Old Guard and New Order, 1940–1944* (New York: Columbia University Press, 2001; 1972 text with new Introduction), p. xxix.

9. Laurent Joly, *Vichy dans la 'Solution finale': histoire du Commissariat Général aux Questions Juives* (Paris: Grasset, 2006), p. 848.

10. André Malraux, *Les Chênes qu'on abat* (Paris: Gallimard, 1971), p. 236.

Chapter 11. The Fourth Republic in Cold War and Colonial Crisis

1. See Stéphane Sirot, *Maurice Thorez* (Paris: Presse de la Fondation Nationale des Sciences Politiques, 2000), p. 40.

2. Annie Kriegel, *Les Communistes français: 1920–1970* (Paris: Éditions du Seuil, 3rd edn, 1985), p. 275.

3. Jean-Paul Sartre, *Questions de méthode* (Paris: Gallimard, 1960), p. 27.

4. Jean-Baptiste Duroselle, *Deux Types de grands hommes: le Général de Gaulle et Jean Monnet* (Geneva: Institut Universitaire de Hautes Études Internationales, 1977), p. 16.

5. François Duchêne, *Jean Monnet: the First Statesman of Interdependence* (New York: Norton, 1994), p. 148.

6. Gilles Férier, *Les Trois guerres d'Indochine* (Lyon: Presses Universitaires, 1993), p. 22.

7. In Eric Roussel, *Pierre Mendès-France* (Paris: Gallimard, 2007), p. 525.

8. In Michel Winock, *L'Agonie de la IVe République* (Paris, Gallimard: 2006), p. 90.

9. René Lefebvre, *Guy Mollet: le mal aimé* (Paris: Plon, 1992), p. 189.

10. *La Bataille d'Alger*, directed by Gillo Pontecorvo, winner of 'Best Film'at the 1966 Venice Film Festival, was originally banned in France but is now available.

11. See Raphaëlle Branche, *La Torture et l'armée, pendant la guerre d'Algérie: 1954–1962* (Paris: Gallimard, 2001).

Chapter 12. De Gaulle's Golden Decade Ends in Tragi-comedy

1. Charles de Gaulle, *Mémoires*, pp. 825–6.

2. Jean-François Revel, *Le Style du Général* (Paris: Éditions Complexe, 1988), p. 17.

3. Jean-Pierre Rioux, *La Guerre d'Algérie 1954–2004: la fin de l'amnésie* (Paris: Laffont, 2004), pp. 18–19.

4. François Duchêne, *Jean Monnet*, p. 361.

5. Jean Fourastié, *Les Trente glorieuses, ou la révolution invisible de 1946–75* (Paris: Fayard, 1979), p. 28.

6. Serge Berstein and Michel Winock, *La République recommence, de 1944 à nos jours* (Paris: Éditions du Seuil, 2004), p. 374.

7. Alain Peyrefitte, *C'était de Gaulle* (Paris: Gallimard, 2002), Vol. 1, p. 279.

8. Ibid, Vol. 3, p. 247.

9. Raymond Aron, *La Révolution introuvable* (Paris: Arthème Fayard, 1968), p. 141.

10. Éric Roussel, *Charles de Gaulle* (Paris: Gallimard, 2002), p. 877.

11. Maurice Agulhon, *De Gaulle: histoire, symbole, mythe* (Paris: Plon, 2000), p. 142.

Chapter 13. Mutations of the 'Republican Monarchy': Pompidou to Chirac

1. Georges Pompidou, *Le Noeud gordien* (Paris: Plon, 1974), pp. 58–68.
2. Olivier Todd, *La Marelle de Giscard, 1926–1974* (Paris: Laffont, 1977), p. 445.
3. Jean-Christian Petitfils, *La Démocratie giscardienne* (Paris: Presses Universitaires de France, 1981), p. 63.
4. Alain Duhamel, *La République giscardienne* (Paris: Grasset, 1980), p. 11.
5. Claude Cancès, *Histoire du 36 Quai des Orfèvres* (Paris: Éditions Jacob-Duvernet, 2010).
6. David S. Bell, *François Mitterrand: a Political Biography* (Cambridge: Polity, 2005), p. viii.
7. Pierre Joxe, *Pourquoi Mitterrand?* (Paris: Philippe Rey, 2006), p. 12.
8. Franz-Olivier Giesbert, *François Mitterrand* (Paris, Éditions du Seuil, 1996), p. 127.
9. Philippe Madelin, *Jacques Chirac: une biographie* (Paris: Flammarion, 2002), p. 800.
10. Franz-Olivier Giesbert, *François Mitterrand*, pp. 13–14, 18.
11. Philippe Madelin, *Jacques Chirac*, p. 775.
12. Jean-Marie Colombani and Hugues Portelli, *Le Double Septennat de François Mitterrand* (Paris: Grasset, 1995), pp. 20–1.

Chapter 14. The 'French Exception': Reality or Illusion?

1. Fernand Braudel, *L'Identité de la France* (Paris: Arthaud-Flammarion, 1986–7), Vol. 3, p. 423.
2. Sue Collard, 'The Elusive French Exception', in Emmanuel Godin and Tony Chafer (eds), *The French Exception* (New York and Oxford: Berghahn), p. 31.
3. François Furet, 'La France unie . . .', in François Furet, Jacques Julliard and Pierre Rosanvallon, *La République du centre: la fin de l'exception française* (Paris: Calmann-Lévy, 1988), pp. 54–5.
4. See Jean Chesneaux, 'La France, un pays comme les autres?', in Michel Wieviorka (ed.), *Peut-on encore chanter la douce France? Les Entretiens d'Auxerre* (La Tour d'Aigues: Aube, 2007), p. 82.
5. Nick Hewlett, 'France and Exceptionalism', in Godin and Chafer, *The French Exception*, p. 8.
6. See Marie-Claude Blais, *La Solidarité: histoire d'une idée* (Paris: Gallimard, 2007), p. 318.
7. Saïd Bouamama, *La France: autopsie d'un mythe national* (Paris: Larousse, 2008), pp. 10, 14–15, *et seq.*
8. Abigail Gregory and Ursula Tidd (eds), *Women in Contemporary France* (Oxford: Berg, 2000), p. 213.

9. Ben Clift, 'French Socialists, *Dirigisme* and the Troubled Europeanisation of Employment Policy', in Godin and Chafer, *The French Exception*, p. 110.

Chapter 15. France in the New Global Order

1. Serge Raffy, *La Guerre des trois* (Paris: Fayard, 2006), p. 20.
2. In Frédéric Charpier, *Nicolas Sarkozy: enquête sur un homme de pouvoir* (Paris: Presses de la Cité, 2007), p. 301.
3. Yasmina Reza, *L'Aube le soir ou la nuit* (Paris: Flammarion, 2007), especially pp. 38–40.
4. Catherine Nay, *Un Pouvoir nommé désir* (Paris: Grasset, 2007), pp. 35–42.
5. Michaël Darmon, *La Vraie nature de Nicolas Sarkozy* (Paris: Éditions du Seuil, 2007), pp. 230–1.
6. In Alexandre Kara, *Ségo, Sarko, qui choisir?* (Paris: l'Archipel, 2007), p. 62.
7. Yasmina Reza, *L'Aube le soir ou la nuit*, p. 144.
8. Catherine Nay, *Un Pouvoir nommé désir*, p. 461.
9. Nicolas Sarkozy, *La République, les religions, l'espérance* (Paris: Pocket, 2005), p. 29.
10. Sami Naïr, *Un Détournement: Nicolas Sarkozy et la 'politique de civilisation'* (Paris: Gallimard, 2008), p. 18.
11. Jacques Monin, *Le Naufrage britannique* (Paris: Table Ronde, 2009).
12. See especially Alan Sokal and Jean Bricmont, *Impostures intellectuelles* (Paris: Odile Jacob, 1997).
13. Thierry Wolton, *Brève Psychanalyse de la France* (Paris: Plon, 2004), p. 239.

SELECT BIBLIOGRAPHY

While the sources cited in the Notes and References are generally works in French, the bibliography is largely designed to meet the needs of the English-language reader and there is an emphasis on the more recent and accessible studies. Apart from general works, which are listed alphabetically, the bibliography follows the historical chronology.

French Sources

Specific aspects or historical figures
See the relevant titles at the appropriate point in the Notes and References.

General Histories

Duby, G. (ed.) *Histoire de la France*, 3 vols (Paris: Larousse, 1987).

Gallo, M. *L'Ame de la France*, 2 vols (Paris: J'ai lu, 2007).

Sirinelli, J.-F. *Dictionnaire de l'Histoire de France*, 2 vols (Paris: Armand Colin, 1999).

See also relevant titles in the major series Nouvelle Histoire de France (Éditions du Seuil), Collection 'U' (Armand Colin) and Nouvelle Clio (Presses Universitaires de France).

Period Histories

Bourdier, F. *Préhistoire de France* (Paris: Flammarion, 1967).

Roman, D. *Histoire de la Gaule* (Paris: Fayard, 1997).

Delort, R. *La Vie au Moyen Age* (Paris: Éditions du Seuil, 1982).

Favier, J. *Dictionnaire de la France médiévale* (Paris: Fayard, 1993).

Bély, L. (ed.) *Dictionnaire de l'Ancien Régime, XVIe–XVIIIe siècle* (Paris: Presses Universitaires de France, 1996; paperback 2002)

Muchembled, R. *Sociétés, cultures et mentalités dans la France moderne, XVIe–XVIIIe siècle* (Paris: Armand Colin, 2001).

Solnon, J.-F. *La Cour de France* (Paris: Fayard, 1987).

Furet, F. and Ozouf, M. (ed.) *Dictionnaire critique de la Révolution française* (Paris: Flammarion, 1988).

Lefebvre, G. *La Révolution française* (Paris: Presses Universitaires de France, 1951).

Demier, D. *La France du XIXe siècle*, (Paris: Éditions du Seuil, 2000).

Dupâquier, J. and Kessler, D. *La Société française au XIXe siècle* (Paris: Fayard, 1992).

Agulhon, M. *La République de Jules Ferry à François Mitterrand, 1880–1995* (Paris: Hachette, 1997).

Becker, J.-J. *Histoire politique de la France depuis 1945* (Paris: Armand Colin, 1998).

Rémond, R. *Le Siècle dernier de 1918 à 2002* (Paris: Fayard, 2003).

Sirinelli, J.-F. (ed.) *La France de 1914 à nos jours* (Paris: Presses Universitaires de France, 2004).

Selected French Websites

CLASSIC FRENCH AUTHORS: TEXTS, RECORDED READINGS, ETC.
In Libro Veritas: www.inlibroveritas.net (over 500 authors)
ABU universal library: abu.cnam.fr (over 100 authors)
Classic works in the social sciences: classiques.uqac.ca

ILLUSTRATED HISTORY AND ART
French history illustrated: www.histoire-image.org (very large collection)
Musée du Louvre: www.louvre.fr (virtual tours, etc.)

CURRENT POLITICS AND STATISTICS
Parliament, parties, etc.: www.francepolitique.free.fr
INSEE (National Institute of Statistics and Economic Studies): www.insee.fr

OTHERS – BY PERIOD

Cave paintings: www.culture.gouv.fr/culture/arcnat/lascaux/fr

Middle Ages: www.fordham.edu/halsall/sbook-francais.html

Renaissance: www.renaissance-france.org (illustrated readings)

Seventeenth century: www.17emesiecle.free.fr (texts, biographies, etc)

Eighteenth century: Voltaire: www.voltaire-integral.com (includes Diderot and Rousseau)

Revolutionary period: www.histoire-image.org (as above); also www.culture. gouv.fr/documentation/archim/revolutionfrancaise.htm

Dreyfus Affair: www.assemblee-nationale.fr/histoire/Dreyfus

First World War, photographic record: www.1914-1918.fr

De Gaulle Foundation: www.charles-de-gaulle.org

English Language Sources

General

Braudel, F. *The Identity of France*, 2 vols (London: Collins, 1988–90).

Clout, H. *Themes in the Historical Geography of France* (London: Academic Press, 1977).

Cobb, R. *A Second Identity* (Oxford: Oxford University Press, 1969).

Gildea, R. *The Past in French History* (New Haven, CT: Yale University Press, 1994).

Hazan, E. *The Invention of Paris: a History in Footsteps* (London: Verso, 2010).

Jones, C. *France* (Cambridge: Cambridge University Press, 1994).

Price, R. *A Concise History of France* (Cambridge: Cambridge University Press, 1993; 2nd edn, 2005.

Todd, E. *The Making of Modern France* (Oxford: Blackwell, 1991).

Tombs, R. and I. *That Sweet Enemy: the French and the British from the Sun King to the Present* (Heinemann, 2006).

Zeldin, T. *The French* (Flamingo, 1983).

France before the Revolution (Chapters 1–5)

Pigott, S., Daniel, G. and McBurney, C. (eds) *France Before the Romans* (London: Thames and Hudson, 1973).

Leroi-Gourhan, A. *The Dawn of European Art* (Cambridge University Press, 1982).

Drinkwater, J. F. *Roman Gaul, the Three Provinces* (London: Croom Helm, 1983).

James, E. *The Origins of France: From Clovis to the Capetians 500–1000* (London: Macmillan, 1982).

Heer, F. *Charlemagne and his World* (London: Weidenfeld & Nicolson, 1975).

Bull, M. *France in the Central Middle Ages: 900–1200* (Oxford: Oxford University Press, 2002).

Turner, R. V. *Eleanor of Aquitaine: Queen of France, Queen of England* (New Haven, CT: Yale University Press, 2009).

Grant, L. M. *Abbot Suger of St Denis: Church and State in Early 12th Century France* (Harlow: Longman, 1998).

Potter, D. (ed.) *France in the later Middle Ages, 1200–1500* (Oxford: Oxford University Press, 2003).

Gaposchkin, M. *The Making of Saint Louis: Kingship, Sanctity and Crusade in the later Middle Ages* (Ithaca, NY: Cornell University Press, 2008).

Allmand, C. T. *The Hundred Years War* (Cambridge: Cambridge University Press, 1989).

Warner, M. *Joan of Arc* (London: Vintage, 1991).

Holt, M. P. (ed.) *Renaissance and Reformation France, 1500–1648* (Oxford: Oxford University Press, 2002).

Hufton, O. L. *The Prospect before Her: a History of Women in Western Europe*, Vol. 1: 1500–1800 (London: HarperCollins, 1995).

Major, J. R. *From Renaissance Monarchy to Absolute Monarchy* (Baltimore, MD: John Hopkins University Press, 1994).

Knecht, R. *Francis I* (Cambridge: Cambridge University Press, 1982).

Pitts, V. J. *Henri IV of France* (Baltimore, MD: John Hopkins University Press, 2008).

Shennan, J. H. *The Bourbons* (London: Hambledon Continuum, 2007).

Mousnier, R. *The Institutions of France under the Absolute Monarchy, 1598–1789*, Vols. 1 and 2 (Chicago: Chicago University Press, 1979, 1984).

Bergin, J. *The Rise of Richelieu* (New Haven, CT: Yale University Press, 1991).

Tapié, V. L. *France in the Age of Louis XIII and Richelieu* (London: Macmillan, 1974).

Lossky, A. *Louis XIV and the French Monarchy* (New Brunswick, NJ: Rutgers University Press, 1994).

Wilkinson, R. *Louis XIV* (London: Routledge, 2007).

Barnwell, H. T. *The Tragic Drama of Corneille and Racine* (Oxford: Clarendon Press, 1982).

Bell, D. A. *Lawyers and Citizens: the Making of a Political Elite in Old Régime France* (Oxford: Oxford University Press, 1994).

McManners, J. *Church and Society in Eighteenth Century France*, 2 vols (Oxford: Clarendon Press, 1998).

Stone, B. *The French Parlements and the Crisis of the Old Regime* (Chapel Hill, NC: University of North Carolina Press, 1986).

Lever, E. *Madame de Pompadour* (New York: Farrar, Straus & Giroux, 2002).

Wade, I. *The Structure and Form of the French Enlightenment*, 2 vols (Princeton, NJ: Princeton University Press, 1977).

Chartier, R. *The Cultural Origins of the French Revolution* (Durham, NC: Duke University Press, 1991).

From the Revolution to the end of the Second World War (Chapters 6–10)

Stone, B. *Reinterpreting the French Revolution* (Cambridge: Cambridge University Press, 2002).

Dwyer, P. G. and McPhee, P. (eds) *The French Revolution and Napoleon: a Sourcebook* (London: Routledge, 2002).

Crook, M. (ed.) *Revolutionary France, 1788–1880* (Oxford: Oxford University Press, 2002).

Doyle, W. *The Oxford History of the French Revolution* (2nd edn, Oxford University Press, 2003).

Furet, F. *The French Revolution, 1770–1814* (Oxford and Cambridge, MA: Blackwell, 1996).

Scurr, R. *Fatal Purity: Robespierre and the French Revolution* (London: Chatto & Windus, 2006).

Asprey, R. *The Reign of Napoleon Bonaparte* (New York: Basic Books, 2001).

Alexander, R. S. *Napoleon* (London: Arnold, 2001).

Lyons, M. *Napoleon Bonaparte and the Legacy of the French Revolution* (London: Macmillan, 1994).

Lough, J. and M. *An Introduction to Nineteenth Century France* (London: Longman, 1978).

Heywood, C. *The Development of the French Economy, 1750–1914* (Cambridge: Cambridge University Press, 1992).

Price, R. *A Social History of Nineteenth Century France* (London: Hutchinson, 1987).

Mansel, P. *Louis XVIII,* (revised edn, London: John Murray, 2005).

Bresler, F. *Napoleon III* (London: HarperCollins, 1999).

Tombs, R. *The Paris Commune, 1871* (London: Longman, 1999).

Mayeur, J. M. and Rebérioux, M. *The Third Republic: From its Origins to the Great War, 1871–1914* (Cambridge: Cambridge University Press, 1984).

Begley, L. *Why the Dreyfus Affair Matters* (New Haven, CT: Yale University Press, 2010).

Cahm, E. *The Dreyfus Affair in French Society and Politics* (London: Longman, 1996).

Shattuck, R. *The Banquet Years: the Origins of the Avant-Garde in France, 1885–World War One* (revised edn, Cape, 1969).

Macmillan, J. F. (ed.) *Modern France, 1880–2002* (Oxford: Oxford University Press, 2003).

Becker, J.-J. *The Great War and the French People* (Leamington Spa: Berg, 1986).

Smith, L., Audoin, S. and Becker, A. *France and the Great War, 1914–18* (Cambridge: Cambridge University Press, 2003).

Johnson, D. and M. *The Age of Illusion: Art and Politics in France, 1918–40* (London: Thames & Hudson, 1987).

Larkin, M. *France since the Popular Front, 1936–86* (2nd edn, Oxford: Clarendon Press, 1997).

Reynolds, S. *France between the Wars: Gender and Politics* (London: Routledge, 1996).

Paxton, R. O. *Vichy France: Old Guard and New Order, 1940–1944* (New York: Columbia University Press, 2001).

Kedward, H. R. *Occupied France: Collaboration and Resistance, 1940–1944* (Oxford: Blackwell, 1985).

Judt, T. *Marxism and the French Left: Studies in Labour and Politics in France, 1830–1981* (Oxford: Clarendon, 1986).

Rémond, R. *The Right Wing in France from 1815 to de Gaulle* (2nd edn, Philadelphia, PA: University of Pennsylvania Press, 1969).

Johnson, R. W. *The Long March of the French Left* (London: Macmillan, 1981).

Mortimer, E. *The Rise of the French Communist Party, 1920–47* (London: Faber, 1984).

Contemporary France (Chapters 11–15)

Kedward, R. *La Vie en bleu: France and the French since 1900* (London: Penguin, 2006).

Gildea, R. *France since 1945* (2nd edn, Oxford: Oxford University Press, 2002).

Hewlett, N. *Modern French Politics: Analysing Conflict and Consensus since 1945* (Cambridge: Polity, 1998).

Rioux, J.-P. *The Fourth Republic, 1944–1958* (Cambridge: Cambridge University Press, 1987).

Duchêne, F. *Jean Monnet: the First Statesman of Independence* (New York: Norton, 1994).

Horne, A. *A Savage War of Peace: Algeria 1954–1962* (revised and updated edn, London: Pan, 2002).

Berstein, S. *The Republic of de Gaulle, 1958–1969* (Cambridge: Cambridge University Press, 1993).

Gough, H. and Horne, J. (eds) *De Gaulle and Twentieth Century France* (London: Edward Arnold, 1994).

Lacouture, J. *De Gaulle: the Ruler, 1945–1970* (Harvill, 1992).

Posner, C. (ed.) *Reflections on the Revolution in France: 1968* (Harmondsworh: Penguin, 1970).

Rioux, J.-P. and Berstein, S. *The Pompidou Years, 1969–1974* (Cambridge: Cambridge University Press, 2000).

Frears, J. R. *France in the Giscard d'Estaing Presidency* (London: Allen & Unwin, 1981).

Bell, D. S. *François Mitterrand: a Political Biography* (Cambridge: Polity, 2005).

Laughland, J. *The Death of Politics: France under Mitterrand* (Harmondsworth: Michael Joseph, 1994).

Maclean, M. (ed.), *The Mitterrand Years: Legacy and Evaluation* (London: Macmillan, 1998).

Keeler, J. T. S. and Schain, M. A. (eds) *Chirac's Challenge: Liberalisation, Europeanisation, and Malaise in France* (London: Macmillan, 1996).

Hanley, D. *Party, Society, Government: Republican Democracy in France* (Oxford: Oxford University Press, 2002).

Bell, D. S. and Criddle, B. *The French Communist Party in the Fifth Republic* (Oxford: Clarendon Press, 1994)

Elgie, R. *Political Institutions in Contemporary France* (Oxford University Press, 2003).

Flower, J. E. (ed.) *France Today* (new edn, London: Hodder & Stoughton, 2002).

Sa'adah, A. *Contemporary France: a Democratic Education* (Oxford: Rowman & Littlefield, 2003).

Godin, E. and Chafer, T. *The French Exception* (New York and Oxford: Berghahn, 2005).

Gordon, P. and Meunier, S. *The French Challenge: Adapting to Globalisation* (Washington, DC: Brookings Institution Press, 2001).

Fenby, J. *On the Brink: the Trouble with France* (London: Little, Brown, 1998).

Rosanvallon, P. *The New Social Question: Rethinking the Welfare State* (Princeton, NJ: Princeton University Press, 2000).

Mendras, H. and Cole, A. *Social Change in Modern France: Towards a Cultural Anthropology of the Fifth Republic* (Cambridge: Cambridge University Press, 1991).

Gregory, A. and Tidd, U. (eds) *Women in Contemporary France* (Oxford: Berg, 2000).

Cook, M. (ed.) *French Culture since 1945* (London: Longman, 1993).

Flood, C. and Hewlett, N. (eds) *Currents in Contemporary French Intellectual Life* (London: Macmillan, 2000).

Badiou, A. *The Meaning of Sarkozy* (London: Verso, 2008).

INDEX